This book is dedicated to my parents

Cherry Diana Heath Wigglesworth 7 March 1923 – 3 April 2006
Gordon Hardy Wigglesworth 27 June 1920 – 13 July 2005

Around & About

Stock Orchard Street

Matthew Barac
Trevor Butler
Adrian Forty
Frances Holliss
Gillian Horn
Martin Hughes
Charles Jencks
Jan-Carlos Kucharek
Katie Lloyd Thomas
Anya Moryoussef
Kester Rattenbury
Paul Smoothy
Jeremy Till
Sarah Wigglesworth (editor)

First published 2011
by Routledge
2 Park Square, Milton Park, Abingdon, Oxon, OX14 4RN

Simultaneously published in the USA and Canada
by Routledge
711 Third Avenue, New York, NY 10017

*Routledge is an imprint of the Taylor & Francis Group,
an informa business*

Typeset in Futura, Baskerville and Courier New by Duffy
Printed and bound in India by Replika Press Pvt. Ltd

British Library Cataloguing in Publication Data
A catalogue record for this book is available from
the British Library

Library of Congress Cataloging-in-Publication Data
Wigglesworth, Sarah.
Around and about Stock Orchard Street /
Sarah Wigglesworth.
p. cm.
Includes index.
1. 9-10 Stock Orchard Street (London, England)
2. Sustainable architecture—England—London.
3. Wigglesworth, Sarah—Homes and haunts—
England—London. 4. Till, Jeremy—Homes and haunts—
England—London. 5. London (England)—Buildings,
structures, etc. I. Title.

NA997.W47A35 2011
728'.372092—dc22
2010031909

ISBN13: 978-0-415-57527-0 (hbk)
ISBN13: 978-0-415-57529-4 (pbk)

Contents

Danger
Overhead
live wires

Foreword

The amazing, funny, serious, demonstration house of Sarah Wigglesworth

Charles Jencks

The architect's own house is a venerable genre, combining at best both the beautiful demonstration of an idea and a wonderful place to explore. Sir John Soane's house-museum is the English touchstone of this bloodline and Frank Gehry's California family home is the last acclaimed version. Such autobiographical buildings, for Frank Lloyd Wright and Bruce Goff, were places for self-experiments, some of which went catastrophically wrong; but as ideas which were later perfected for other clients, they provided a necessary springboard. Without risk there is no invention, no character and then no identity. Auto-buildings, to give the genre an odd name, can be extreme and obsessive, the working through of an architectural concept without compromise. Le Corbusier's wife famously said of her husband's self-experiments in the sun-drenched building, 'All this light is killing me, driving me crazy.'

Sarah Wigglesworth's house and studio for her office, and partner, Jeremy Till, takes its place in this continuous tradition as an explosion of architectural wit, from the front door to the top library, a little eyrie that peers out of its quizzical tower. This shed of a head looks over the bleak Islington landscape like a periscope from another world. Is it a defence against the world, and noise, pollution, and squalor; or just a cheap, vernacular shed?

Although, perhaps, not intending the 'Straw Bale House' (among its several names) to be seen as a series of amusing and relevant quotes on the history of architecture, it encourages such a reading because of its archetypes, as well as illustrating the intended lessons about sustainable living. Didactic buildings can be very funny, as James Stirling showed, either intentionally or by accident and, whichever way, humour is not a bad teacher. A gentle smile follows one throughout the Wigglesworthing narrative, the suggested story-line that starts on a late Victorian street of row-houses and ends in a library to contemplate the experience.

The immediate streetscape sets the scene as a typical compromise of peaceful London. It is domesticity versus grinding metro-traffic; a grand maple tree hovers to one side against the commuter trains. This opposition is picked up in the front wall and on the rest of the journey, as a dialogue between light-touch organic and heavyweight industrial. The sophistication of this high wall with its bay rhythms immediately reminds one of an Italian palazzo, but here it is the grid of a grey Miesian frame holding up galvanised panels set below a rich weave of willow wood taken off the peg, *ad hoc*. Yes, ruddy-brown wickerwork is playfully turned on its side, and it transforms the palazzo into an outsize basket or a seat. Any designer who doesn't get this double reference, with its high front door, should retake Arch 101.

The rustication becomes much more protective on the railroad side of the building where rotting sandbags, filled with concrete, slowly decay only to sprout a new skin of urban weeds amid their cellular units. These horizontal courses serve as heavy, acoustic baffling. But it is their expression that counts. They bulge slightly and hang over the side of the exposed I-beams like the flaccid clocks of Salvador Dali; they squeeze tight the black railway sleepers that frame the windows. Brunelleschi felt this way when he designed the massive rustication of the Pitti Palace, but here it is offset by a silver-blue wall, held in place by buttons! A quilt of bulging and ruckling pillows. This is an extraordinary and, I suppose, a feminine contrast. It gives the rustication of the Second World War sandbags, the trench architecture, a metaphorical presence not seen since the seventeenth century, and those aggressive rusticated diamonds punching their pyramids at passing gondolas on The Grand Canal in Venice. Tourists still admire these. If only harried commuters would look up from their papers as they sped past the Wigglesfort, they'd get an even funnier thrill.

Holding this façade and the studio above, at least symbolically and visually, are gabions made from recycled concrete, the third *ad hoc* use of ready-made material. Inside these fat piers are the *real* concrete columns. The Mannerism of heavy rectangular piers holding the massive Sandbag Order makes visual and semantic sense. It also harmonises with the raw concrete beams overhead and the pebbles and stones underfoot. And it allows a kind of stately Egyptian procession towards the studio between paired piers that, cleverly, work their rectangular logic on both the side and the front axis. They are not an avenue of double sphinxes, of course, or the monumental pairs of animals that lined Ming tombs, but the feeling of being in such a hieratic space is unmistakable. As if to send up the very quote she invokes, the white logo 'Sarah Wigglesworth Architects' is displayed straight ahead. But it now runs vertically at right-angles to expected logic (like the front wicker hurdles, also set the wrong way). And in case you miss these contrasts and inversions, they are displayed on a magenta-pink door of impeccable modern taste.

In effect, it is warfare architecture set against the pleasures of the pillow, counter-moods that set the tone for all that follows. If a façade deserves listing as the primary example of *ad hocism* in Britain, it is surely this one, though preservation would go counter to its message of pleasurable decay.

After confronting us with so much architectural firepower at the beginning of the drama, Wigglesworth would seem to have created a difficult role for the second act. But in the garden to the left of the entry the mood relaxes, and changes to the light and airy. In place of the primitive classicism, one finds Japanese bamboo and picturesque planting. A window-wall of asymmetrical panes opens on to a typical back garden of vegetables, flowers, washing and two ornamental birch trees. It is a somewhat messy and relatively undesigned space, like the other gardens one can see extending down the row. Yet placed in opposition to this expression of the everyday are several intense elements of architectural order. A row of steel columns again holds the cornice of grey I-beams. A corner inglenook juts out above the garden like a late work of Frank Lloyd Wright. And then one flourish ends the route, the straw bale corner that gives the house its usual name. Like the famous Miesian corner at IIT in Chicago, on which an epochal debate took place in the 1960s, one realises that a statement is made.

This corner pavilion, enclosing the bedrooms in protective insulation, is the culminating piece of didactic English wit, also in the tradition of arts and crafts, and of James Stirling *dimonstrazioni*. No wonder it appeared blown up in size on the cover of *The Architectural Review* in 2002 for all architects to take note. It demonstrates, indeed laughingly proclaims, its green credentials to the Age of Sustainable Rhetoric. The first modern use of huge straw cubes for 200 years – 550 bales of super-insulation gathered from a West Country farmer for £825, another victory for *ad hocism*. 'So there, you high-maintenance claimants to the prize of most-sustainable; so there Lord Foster, Sir Michael Hopkins and other be-knighted peers of the architectural realm. Look on my corrugated metal and polycarbonated sections with despair, and note the way I have layered and revealed them just so, to let your eye in on the secret and keep the rain out. The green lessons lie in the pleasures of clever reuse, those that create high-architecture not expensive high-tech.'

If buildings could speak, Wigglesworth's commendable bedroom corner would say something like this: that the most sustainable is not necessarily the cheapest or most ecological or most recycled, but any of this combined with architecture that people want to sustain because they love it. As it is, her house and studio have many other accessible *and* esoteric messages embedded in their architectural language. And this brings up the questions of intentionality and communication, whether the many quotes are conscious or accidental. How much of all this is in her authorial voice, and how much is it in the heightened language of architecture itself? Next to the didactic straw bale corner (which is foreground, also on the cover of *AR*) is the trunk of a tree sporting its knots and branch scars. It (visually) supports a steel beam and acts as a transition point to a miniscule Japanese garden. Bramante and Philibert de l'Orme are behind this Tree Trunk Order, as are many others back to Vitruvius and beyond. I have no idea if their memory is being invoked. But here, stripped of bark and elevated on a real concrete base and gently showing its non-structural truth like a good postmodernist, it is one more amusing and sensuous touch that shows the building to be a worthy exemplar in the great game of the architect's own home.

Introduction

Sarah Wigglesworth

We have grown familiar with the building's character, learning how to live with the train noise, where the sunny spots are located and how often the gravel path needs raking

9/10 Stock Orchard Street was the first new building we built. It was also the culmination of ten years' thinking. In the decade since the building contract finished, it has, for better or for worse, come to define the direction of my architectural practice. Despite the building's profile (*Grand Designs* is regularly repeated), we have received only one subsequent commission for a private house. Rather, during those ten years the office has established itself as a small practice working in the public sector and the projects that have come our way have allowed us to develop our approach to building ideas, aiming to make work that is both provocative as well as playful and which approaches green architecture with a critical eye. In parallel, as owner-occupiers we have completed substantial portions left unfinished when we moved in. We have grown familiar with the building's character, learning how to live with the train noise, where the sunny spots are located and how often the gravel path needs raking. The garden has grown up. To quote Kester Rattenbury, 'Time has settled around it.' As we have adapted to the building, so we have retold the stories surrounding it – to guests, to journalists, to the public – and found an eager and questioning audience hungry for relating the narratives about what a building – as action and artefact – means. This book is a response to that call.

9/10 Stock Orchard Street was first published in the UK in 2002 but has continued to be published around the globe ever since, and has featured in several exhibitions in the UK, USA and France. It has been referred to in academic debate. The project reached a national audience after featuring in the first TV series *Grand Designs*, subsequently being chosen by the public as one of their six favourite buildings from across all series. Regularly re-broadcast, each screening elicits comment, recognition and opinion from every quarter and a fresh line of visitors spotted taking photos. Since the

North (bale) wall, 2009

1

project's 'completion' we have had requests for information from a number of schools of architecture that have set the building as a case study, queries from other architects about the construction details, researchers asking to carry out studies, and enquiries from the public regarding sources of equipment and furniture. We have been invited to speak about the project at conferences on a diverse range of subject matter, given seminars at Grand Designs Live, and have spun the project every which way for different purposes and intentions (Critical Practice conference at The Bartlett, Ecology Building Society AGM, etc). Since we first let the public into the buildings during Open House in 2003 and were confronted with a queue of 1200 people, we have opened our doors to groups of interested visitors from all over the world. This has now settled into a pattern of two open days a year when we offer an hour-long tour of inside and outside to between fifteen and forty-five people. In 2001 we published an illustrated description of the project in the form of a small guidebook that continues to sell steadily. The ongoing interest in the building suggested that there could be purpose in making information on the project available in more permanent format, including many of the key construction details.

As the title *Around and About Stock Orchard Street* suggests, this is a book about architecture, but it does not deal principally with the building as a visual or historical object. Rather, it tries to situate the building in a broader cultural context, exploring the many conversations engaged by architecture. It aims to open up and examine the extended field in which architecture is situated and produced, which includes the philosophical, economic, social, technical, historical, ecological and discursive contexts encompassed by buildings in general. It uses 9/10 Stock Orchard Street as the starting point for the exploration of these issues, but the approach used could be applied to any building at all. In that respect it situates all buildings in a shared commonality, an accepted ordinariness. At the same time 9/10 Stock Orchard Street is not an ordinary building; moreover, it is very much part of its

time, its authorship and its place. Thus, the book seeks to access generic lessons by engaging in the specific context and subject matter of a single building project. Designed and constructed at the turn of the millennium, the building captured a moment in the history of architecture when the ethics and values of mainstream modernism were, not for the first time, being challenged, particularly as climate change was beginning to ask architects how to respond to its implications. As a live/work building by and for two architects on a site in inner London, the project was intended as research-in-action, an ongoing exploration of built ideas pushed to their extremes. Based around passive ecological design and exploring new living patterns, the approach resulted in a building characterised by its experimental materiality and hybrid qualities. Its aesthetic combined recycled materials and craft techniques with state-of-the-art components and technologies to create a collage of technical solutions, and its design drew on a series of references from art, architecture, self-building and popular culture. As some of the chapters in this volume confirm (Barac, Rattenbury), it is its resistance to categorisation that has challenged and continues to challenge many critics and observers.

We finally took occupation of the house at Stock Orchard Street in December 2000, so the publication of this volume celebrates the tenth anniversary of the end of the building contract. I have avoided using the description 'completed building' because the building is still 'incomplete' and construction is purposefully ongoing, as each year witnesses the installation of a further element of the design omitted from the main contract; these elements now already overlap with the sabbatical maintenance programme. This book looks back to survey the genesis, conception, building and inhabitation of Stock Orchard Street, assessing why and how we did it, what issues were engaged in its conception and design, how it took shape, what took place, and what changed as a result. It is based on the premise that architecture has many dimensions and may be understood and approached in multiple ways.

As a practising architect I am only too aware of the prosaic nature of much of what we do, yet I am also inspired by the potential for architecture to communicate in profound and moving ways. It is the oscillation, between the extremes of banality and pleasure, between bureaucracy and intellect and between shapeless matter and meaning that this book attempts to portray. The copious illustrations provide another way in to understanding the buildings, not as perfect products but as messy, changing, weathering, growing organic beings in their own right.

The title of this book deliberately implies that it is about more than just the project, and indeed, some chapters hardly discuss the project at all (Horn, Forty). In this book the building is the framework around which gathers a wider set of ideas about both the present state of architecture, and the design, construction and inhabitation of a building. In this way it is intended not as a conventional building monograph, but, rather, to extend the ways in which the subject of architecture can be communicated, debated and understood. It consciously avoids a discussion of style and appearance that adheres to the majority of built work in favour of telling a set of tales, warts and all. Some are descriptive, some are fables, some are analytical and some deliver information. In keeping with the spirit of the building, my aim was to set out deliberately to cross the divide between scholarly literature and popular books on architecture, engaging an audience at all levels of interest, curiosity and expertise; in offering data for evaluation and analysis, a rare degree of transparency has allowed us to assess the claims for the ecological principles behind the buildings.

The work of the architect involves many different skills. Among those that might appear on a university curriculum are design creativity, technical knowledge, numeracy, time management, literacy and administrative skills. But twenty-five years in practice has taught me that these are just the basics. Other really important attributes are the 'soft' skills that include vision, persistence, determination,

advocacy, good communication, getting along with other people, confidence building, leadership, conviction, humour and thick skin. The experience of realising a building engages a wide range of emotions, swinging from triumph to despair, seriousness to comedy, worry to relief. No single narrative can capture the entire picture. The book attempts to relate the numerous parallel and complementary ways of understanding what makes up a project from different perspectives and interests. In this respect the subject of the endeavour is less important than that a piece of architecture should be presented in this way. That Stock Orchard Street has been chosen as the subject of this book is principally because, as author, as client and as occupant, I have been involved in it from several sides of the project. This has provided access to all the relevant archive material and offered privileged knowledge about the process from several different viewpoints.

In narrating the myriad narratives that spin off from the project I have selected a group of people whose work I admire and who have, in different ways, been important to this project. Each author was given the same brief: to use the building as a foundation for an argument related to their interests in architecture. The resulting texts and images reflect their particular specialism and the relationship they hold with the project. Although I have approached the authors because of their interests and have told them why I have made my approach, the subject and style of each contributor's work is theirs alone; my involvement has simply been to offer comment and encouragement. If the book feels uneven, this is my responsibility, but one that I will defend, inasmuch as it reflects the openness of the relationship and the trust I have invested in such a diverse group of authors. One of these is Jeremy Till, my partner, co-author, co-designer and collaborator, who was my constant companion through design and construction. His chapter describes the effects of opening a house – and all that it represents as privacy – to the public. In this chapter he takes a look in the mirror to ask what is involved when an architect builds their own home and then offers their lives up to public scrutiny. What revelations are given? What is taken? What is learned and who learns it? Jeremy explores the intent and provenance of some key ideas and techniques behind the design of 9/10 Stock Orchard Street, comparing them to more ubiquitous methods. In asserting the impossibility of fully comprehending what is being said in a 'first building', he conveys the project's ambiguous character over the conventional architectural virtues of consistency and clarity. This refers to a second chapter, jointly authored with myself, which publishes for the first time a lecture we gave in 1998 on the eve of commencing construction. Entitled 'Telling Tales', it describes the humorous and anecdotal side of trying to get the building underway and it takes the form of an illustrated drama.

Apart from developing the concept for this book, my own contribution consists of two chapters. The first, 'The Client's Tale', is factual and narrates the client's view: the story of the genesis, design, construction and occupation of the building. It simply records the events that took place and introduces the main characters, some of whom author their own chapters later in the book, relating their version of the same events.

As a designer and teacher I am interested in where creative ideas originate and how to approach a project when confronted with a blank sheet of paper. I never conceptualise design as a scientific process or singular method, though it involves data gathering and relies on accurate research; but neither is design simply wilful, individual whimsy, a private dialogue with personal obsessions. Rather, design is a conversation with ideas and culture that speaks and is received in ways that are dependent upon context. It is mediated through the interests and identity of the designer who, in designing, makes sense of the place and the brief in meaningful ways – that is, ways that contribute to the cultural conversation. Accordingly, my second chapter, 'Ordinariness and Perfection', deals with how we commenced the design for the Stock

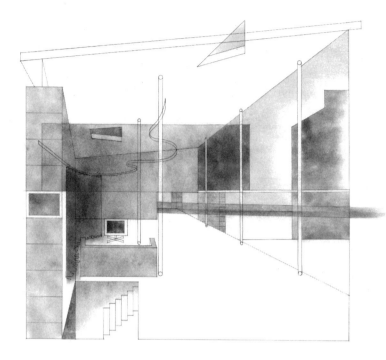

Living room study, Sarah Wigglesworth

Orchard Street site, explaining what issues and ideas became important for the development of the project and how they shaped our approach to space, material and technology. This provides background material against which to frame other authors' contributions.

A great deal has changed in life and in the construction industry over the past ten years, and Gillian Horn's chapter looks at these through documenting the changes that have taken place in her life since 1999 when she left her role as Project Architect for 9/10 Stock Orchard Street to join Penoyre & Prasad Architects. Her chapter paints a picture of the social context of the mid to late 1990s and tracks how architecture and construction has altered in the interim period. Paralleling the digital revolution that has played itself out with full force in social life as it has in the building industry, Gillian describes how, on a personal level, our idealistic rebellion against existing structures has been replaced by an embracing of mainstream procurement methods and an engagement in the large construction programmes initiated by the Labour government in the wake of the 1997 election. In her analysis Gillian considers the development of new building delivery systems (PFI, DBCM, D&B) aimed at transferring risk (including financial) to the major contracting organisations, showing how these effectively relegate architects to the status of subcontractor and building users to processual data. She considers the effects that this has had on the 'product' – architecture – and muses on what sorts of alternative public buildings we might expect should they be procured in the manner of the Stock Orchard Street buildings.

Adrian Forty's contribution is sparked by a chapter on architecture among the work of Sir Francis Bacon (1561–1626). Drawing on the essay 'Of Building', Bacon's only commentary on architecture, Forty raises the issue of whether 9/10 Stock Orchard Street is ethical architecture, and if so, in what way. Bacon's essay engages architecture's relationship to process ('procedures and results') as opposed to those of representation, or its formal meaning. He points out that in its visual appearance architecture can lead us astray, suggesting to us that the world is more ordered than it really is. Bacon reminds us that architecture resists over-systematisation and completeness and, accordingly, a philosophy applied to it should reflect this. Forty asserts that Bacon's essay is the first piece of critical writing on architecture, using theory to turn architectural thought on itself, making it question its own principles. In raising the issue of ethics, Forty argues that Bacon's approach means that transparency of process is preferable to the blind application of principle and that this is what an ethical architecture should be. He concludes by arguing that in the manner in which 9/10 Stock Orchard Street asks questions of architecture, it could be regarded as ethical.

Katie Lloyd Thomas picks up on the representational theme. She uses Elizabeth Grosz's definition of 'excess' to discuss ideas and processes in the employment of specific materialities found in 9/10 Stock Orchard Street. Delving into the contractual communication generated during its construction phase she argues that the Building Regulations inhibit but do not wholly restrict the propensity of architecture to push things to extremes. She

picks up four materials in particular – cloth cladding, sandbags, straw and gabions – and explains how each in their turn leads 'to openings, contestations and invention within otherwise prescribed processes'. In doing this she argues that the transgressions may be read as a feminist interpretation of excess in the context of architecture.

The issue of female space is picked up again by Frances Holliss in her chapter 'House with Associated Office?'. Her work addresses the history of what she terms 'workhome', a hybrid building type containing both a dwelling and a workplace. Examining this building type she shows how prevalent it has been in history, especially in women's lives; and that it is relatively recently, with the advent of zoning and planning law that single-use types have predominated, rinsing the city of richness, activity and ambiguity.

Trevor Butler authors two chapters in this book. An environmental engineer, his chapter 'From Innovation to Commonplace' places 9/10 Stock Orchard Street in the context of the evolving definition of 'green' buildings, tracing the debt owed to the pioneers of the green movement. This chapter describes the environmental features of 9/10 Stock Orchard Street, concluding that its key innovation is in addressing the aesthetic of green, with its recycled and low embodied energy materials. His second chapter, 'What Do We Mean by Green?' is an analysis of the energy consumption of the buildings. Using data gathered through five years of occupation, this shows that the anticipated calculations of energy-in-use were optimistic and that what was environmental good practice in 1997 under the 1995 Building Regulations is now well below the benchmarks taken for granted in new developments in 2010. Trevor reminds us that environmental claims for buildings made before they are occupied for a period of time should be regarded with suspicion, and post-occupancy evaluation should become the standard for all buildings. Furthermore, he posits that the field of green is converging around a consensual position based on BREEAM and other templated procedures. While these have the effect of ratcheting up the criteria for achieving stated energy targets, aiming, with user knowledge, to reduce energy consumption, the debate about different ways of being green is undergoing a concomitant closing down.

Martin Hughes is a remarkable building contractor. As KOYA Construction, he managed the construction of 9/10 Stock Orchard Street. Without Martin, the project would, quite simply, never have been built and we were exceptionally lucky to have been introduced to him. His experience in self-building projects (especially ecological building) and his wide knowledge of how to realise other people's work were critical factors in enabling the completion of this project. Combining an impressive level-headedness with a conviction that such a crazy project could be built at all, let alone for our budget, he allowed us to invest our faith in his demonstrable abilities while getting on with our own crises. Martin's chapter describes the relationship between key issues pertinent to all building contracts: time, and the interface between trades and money. Martin explores what are essential matters to understand in order to concretise any project. Contrasting building contracting with product manufacture and factory fabrication, his chapter addresses an area infrequently discussed in books on architecture and is a welcome contribution from a very different perspective.

Matthew Barac's chapter comes closest to a critique of the building. His contribution is an exploration of the co-dependence of practice and theory, and specifically examines the 'thoughts and references that make up the conceptual framework of "house"'. His mission is to define how we might recognise that special something which sets one house apart from others, defining this distinction as research-in-action. In defining what this might mean he draws a distinction between novelty, such as might qualify a project for magazine publication, and genuine innovation or originality.

This theme is continued in Kester Rattenbury's contribution. Part building critique, part historical documentary, Rattenbury considers the reaction – by public, print media and broadcasting – to 9/10 Stock Orchard Street. She draws broader conclusions about what motivates publication and considers how the communication of architecture is framed in specific ways. She shows how this is an evolving situation, especially since the advent of television as a medium for presenting architecture to the public in an accessible way.

Short stories punctuate the longer chapters. Anya Moryoussef writes a poetic description of working in our office, where she was an intern for two years. Jan-Carlos Kucharek describes building the model of the project even as we were still designing it, and reveals its sad demise. Letters to the *Architectural Review* commenting on the building are reprinted. Also reproduced here is a discussion between ourselves and Tony Currivan from *Building for a Future* magazine (now called *Green Building* magazine, www.greenbuildingmagazine.co.uk), addressing the orthodoxies of ecological building. Between these texts are photo essays by Paul Smoothy, documenting a year in the life of the building commissioned by me to celebrate its tenth birthday. If this is all you do with this book, enjoy these pictures.

It was in 2006 that the idea of doing a book on Stock Orchard Street was first planted in my mind. The book is lucky to be in print at all. Before Routledge expressed their interest, a number of other publishers with which I took soundings declined to get involved. Most wanted a coffee table book featuring 9/10 Stock Orchard Street among a selection of other projects of a similar genre. None of them could understand the idea of exploring the issues surrounding a project for a single building. Even reviewers had mixed feelings. Some (mostly across the Atlantic) thought it sounded like a plausible idea but were not familiar with the project, while the UK practitioners accused the proposal of being blatantly self-publicising. Academics said the proposal was unrigorous and lacked method. One said it was self-aggrandising, since the building clearly didn't merit this much attention. One publisher wanted to cut the length of the text in half and model it on an existing title within their stable. As ever, by deviating from existing conventions my work has fallen through the cracks, located somewhere in the messy divide between practice and theory, an irritating bedfellow in both camps.

Deflated but not entirely put off, I have pursued my vision because I felt this book was trying to express a different understanding and engagement with architecture. Part personal memoire, part professional document, part technical manual, part intellectual reflection, part picture book, the volume attempts to portray the numerous routes to produce, read, understand and enjoy architecture. It drills down into the subject rather than skimming the surface. It does not attempt to make judgements on the relative value of these different aspects. I stand by this approach, even if it comes with the potential charge that it is overtly self-referential. As with Adrian Forty's description of Bacon's 'Of Building', this publication may well be 'considered "weak", disjointed, lacking coherence, without a conclusion'. Like Bacon's *Essays*, it is not meant to endorse any particular rules, but rather to raise questions about architecture from within the discipline. I therefore extend my sincerest thanks to Routledge for taking that leap of faith in supporting its publication and would like to extend special gratitude to Fran Ford, Commissioning Editor, for her empathy and encouragement during even the most difficult moments.

I would also like to extend my sincerest respect and thanks to my authors who have stuck by the concept of this project throughout the three years of its gestation. Their willingness to participate in this project, their encouragement and their professionalism has been a joy to witness. Keeping faith with this project, I hope they are pleased with the final result. Further thanks go to Ellie and Katya Duffy of Duffy Design whose design for this book has captured and interpreted its contents so eloquently. It has been a pleasure to collaborate with them and witness their insightful understanding of the book's intentions.

Finally, I extend my gratitude and love to Jeremy, my best friend, worst critic and fellow-traveller in this extraordinary journey that has been such a shaping force in our lives. His confidence in my ability to carry this through has made it all possible.

Part 1

The client's tale

Sarah Wigglesworth

1

We began looking for a site in the summer of 1993. We had returned from our Fulbright Fellowship in the USA at the end of 1991: Jeremy to The Bartlett, while I returned to my small practice and my part-time teaching post at Kingston University. A spirit of change blew through London's young architectural community; the targets of our frustration were tired ideas, self-serving professionalism and the commercialisation of the building industry. Many of us saw an outlet in redefining our praxis, seeking a more fluid, responsive, collaborative and self-reliant way of working. This included any or all of the following: debate, community action, self-build, teaching, writing, making things as well as designing and/or building our own project. Everyone we knew seemed to be doing the same: looking for a small patch of land where they could give free reign to their personal ambitions.

I had been running my practice for five years: modest domestic extensions, kitchen and bathroom renovations. Nothing special, but a good way to cut one's teeth: learning through doing, finding out the hard way. Practice offered autonomy but all too often the promised vision was squandered: absurd expectations for small budgets, a client's lack of confidence, failures in communication or a builder's incompetence. In parallel, teaching was full of hope in the possibilities offered by architecture. We were leading studios at several universities and it was an exciting time for theory. We were especially interested in making critiques of conventional practice, looking at new processes and associations to develop a redefined profession and a revisionary form of architecture. The gulf between the aspirations discussed in our teaching and the reality of everyday practice seemed very wide and hard to bridge. Gradually, we formed the idea of a project that would explore how close we could bring theory and practice. We fixed upon the idea of buying a site and building a house for ourselves that would test this idea to the limit.

Fresh shoots

The USA changed us in many ways, propelling our praxis in new directions. One shift was significant: the urgent need for architects to take more responsibility for what is now called climate change. We wanted to design more ethically, more ecologically, helping 'green' design to gain greater mainstream acceptance, but more importantly, we wanted to adjust the way in which architecture, the profession and the product were considered, discussed and evaluated. As part of this critique I became involved in two defining projects: Desiring Practices, and in parallel with the design of 9/10 Stock Orchard Street, editing an edition of *Architectural Design* entitled *The Everyday and Architecture*.

Desiring Practices: Architecture, Gender and the Interdisciplinary arose as a feminist critique of mainstream (patriarchal) structures of knowledge, business practice, professionalisation and production. Our critique centred on the ways in which female knowledge had been apparently erased from design and the ways in which women had been excluded, through role and hierarchy, from influencing the built environment as both clients and users. We also considered the effects that alienation had had upon the experience of women in the city. Conceived by Duncan McCorquodale, Katerina Rüedi and myself, it took the form of a two-day symposium (held at the RIBA in order to penetrate the heart of the establishment) and an exhibition in twelve London venues. With large numbers of helpers we managed these events on a shoestring budget, subsequently publishing both the symposium papers and the exhibition catalogue as one of Black Dog Publishing's earliest titles. This project was a defining one for me, helping me to make sense of my personal situation while also establishing a theoretical basis for a critique of the milieu in which I worked.

Architectural Design: The Everyday and Architecture evolved from this thinking. Its aim was to consider the ideas and product that resulted from a critique of conventional values with its emphasis on the beautiful, the one-off, the monumental and the perfect, concentrating instead on the overlooked aspects of the built environment that are the background to our everyday lives. As part of this exploration we began to reassess the role the architect plays in enabling changes to the built environment, reliant as most are on patronage and funding provided by public or private corporations. Notions of autonomy and altruism seemed absent from this scenario and we were looking for ways in which to understand this, seeking examples from across the globe of how this situation had been overcome. It was during this time that we came to know and admire the work of Sam Mockbee and the Rural Studio.

Right up until the late 1980s I had found it hard to get excited about ecological architecture. Dull and worthy, 'green' was, I believed, a strait-jacket on individual expression. However, while at Kingston University I had become aware of the work of Short, Ford and Partners, and I taught for several years with Peter Sharratt, then working on the production information package for their Queen's Engineering Building for De Montfort University. This firm's appreciation of the arts and crafts, rooted in an architecture responsive to place and environment, combined with a knowledge of naturally ventilated buildings (especially the expressive qualities of wind towers) to offer a new model for sustainable architecture, one which possessed a distinct appearance that was both articulated and functional. For me, this was an exciting moment in which the possibilities for green building began to emerge with greater clarity.

So whatever we built was an attempt to contribute a new sensibility in design, a different way of collaborating, a vastly expanded material language and a new green aesthetic, one that moved away from the image that attached to its pioneering exemplars.

Going, going, gone…

The first auction we attended that caught our eye was selling a site in Cromer Street, off Gray's Inn Road. Adjacent to a nineteenth-century house, it was a bomb-damaged site, with several large plane trees growing on it, and it was being used as a car-park. The trees were listed, and building on any part of it would have been difficult. It was acquired by a nearby office for far more than our finances would stretch to, and remains a car-park to this day. But simply going to the auction emboldened us to the bidding race, and we were hooked.

The site in Stock Orchard Street came to auction on 15 February 1994. We set ourselves a limit of £92,000. It was far more than we really wanted to pay but the previous auction had steeled us. We had worked out what our house was worth, what we could borrow, what we could scrape together from savings, parents, premium bonds, PEPs and ISAs. It was not very optimistic, but it was all we could get and all we believed we could justify.

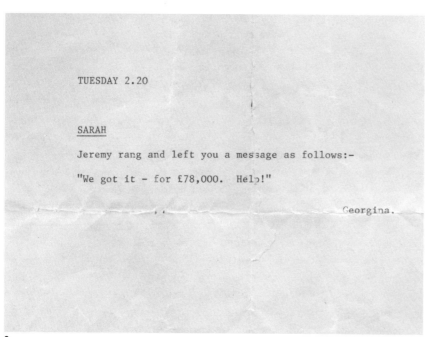

4

5

6

Jeremy attended the auction alone, because it was my teaching day and I had a studio review. I was sitting in the large Crit Room over the entrance hall at Knight's Park in the middle of the afternoon when the school secretary, Georgina, thrust a green paper note into my hand. It read: 'We got it – for £78,000. Help!' [Fig 2 green note] That was all. I can't remember anything about the students' work that day.

Few developers attended the auction, perhaps because 1994 was the tail end of a recession and nobody was looking for opportunities. Perhaps nobody spotted the potential; perhaps they knew something that we didn't. Whatever the reason, we were lucky.

We visited the site only once before the auction. It was visible from the street, but there was a great deal more to it than could be seen from the outside. I can't remember whether we ventured in, braving the suspicious glances of the tenants. I don't think we did. However, we did make enquiries with the Local Authority's Planning Department. The site sat on the boundary of a conservation area that included the semi-detached cottages on Stock Orchard Street, to the south of the site. To the north and west stood an estate of houses constructed in the 1980s on former railway sidings, while to the east the main railway line leaving London for Scotland bordered the property.

The auctioneer's details were vague about whether the rectangle of land closest to the railway, which was shown hatched red on the sale particulars, formed part of the property [Fig 3 the auction catalogue]. It stood to the railway side of a high wall bisecting the site, immediately to one side of the old gateway, an arched brick structure that terminated the street. When we visited, this area was full of buddleia and discarded objects, impossible to access behind a new brick wall in a semi-ruined state, patched with chain link fencing. We could just about make out a concrete ground slab suggesting that there had been a building there at one time [Fig 4 the site].

The main part of the site was occupied by a forge making leaf springs for motor vehicles (mainly for taxis but also for veteran and vintage cars). The forge was in the centre of a run of buildings stretching down the length of the northern boundary. At the far west end was a small smithy, and between these two buildings lay an area where the leaf springs were painted with tar to stop them rusting [Fig 5 the site from across the railway, Fig 6 the site looking east, the site's north retaining wall]. The forge roof was spanned with a set of trusses made of large timber sections and was covered in corrugated fibre-cement boards, with clear plastic roof windows let into it. A fern was growing from the eaves. There was hardly any light and the place was filthy. None of the structures had doors because the spaces surrounding the furnace were so warm.

To the south, a lean-to along the garden wall adjoining No. 8 Stock Orchard Street was empty except for some discarded springs and the mess room, adorned with clothing hanging out to dry. In the cobbled driveway sat a huge guillotine, which cut the strips of steel ready for inserting into the oven.

7

Once hot, they were bent into the correct shape over formers (different shapes for different models of vehicle) and bound together to create the finished spring. These were fitted to the underside of the chassis in two curtained bays opposite the gateway. This would often be the final stop in a journey through the small taxi-servicing industrial zone that still exists in Stock Orchard Street, starting with the body shops, respray yards and service garages at the top of the street and finishing in our site.

Proud new owners, we visited the site to introduce ourselves. I think the tenants were a little surprised to see who we were – two thirty-somethings who didn't look like developers. They were understandably suspicious. 'Why hadn't they bid for the site?' we asked them. Their surveyors had advised that the rear wall of the property, a 4.8m-high Victorian retaining wall, needed rebuilding. We gulped. Had we missed something crucial? A closer look suggested it was fine [*Fig 7*] but then again we hadn't asked a structural engineer to take a look. The conversation focused around our plans; clearly they were preparing for eviction, but there seemed little point in losing our tenants until we had a firm vision for the site: the rental money would come in handy and we had no wish to destroy their business. We also felt that finding alternative accommodation for the forge in Islington might support our planning application. It was agreed to renew the tenancy on a year-long lease while we clarified our plans and looked for alternative premises for the forge. We figured that in the worst case scenario we might achieve a planning permission for something new there, even if it wasn't our dream home.

When the deeds arrived they showed that we had indeed acquired the part of the site adjacent to the railway. Suddenly our plans to build a dwelling began to expand. With 25 per cent more space than we had bargained for we realised we could construct not just a house but also an office for the practice. Although this would stretch our budget, it would mean the freedom to work without paying rent, allowing the practice to undertake interesting work that did not pay well. The freedom to redefine our working arrangements was tantalising, and the additional expense could be justified by the option, if everything went wrong, to sell or lease the office (as well as providing an income in retirement). We also began to enjoy the idea of a hybrid building that would combine the living and working elements of life, just as our existing house did. This was the seed from which the programme for the building began to grow (see 'Ordinariness and Perfection'). Oddly enough, naïve and so hungry were we to realise our project for an experimental architecture that at no point did we ever seriously consider developing the site for immediate financial gain, even though it was clear that the site could have accommodated up to six small live/work units and an access road.

Telling stories

While we looked for a new home for the forge we began thinking about the design. However, before drawing anything we had to agree some rules for how we were going to work on the project. Experience had taught us that when two architects are working together the one that makes the first mark

8

claims the project as their own. If this was genuinely going to be the collaborative design we wanted it to be, and if both were to have an equal input into the design of their future home, we had to be equal partners. So we decided that we would not draw anything until the agenda for the building had been agreed between us, and this meant conjuring the design in another medium: narrative.

For two years we drew nothing, but we talked endlessly about the possible building we would design. We raided our memories for our favourite building moments, great and small, grand and humble. On summer holidays we would see something and decide that it should be incorporated. We talked about how we wanted to live, what sort of feel the place should have, where the bits should lie on the site. We referenced our heroes' works, new and old, and told others about our plans, taking on their comments as they were offered. Following such a long gestation, when the design was finally born and we put pen to paper, it popped out, pretty much fully formed.

Then we got scared. How on earth were we to get this through planning? Sited on the boundary of a conservation area in a borough with a poor reputation for supporting modern design, we suddenly had a reality check. We convinced ourselves that our planning application would be rejected out of hand. Desperate, we approached a planning consultant to help us.

Peter Kyte's advice astonished me. While the conventional wisdom is to engage the officers in the Planning Department in a dialogue before making an application, Peter advised us that we should not talk to them at all. All this would achieve, he argued, is a bargaining position for the Department. Instead, he suggested that we should design precisely what we wanted, prepare a complete set of drawings fully describing the scheme, and he would support the application by writing a report setting out the grounds, under the UDP, on which the Authority should pass the plans. I was sceptical and thought this couldn't possibly work; but something nagged away: he was the expert; perhaps we should trust his judgement. After all, what could we possibly lose except time and his fee? That didn't seem a high price if the strategy worked.

Our deadline for completing the planning drawings was 1 May 1997 – the date of the General Election. We placed our drawing boards in front of the television in our living room and in time-honoured fashion, settled down to an all-nighter, complete with a crate of beer to celebrate the highly anticipated Labour victory [*Fig 8* TV during the election results, 1997]. We didn't finish the drawings that night because the longed-for victory came too early.

More than three years and several rental renewals after we had bought the site, Brost Forge found alternative premises near Pentonville Prison and moved out, taking the furnace apart firebrick by firebrick. We celebrated my fortieth birthday in the ruinous site with a surprise party organised by Jeremy [*Fig 9* birthday meal in the old forge].

9

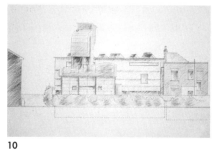

10

To help the planning process run smoothly we held an open evening on site to show our neighbours our intentions. The sad, empty spaces of the former forge were used as the setting for a small exhibition of coloured drawings fixed to panels, balanced on straw bales. We thought the bales were a nice touch [*Fig 10* planning drawing]. We offered wine and were on hand to explain our designs. A surprising number of people turned up. Nobody criticised our scheme. They seemed glad that the forge was gone and that a new house was about to replace the dilapidated sheds.

A planning permission has to be decided within a statutory period of eight-weeks. Seven weeks after the Council notified us that our submission was valid we had still not heard anything from the Planning Department. We convinced ourselves that this heralded bad news, and that we would be forced to appeal their decision. With a heavy heart, we braced ourselves to telephone our allocated case officer, Akis Didaskalou, to request a meeting. This was our last chance to try and stay a refusal before the decision deadline expired. When Akis told us it was being passed under delegated powers I was speechless, convinced he must have the wrong scheme. No, it was the one with the wild strawberries on the roof. 'We've had a few letters in support, nothing negative.' A week later we received the planning approval letter. Peter Kyte's strategy was vindicated: we were free to start working in earnest.

14

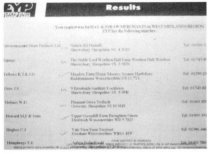
11

12

13

15

Modules and regulations

We began by setting out the building on the site. The key component in the setting out was the size of the bales. Not only were they large, modular elements determining the scale of the house, we had no idea what size a bale was. To find out, there was no reaching for the RIBA Product Selector. *Yellow Pages* had a section entitled 'Fodder Merchants' [*Fig 11* fodder merchants]. After a few calls we located a dealer near Cirencester, and in August 1997 we made a trip to the farm where the straw was being reaped and baled up [*Fig 12* baler machine], and inspected a barn full of the product of several years' harvests. We studied a range of different types of straw (wheat, barley, rye, flax) and noted down dimensions to establish a median bale size [*Fig 13* SW measuring bales]. It was clear already that we would have to deal with huge tolerances. This was going to prove something of a challenge.

There were endless discussions about whether we should use a timber frame (we considered telegraph pole columns) or opt for a steel frame. Eventually our decision coalesced around steel because it seemed the most cost-effective choice for the spans we were considering. We now started working on the office. This was a simple two-storey volume but it lay close to the railway line so it had specific acoustic issues that needed addressing. We began researching system building, looking closely at prefabricated concrete-based panel systems for both the floor structure and the walls. This had the advantage of swift erection and noise abatement but systems rely on repetition for their economy, and after lengthy testing it was clear that the building was so bespoke that a more forgiving system would be preferable. We decided on a simple beam-and-block floor, and roof and walls composed of timber studwork.

In May 1997 we had attended a straw bale building course at the Centre of Alternative Technology in Machynlleth, Wales, led by Barbara Jones [*Fig 14* straw building workshop]. We learned how to build a single storey load-bearing bale structure held together with hazel stakes [*Fig 15* JT & SW building with bales at CAT]. This method was rather different from our own intentions but it was useful as a starting point to understand the issues and gain hands-on experience working with bales.

In October 1997 we received a call from our engineers, Price & Myers, asking if we would like to participate in a stand at Interbuild in Birmingham. Someone had dropped out of a feature called Façades of the Future which, we were told, included a panel from Future Systems' media stand under construction at Lord's Cricket Ground. The proposition was to build part of the straw wall, a low-tech counterpoint to the Future Systems exhibit. With less than two months to go to the event, we felt that this would be a huge challenge, but that it would give us a unique opportunity to do the R&D on bale construction that would be helpful in detailing the building. Accordingly we set about designing the exhibition.

16

17

18

What we evolved was a two-sided structure comprising a floor and two walls set at right-angles. The walls were built out of straw and had a window and a plasterboard interior. We developed a cladding for the bales that made the bales visible on the exterior. The cladding was a rain screen consisting of tongued-and-grooved twin wall polycarbonate sheets held at a distance of 100mm outside the bales by a system of purlins.

We managed to obtain sponsorship for the bales, flooring, windows, structure and plasterboard; quite an achievement given the unorthodox construction techniques. Gillian, Jeremy and I drove to the NEC in Birmingham in a hired van and spent a week building it [*Fig 16* Gillian at Interbuild]. Surreally, we stayed in a National Trust property twenty miles away. The completion of our exhibit was received by the trade with a mixture of scepticism and incomprehension but we felt a special sense of achievement [*Fig 17* finished exhibit – interior, *Fig 18* finished exhibit – exterior]. After an immense amount of R&D we had basically worked out how we were going to build with bales. Once that was established, the production of information for pricing and construction could progress.

Money

Having achieved an ambitious planning permission and worked out the building size and its strategic construction methods, the moment when we were to see if it could be built crept closer. A pre-construction estimate is a reality check and this seemed the right moment to test the scheme against our budget. We had been recommended a trusted QS. In February 1998 a cost plan was drawn up. When the estimate was presented – £1.3 million – we were incredulous. This was serious because we didn't have anything like that sort of money. Frustrated at the mismatch between their vision (main contractor, JCT contract, traditional tender, good finishes, risk management) and ours (self-build, partnering, open-book accounting, cheap and cheerful), we sent the team back to their spreadsheets for another look. We met to discuss a way forward, including considering procurement and self-building. New estimates were returned: £1.1m, later revised down to £880,000.

Naïve though we were (and we were certainly not cost consultants) we were convinced that the QSs were wrong in their predictions and began to think of different procurement options that could help bring costs down. We felt we might get a more accurate assessment by appointing a contractor at this relatively early stage, working together with them to design the scheme to meet our budget. We thought a contractor's estimate might more accurately reflect current market prices and bring real building knowledge to the project. We discussed the building with a few contractors, but none of them felt confident in handling the unusual materials and techniques we had envisaged, openly advising us that greater risk meant higher costs. The building was more complicated than a single house, since now it also involved an office, and its proximity to a railway line where work needed inspection provided additional problems for a contractor.

Then Howard Meadowcroft, who at that time was working for Architype, suggested we contact Martin Hughes. We knew Martin as the man who had constructed Architype's extension to the Horniman Museum in south London. When it was published this project had caught our eye owing to its clever approach to procurement as well as its ecological design. We approached Martin and he came to see us. Always ready for a challenge, he didn't seem fazed by the project and said he would be interested in building it. He went away to price it and came back a month later with a cost plan totalling £637,000. This was still way over our budget but was at least looking as if it was within striking distance. So we set about making radical cuts, paring it down to its essentials – at one point, in desperation, putting the plans on the photocopier and reducing the area by 10 per cent. We cut out everything extraneous while we worked closely with Martin, exploring comparative estimates for different construction methods that might bring the project closer to our budget. After four months, the building was down to 430 square metres (not counting the unoccupied ground levels) and the cost plan stalled at £480,000: we could find nothing more to economise on. It was still above our budget but it did include a contingency. We felt nervous, but without redesigning the building in its entirety we had arrived at the moment when we had to make an act of faith. We needed to begin construction now or we would never do so.

Builders

Throughout May and June 1998 we worked alongside Martin to adjust the cost plan as we progressed with the working drawings and identified our supply chain. Martin proposed taking the role of Contract Project Manager, using a very lean team of four or five carpenters as the core labour force while procuring specialist subcontracts package by package as information was issued. We agreed to an arrangement where we, the client, and he, the contractor, would take equal risk in managing the project's cost. This meant splitting equally the cost of overspending or the benefit of underspending. The idea was that this would be a non-adversarial arrangement (a 'partnering contract') where we acted in tandem towards the common goal of completing what was, after all, a challenging project for both of us. Martin wrote the contract, since no standard contracts were available at the time. It was eventually delivered to us in May 1999, and remained unsigned and un-referred to. Notwithstanding a few frustrating events we remained on good terms, true to the spirit rather than the letter of the contract.

The programme Martin drew up showed a three-month demolition contract followed by a year on site. It was agreed that we should start working on drawings with a view to issuing packages for pricing in an order determined by Martin. Gillian Horn would act as Project Architect, distancing Jeremy and myself from the day-to-day involvement of running the contract while attempting to maintain the distance required of a client/contractor relationship. Jeremy reduced his teaching to 0.5 full-time for six months so he could stay close to the design development. This allowed us to research the project's complex technical solutions while Gillian managed contractual relations face to face. In reality relations were not quite as clear-cut as this.

Jeremy took on the Building Regulations submission, making a set of annotated drawings that addressed each of the Approved Documents. The drawing submission made, we awaited the response with great anticipation. When it came, the main concerns were the bales, the composting toilet, the gabion cages and the fire escape from the tower. Prem Seyan, our Building Control Officer, asked to see all the evidence for the performance of bales: Agrément Certificates, manufacturers' standards and so forth. Needless to say, as an agricultural by-product, such evidence did not exist. We agreed to forward all the paperwork we could find where bales had been used successfully elsewhere, and downloaded masses of information from bale building websites across the USA, justifying our own approach with reference to the British climate and regulatory structures. Mr Seyan accepted this evidence and approved their use, principally, he told us, because the bales were not load-bearing. We manoeuvred around the issue of the composting toilet (whose existence was not recognised under Building Regulations) by providing a standard WC, which did conform, in the second bathroom.

The gabions and the fire escape were more problematic. Essentially Mr Seyan did not accept that the gabion cages were of sufficient robustness to support the office, despite Price & Myers' calculations and the manufacturer's test results that proved otherwise. His argument was that, located so close to a railway line, a fire could occur in the undercroft or the building could be ram raided, causing the wire to melt and the rubble to be released, sending the building crashing down on a passing train. We thought this highly unlikely but he did have a point about disrupting a public utility; we did not want to be responsible for causing the deaths of unsuspecting commuters. And since we didn't feel precious about 'truthful' building construction, we agreed to build a concrete column within the gabion cages. This way, if the gabion fill proved sacrificial, the building would not collapse.

Finally, after lengthy arguments about the method of escaping safely from the tower if the house caught fire, we settled on providing a fire door at roof level below the landing and directing an escape route across the roof garden and out via the office stairs.

Raiding the bank
Things were getting real and we needed to realise our assets as well as to borrow enough to finance the project. We approached all the high street banks with our business plan, including those with whom we had been investors for many years. None of the banks would advance us any money for the project: it was too unusual, too risky. It looked as if we were going to be stuck. Then we spotted an advertisement for the Ecology Building Society. They made a positive point of supporting sustainable buildings (including ones built out of bales). Without much fuss and for very little additional cost they agreed to lend us the requisite funds to see the project through.

Meanwhile we needed to sell our existing house. This was our first home, in an unglamorous location in north London, but we had lavished a lot of attention on its refurbishment over the course of eight years, including carrying out all the plumbing and electrics and a lot of the building work with our own hands. It was a wrench to let it go. The estate agent put it on the market for what we thought was an absurdly high price, but we were assured this would be realised in time. We needed enough money in the bank by March 1999 in order not to delay the contract. The market was rising, so things looked good.

The demolition contract began on 12 October 1998 [*Fig 19* demolition]. Not long after we put our house on the market we received an offer. Worried that we might not get another such offer again and determined to avoid a bridging loan, we accepted it. Soon we would have nowhere to live and no office to work from. In haste we moved the office to the smallest possible unit in the Omnibus Workspace in North Road, five minutes' walk from the site. We took a three-month lease on an apartment in Bloomsbury, on the assumption that this would allow us to find a permanent rental property in due course. By now Jeremy and I had appointments at Sheffield and Jeremy was spending most of the week in Yorkshire.

In January 1999, in the pouring rain, the actual construction got going, commencing with the bedroom wing. The plan was to complete this end first, then complete the office, which would allow us to move in and save us our office rental; then finish the infill section which comprised the main part of the house. The building was set out on site by Martin with a laser and the

19

20

21

22

drainage runs were dug through the mud to connect into the existing manholes at the correct invert levels. It still remains a mystery to me how anyone can work through so much primordial mess to determine dimensions with any degree of accuracy.

Work on the bed wing was different from the remainder of the building because it was the only section where the structure was built off a ground-bearing slab. I remember Martin phoning me at 7.30 a.m. in early January to ask for the details of the slab-to-wall junction. We had been so involved in designing the complex and improvised elements of the building – the bale wall details, composting toilets, gabions and roofing details – that we hadn't even thought about the simple junctions with the ground. The clock was ticking. Every hour men stood idle on site was costing us money. As I hurried into the office that day I was panicking hard and I seemed to be in a permanent state of panic from then on, racing as we were against the clock. But the details were sent out before lunchtime and they seemed to work. At one level this felt easy: issue a drawing and a couple of days later it was being built; at another, building followed so fast on drawings that there was no room for error. For a long time we were only just ahead of the contractor [*Fig 20* site with slab].

The environmental design had progressed with advice from a number of sources that had given us their time for free: Randall Thomas at Max Fordham's; Tadj Oresczin at The Bartlett and Michael Popper. We had read everything we could lay our hands on about how to design passive ecological buildings but we could not afford a services engineer. Predictive modelling software was not readily available and even if it had been, we could not have afforded it. The aim of the project, to design a passive environmental building, meant a fair degree of guesswork, and in many ways the building is a built experiment. We designed the building as a breathing wall structure, which was the current vogue at that time. An airtight building was not a major consideration. We did the heat loss calculations (which were radically underestimated) and sized the radiators ourselves; we planned the routes of the services runs and specified the boilers. Richard Pearce confirmed the sizes of our pipe-work.

The bed wing went up quickly with the men on site being tutored by us in bale construction. They were masters at working in timber, and things progressed at a swift pace [*Fig 21* bed wing studwork]. Confidence rose. Before long we had a small stand-alone structure the size of one of the small cottages on Stock Orchard Street at the far end of the muddy site. This would contain the two bedrooms, one on each floor, a hall, utility room, a small office, two bathrooms (one yet to be installed) and two closets. Next it was the turn for the foundations of the office element. I was in Montreal giving a lecture at the Canadian Centre for Architecture when I took a call from Gillian: the diggers had exposed a huge circular brick structure which disappeared into the earth under where the office was going to be [*Fig 22* underground structure]. What should we do? Desperate to keep the work on track I advised that they simply fill it with concrete and keep going.

23

24

25

At the end of March 1999 we had to move from our temporary accommodation in Bloomsbury and the question was: where to? Then there was an arson attack on site. It destroyed the contents and structure of the carpenters' workshop that had been constructed against the flank wall of No. 8. We were lucky not to have lost more. Suddenly things looked grim. Despite insurance, building sites attract mischief and the contractor had already had a number of tools stolen. We could not afford to lose the building halfway through construction. The timber and bales of the bed wing were exposed and especially vulnerable, and all the while the site stood unprotected at nights and weekends. We certainly had not factored into our calculations round-the-clock security and, if we paid for this, something drastic would need to be omitted from the contract.

It was decided that the only way we could secure the site was by inhabiting it, so we bought a second-hand mobile home and Martin's men connected it to the electrics and drainage, positioning it at the far end of the site adjacent to the bed wing. Thus, during the week, I became the sole site security operative. It felt vulnerable but I had to put this out of my mind because there was no alternative [*Fig 23* mobile home]. At least I was on site to monitor progress and discuss things with Martin and the crew when they arrived at 7 a.m. each morning.

Working adjacent to a railway line brought its own issues. Everything we did within six metres of the line required the permission of Network Rail. We had wanted to extend the building up to the railway line but were told we were not permitted to build within 5m of the boundary. After some negotiation it was agreed that we would build no closer than 3m. Network Rail now required a full-height, completely covered scaffold to the railway side held down with ballast, to prevent anything falling on to the track [*Fig 24* scaffold along railway]. Finally every activity we carried out within 3m of the line was monitored by at least one inspector, at our own cost. This sent expenses through the roof.

Moreover, the trains vibrated through the site and the noise was disturbing. While we could mitigate the latter by locating the bedrooms to the rear of the site and detailing the office to address the acoustic issues, the only way to deal with the vibration was to put the building on springs. Paul Gillieron took readings across the site at different distances from the railway lines and made his recommendations. A German firm, GERB, submitted a quotation for the springs which were to be located above the gabion columns (for the office) and underneath the columns of the main house. The cost came to £10,000. Our budget had not allowed for this. An agonising choice confronted us: if we opted for the springs we would use up all of our contingency at an early stage, but retro-fitting was not an option. If we did this now, it was likely that we would have to omit something else. In December 1998 we reluctantly accepted the quotation. As it turned out, this was a wise decision [*Fig 25* spring at the base of house column].

The steelwork package was procured and a major leap forward took place when in May 1999 the trucks delivered all the pieces in several loads, starting

26

27

28

with the house frame, then moving on to the tower and finishing with the office [*Fig 26* house steel frame being installed, *Fig 27* base frame for office on top of gabions]. The tower was assembled in three flat panels by laying all the parts out along the length of Stock Orchard Street and bolting them together [*Fig 28* tower frame being assembled]. An 80ft crane lifted the panels up over the building, slotting them into place between the roof beams [*Fig 29* tower frame being installed]. Since we were forbidden to use any equipment that came closer than 5m to the railway, the pylons had to be swung up over the roofs of the cottages. That was a really exhilarating moment [*Fig 30* tower and house frame].

Once the steel frame was up, we were ready to build the remaining bale wall. We invited a group of about fifteen friends, students, enthusiastic acquaintances and family to a communal building weekend and watched, delighted, at the incongruity of it all, as the overloaded truck trundled on to our urban site laden with beautiful, golden-yellow barley bales, shedding whisps of loose straw as it went. It was a hot weekend and we worked hard, but by the end we had finished the entire wall, a length of about 20m, and felt really proud of what we had done [*Fig 31* bale wall weekend]. At the end of July the office steelwork was completed and we were able to progress with the beam-and-block floors, then the studwork infill [*Fig 32* office steel and timber frame].

The plasterers turned up and rendered the wall with lime render. It was very hot and nobody thought about hanging wet hessian sacks over the render, so it dried out too fast and cracked. This had not happened in the bedrooms which had been rendered in cooler, damper conditions. We were annoyed. Martin and his crew disappeared from site to attend to another job nearby that they were running in parallel with ours. Initially this seemed a relief, since it gave us more time to work up our drawing packages. We then endured the wettest of summers. Did it rain every day? I can't be sure but it felt like it. Water cascaded down the poorly protected bale wall. Before the end of the summer the bales had rotted and had to be replaced. My beloved bicycle was stolen from outside the trailer. Then thieves broke into the trailer and took the few precious possessions that I had not put into storage. The odd workman showed up now and again and carried out a desultory amount of work. The larder was built around its hardboard-clad formwork and masonite floors were installed in September, but progress on the remainder of the building seemed to have slowed to almost a halt [*Fig 33* house with larder and bale wall]. It was evident that the building would not be complete by the end of the year. The glacial pace, combined with living in the confined space of the caravan in the bad weather depressed us, and as the bales rotted away frustration and anger grew. Autumn arrived and the weather turned cold. The mobile home was damp: the electric blanket needed to be on for four hours to remove the moisture from the bed before I could get into it. My clothes began to smell of mildew.

By November 1999, things were at a low ebb. I gave Martin an ultimatum: make the bed wing habitable within a week. Two weeks later I was living there. At last I had a warm, dry, secure place to inhabit. We sold the trailer

29

30

to a construction company and celebrated the new millennium living in the new building. But the practice was struggling to stay afloat, with such an all-engrossing project that provided no revenue on the go. First, Michael Richards departed; then, unbelievably, Gillian, who had been loyally helping us build the practice for four years: we were not earning enough to pay her salary. Deflated and miserable, I moved the office into the bed wing, took over the running of the project and worked there alone, climbing up a builder's ladder to the first-floor bedroom to sleep and cooking on a second-hand Baby Belling in the utility room [*Fig 34* temporary working from the house lobby].

By now it was clear that the building was going to be, at the very least, six months late. We had sold our house far too early. This was galling, as house prices were rising fast, and, had we waited, we could have avoided caravan living and at the same time had more money for building. Construction prices were spiralling upward and it was becoming increasingly difficult to procure our work packages for the tight budget Martin had been hoping for. The same packages of work were tendered several times, simplifying the details with each go. We made cut after cut: now the tower was in place it would have to be weatherproofed but we could not build the staircase and library; the light shelf over the house windows was omitted; the handrails to the roof, mezzanine and deck were lost; the floor finishes to the ground floor were in abeyance and we decided to complete several of the finishes ourselves. The entrance to the office was left without an enclosure and treads to the office stair were abandoned. Our dreams of fitted furniture evaporated. The garden would have to wait.

32

34

31

33

35

36

In February 2000 Warmcell insulation was sprayed into the office walls and finally the underfloor heating pipe-work and screeding took place [*Fig 35* screeding the office floor, February 2000]. Time moved on and the roofing membranes were installed in March [*Fig 36* house roof].

There were small moments of joy among the challenges. The builders came up with a simple system for gauging the sand/lime/cement mix for the sandbags and then filling them. We found ingenious ways of fixing the bags and the finished effect surpassed our dreams. The cloth cladding, which everyone told us was impossible to make, was fixed by consummate craftsmen from Martin's team and its appearance was gorgeous [*Fig 37* mounting the cloth cladding April 2000].

Work continued. By the end of August 2000 the office was finally ready to occupy; shelving and desks were installed in the mezzanine storey and we moved in. September came and, to mark the completion, Siobhan Davies celebrated her fiftieth birthday with a huge dinner served on long tables on the lower level of our brand-new space. The autumn dragged on and the house progressed slowly. The tower was clad, the soil for the roof garden was dumped in place and the windows and doors finally went in after a lengthy period of anxious detailing to avoid cold bridging and improve buildability [*Fig 38* the house, October 2000]. Having rejected our preferred boiler and replaced it with his favoured state-of-the-art model from Germany, The M&E subcontractor disappeared and could not be enticed back. The front fence went in and the site was, at last, secured. Two steps forward and one step back, the frustrations continued to mount despite the halting progress. I was exhausted, as much from loneliness and frustration as from the mental strain of the slow grind of trying to get the job done.

The end of 2000 approached and we had run out of money. Making last-minute decisions to lose anything inessential, we had to stop because we had spent everything we had and could borrow. Christmas loomed and Martin's men made a heroic effort to complete the house. We spent our last remaining money on a wood-burning stove that would keep the house warm. The plumber returned in the nick of time, only to disappear again without fully commissioning the system or explaining to us how it worked. The roof was still leaking, the floor was incomplete and plasterboard was missing from one area. The entrance to the office was open to the elements and all the external works were omitted.

On the verge of taking possession we had to arrange building insurance. It was a surprise to find that AXA was prepared to quote only slightly over the odds. Perhaps this Swedish company was used to houses full of cellulose materials! Perhaps the construction was so far from the norm that it was all the same to them. Or perhaps it was our postcode that proved the defining factor.

Mr Seyan, the Building Control Officer, visited the site for the final time. At this stage we were missing decks and handrails everywhere, one bathroom and the entire tower were incomplete, the garden was a mess, the solar

37

38

thermal heating wasn't working and the solar shading had been abandoned long ago, but as far as his remit was concerned, he was satisfied. Final sign-off would have to wait until later. Tentatively, at the end of the visit, Mr Seyan confessed to being a fan of ecological building.

We arranged for our stored furniture to be delivered to the new house just before Christmas 2000 and celebrated the end of the contract by inviting the builders to Christmas dinner at the dining table we had not set eyes on for twenty-seven months [*Fig 39* after Christmas Dinner, December 2000]. We cooked lunch in the new kitchen for Martin and his core craftsmen, with whom we had lived twinned lives for more than two years. They had done a wonderful job but I was worn out and I couldn't wait to get my life back. The house felt empty without them, but a new chapter was opening up. After all the agony, I had to learn to love the building. It would be a further two years before I was able to admit that I did.

Having reached some sort of finality we settled back into everyday life. My sleep pattern had been permanently altered after getting up at 6.30 a.m. for so long, and Jeremy was spending most of the week in Sheffield, so I had a chance to observe the buildings at close hand. It was interesting watching how the building responded to the views, the changing seasons, the light and the weather. It was torture hearing the rain drum on the polycarb roof of the entrance hall in the full knowledge that the roof was still leaking. But the bedrooms, enveloped in straw and with their solid shutters offered respite, and we realised that we had overlooked their beneficial acoustic properties. Islington's Council Charge Officer made a visit, declaring the house a 'First Floor Flat (unfinished), Band D' and gave me a single occupant's discount.

39

We set to work on the garden, designing a scheme that had a detectable geometry when viewed from the living room but which could still accommodate variety. The garden would be a form of potager, combining productive and ornamental plants so that we could take pleasure in every sensory aspect it could provide. The first year we had no slugs, and the potatoes were prolific.

Year on year we made progress in completing the building: the office staircase was enclosed, its timber stair treads fixed in place, the solar shading installed, the roof leaks mended, the solar water heating got working, the tower with its library shelving constructed, furniture commissioned, the pond waterproofed. Little by little things have taken on their intended shape, and order has returned. We have learned how to live in this building and it has taught us many things. Most important of all is this: a building is not a car, the perfect product that functions to predictable criteria. Rather, it is a living organism that has a character, a life and a set of responses all of its own. The occupation of a property is a process of developing a shared intimacy and respect. It takes time, care, maintenance and learning, but it rewards with surprises and insights.

It has been a while since we reckoned up but at the last count we think we have spent close to £680,000. Thus the cost has stabilised midway between Martin's and the QS's last estimates. On the other hand, without Martin's more optimistic calculations, the project would probably never have been constructed. This goes to show that, sometimes, a little fantasy goes a long way…

Autumn colours, 2008

Previous page **Over the Caledonian Road railway bridge**
Above **Towers, June 2008**
Right **Jeremy giving Open House Day tour, May 2008**

Garden, March 2008

Above **Garden in the snow, February 2009**
Right **Bed wing, winter 2009**

Left **Planting, May 2008**
Above **Lawn clipping, May 2008**

Below **Seedlings, May 2008**
Right **Newly pointed wall, 2008**

Left **Compost heaps, April 2009**
Below **Roller, April 2009**

Tower study, Sarah Wigglesworth

44

Telling tales

Jeremy Till and
Sarah Wigglesworth

January 1994

Architects find something compelling about auction catalogues. Those red lines around sites marking out territories waiting to be filled with projects, catalysts for dreams. We have been catalogue aficionados for years and have recently ridden the thrill of the auction itself, building up hopes, only for them to be deflated in the instant of the hammer.

February 1994

This is our third attempt. Hopes built less high. The site is in North London next to the main east coast railway line and is being sold by British Rail to realise their capital assets prior to privatisation. The site is currently occupied by a forge whose lease expires in six months. Surrounded by undistinguished housing, the site – at twenty metres by forty metres – could accommodate five new houses or ten apartments. Expecting a lot of competition for it, we make a desultory visit a week before the auction (grudgingly shown round by a glowering tenant), do the barest planning enquiries, back-of-the envelope financial calculations and set a spend limit around the guide price.

1.00 pm 15 February 1994

Auction tactics: (1) Set financial limit and stick to it. (2) Avoid rush of temptation to the heart and then head. (3) Only enter bidding when it is down to three people. (4) Worry about all those stories of being landed with an uninhabited island in the Shetlands while picking one's nose – gesture clearly. (5) When down to the last two, if the other person looks frantic, act nonchalant. If the other person looks nonchalant, appear firm but not desperate.

2.14 pm 15 February 1994
Tactics work. We get it for less
than we expected. Jeremy leaves a
message for Sarah at Kingston. He
is lightheaded, but worried about
the lack of other interest (do
they know something that we
don't?).

15 March 1994
Final legal paperwork in
transferring the site. A detailed
reading of the covenants reveals
potential problems as to how
close to the railway we can
build.

23 March 1994
Auctions are very efficient
methods of buying. A month later
we own the site. We phone the
tenants, announcing ourselves as
the new landlords. A difficult
conversation ensues. They have
been on the site for fifty years
and have no intention of moving.

26 March 1994
Visit the site to force a
confrontation between our liberal
leanings and the realities of
property owning. Chris, the
owner, shows us around. The forge
is one of the last in the country
making leaf springs for classic
cars. It is brutal, Victorian
work. We leave having agreed to
extend their lease for twelve
months while they find
alternative premises. In the
meantime, we hold back from
making designs for the site until
its future is more certain.

December 1995
After eighteen months, Brost
Forge have still to find another
site. We extend their lease by a
further six months and start our
own search on their behalf.

27 January 1996
The long period of undrawn
gestation has meant we have
first talked the building into
existence rather than drawing it;
sitting alongside each other in
a conference, Sarah draws the
first sketch which captures
those tales.

26 June 1996
Extend Brost Forge's lease for a
further six months. Commission
Christine Sullivan to photograph
the site and its working.

July 1996
The designs of one's own house
set up inescapable tensions –
between hopes and reality,
between role of client and role
of architect, between pushing
the boat out and yanking it back
in. The first moves are therefore
a kind of therapy to ease us
into an acknowledgement of
these tensions.

August 1996
Generic principles of
the design begin to emerge:
...a confusion of home and work...

...the idea of the house as
a domestic equivalent of the
Bürolandschaft...

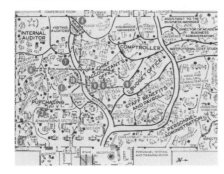

...with a regular grid interrupted
by domestic difficulties...

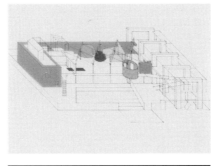

...and the pervading image of the
house as a dining room table.

6 September 1996
Walk out of Salisbury and see
a straw temple.

September 1996

The building begins to settle
on the site in plan.

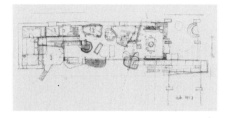

November 1996

First contact with Keijo, our
partner in our EU research grant
application. Keijo has been
quietly building straw bale
buildings in Finland for the past
ten years, pioneering the method
on his own. To date his buildings
are the only ones in Europe to
use bales.

December 1996

Reluctantly extend Brost Forge's
lease for another six months.

26 February 1997

The undistinguished houses
abutting the site in fact form
part of a conservation area.
Decide to employ a planning
consultant, Peter. At our first
meeting with him, we decide to go
for an all-or-nothing strategy,
with no prior consultation with
the planners. We will hit them
with a full document and
drawings.

1 March 1997

Achieve breakthrough with the plan, bringing back the landscape
of the dining room table littered with domestic artifacts.

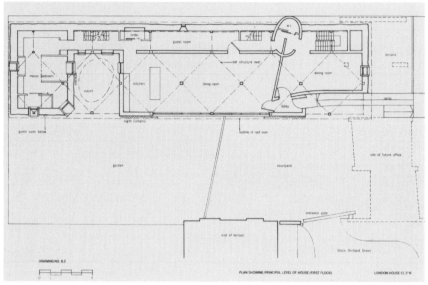

4 March 1997

In a snatch of conversation over supper we finally ditch our
attachment to the wavy roof and move to a titled flat plane.
It feels as if a burden has been lifted.

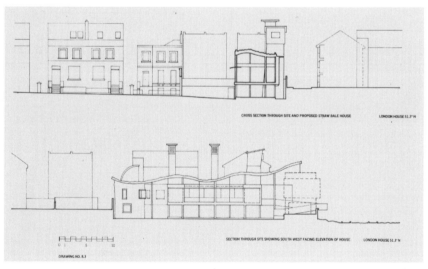

17 March 1997

Brost Forge finally move out of the site. They have found a smaller
building on an industrial estate half a mile down the road. The
exchange of keys is awkward; they are convinced that we are going
to sell the site on at a huge profit.

19 March 1997

Thus far we only have sketch models of the house. For our submission to the *Best Young Practices Directory*, we ask Carlos and Steve to build a new model. The briefing session on the model turns out to be more like a review, with Carlos and Steve musing over cups of coffee as to which parts of the project they like or do not like. We remind them that we are paying to have a model made, not to get angst.

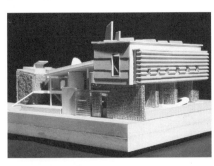

23 March 1997

Spend the day on the site tidying up. Traces of Brost Forge remain - sad and accusing.

3 April 1997

Postcard from Carlos thanking us for payment. He writes: 'We grew to like the building a lot, gawky junctions and all.'

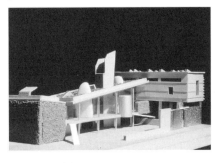

4 April 1997

Ring Carlos. 'What fucking gawky junctions?'

April 1997

Show model to Peter, our planning consultant. He goes strangely quiet and looks worried. It is clear that this is the first time he has realised the true extent of the challenge that he has taken on. We decide not to include the model as part of the planning submission.

10 April 1997

Meet Keijo in London. It turns out that he is a sports teacher in a small town in the middle of nowhere in Finland. He is straw bale mad. His ambition is to build a straw bale sports hall for his students. We show Keijo the site. His face drops; it is so far from the plains of middle Finland. We repair to the pub. Keijo sits brooding over his beer and then suddenly a smile spreads over his face. 'I have an idea,' he says, 'straw bale pub.' And suddenly the world is OK again.

10.00 pm 1 May 1997

Election night. We set up drawing-boards in front of the television in a final push to finish the planning permission drawings.

11.00 pm 1 May 1997

A Labour landslide looks likely. We start to drink.

1.00 am 2 May 1997

Lines start to waver.

3.30 am 2 May 1997

Tory Minister Michael Portillo loses his seat in the biggest upset of the night. Drawings by now completely abandoned.

12 May 1997

Our self-imposed deadline to get the planning drawings finished expires tomorrow. We still have to design the tower and spend a frantic day and night struggling with ugly versions. We are still not satisfied, but decide not to worry because the tower is part of our sacrificial strategy with the planners - at five storeys we do not expect it to be accepted. It is intended to form our first point of negotiation and if necessary be given up. We have also put in some completely hopeless car-turning circles as a diversionary tactic.

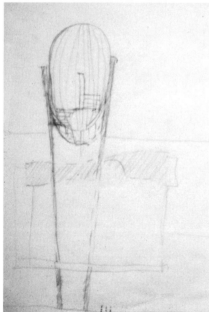
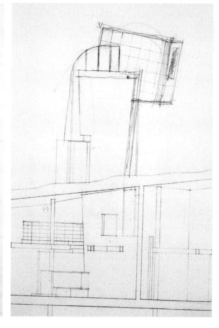

16 May 1997

Sarah's birthday. We finally submit the planning application. On the assumption that it will go to appeal, we may get a decision by January 1998.

31 May 1997

Straw bale building workshop at the Centre for Alternative Technology. The course is run by Barbara Jones, Britain's expert on the technique. She appears suspicious of us as architects, believing straw is the domain of the non-expert.

10 June 1997

Send forty letters to all our neighbours inviting them to an open day on the site to show them the planning drawings.

23 June 1997

Open day on the site. We have prepared some cute crayon drawings and have made an unthreatening model in white card showing the building in relation to its surroundings. We build a straw bale wall and mount the model and drawings on it. About fifteen people turn up, all glad to be involved. Comments centre around the colours on the drawings (liked), the mess of the present site and buildings (disliked), the proposed chickens (already adopted by the kids) and the wine (appreciated). Generally people are very positive. They feel anything is an improvement on having industry at the end of their road. Straw bales and towers are low on their list of worries. We realise at the end that the drawings have been completely superfluous, but the event essential.

6.30 pm 23 June 1997

N is one of the last to leave the site. He is six years old, pug faced with a snub nose that looks like it has already been in fights.

'He is really a little softy underneath that,' his mother says, 'He's got a Lego set.'

'You going to have a party when the house is built then?' N asks.

'Sure,' I say.

'Can I come?'

'Course you can.'

'What time will it be?'

'What time is good for you?'

'Well, I get back from school at three thirty, so about four.'

'OK, four it will be.'

N smiles.

'When's the party going to be then?'

'About two years' time.'

His face falls and he turns to walk away, shoulders dropped, disbelieving of a time-scale which is so far beyond that of his Lego.

3 July 1997
Ring the planner. Nervous, because this is our first contact with the Planning Department.
'I was ringing to see how you are getting on with the application for 9 Stock Orchard Street.'
'It's fine, we have no problems with it,' he replies.
'I was wondering,' I reply, slightly disbelieving, 'if we should have a meeting to move it along?'
'No, we don't need one. I will be recommending to the chief planner that we approve, and if he agrees we will do it under delegated powers.'
'We *are* talking about the same scheme here are we?'
'Yes, it's the one with the wild strawberries on the roof.'
'So is the consultation period over?' I ask.
'Yes, and no objections, just a few letters of support from your neighbours.'
'...and you aren't going to conservation advisory panel?'
'There's no need. We are very excited about the scheme and I guess you are too.'
'Certainly am,' I reply.
Now it is his turn to sound disbelieving. 'And are you really going to build it?'
'Yes.'
'Well you should have the permission with you in a couple of weeks' time.'
I put the the phone down. The others in the office are looking at me in shocked disbelief.

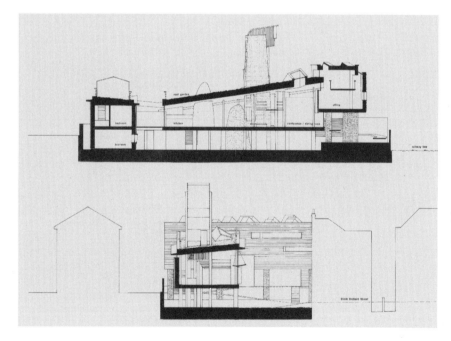

16 July 1997
An unconditional planning permission arrives within the eight-week statutory period. Ring Peter. He says it is the greatest success of his career.

1 August 1997
Meet the Railtrack surveyor on site to discuss the way forward. He brings with him a massive book on working methods for buildings on sites next to railways. He also has a measuring tape, which he wields like a weapon.

15 September 1997
First publicity on the house comes out in *Perspectives on Architecture*, the journal funded by the Prince of Wales.

16 September 1997
Redesign of the office, which at first sight looked a real problem, results in a major improvement in the scheme.

2 October 1997
The *Daily Telegraph* has picked up on the *Perspectives* piece and wants to do an article as a scoop. A photographer is dispatched to take pictures of us on the site. Four rolls of film later he leaves, musing with us over issues of sustainability. 'I mean,' he says, pointing at his photographer's little red sports car, 'it's a disgrace, they could make those tyres last forever if they wanted, but they make them with built-in obsolescence. It's such a waste,' he says, kicking the hub caps, and then noisily spurts off up the road.

9.00 am 3 October 1997

Telegraph piece comes out in the main news section. Sarah annoyed at the photograph with fat neck, Jeremy upset that of 144 shots taken not one is good enough to include him. Article quite fair.

9.30 am 3 October 1997

The telephone goes ballistic. BBC News wants us on site in two hours. Three radio interviews fixed up in the next twenty-four hours. *Islington Gazette* sends around hardened journo, who opens his questioning with: 'This is just a gimmick isn't it?'

12 noon, 3 October 1997

Meet the BBC on site. Overhear the reporter talking to her editor on her mobile phone: 'No they aren't a bunch of eccentrics, so we can't pursue that line.'

5.45 pm 3 October 1997

Douglas Cameron, LBC News radio: 'And we have all heard of three little piggies, now architect and lecturer Jeremy Till is planning to build a straw house in London. Jeremy, isn't this a very *stupid* idea?'

4.00 pm 7 October 1997

At the end of a lecture at The Bartlett on architectural plans, in which I have debunked their status and utility, Jonathan Hill pointedly asks how we have designed our house. Of course, despite all the other tactics we have used, the plan has always been there and we can trace the lineage of the design as it unfolded through plans alone.

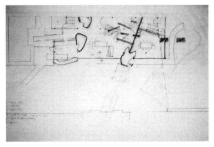

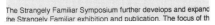

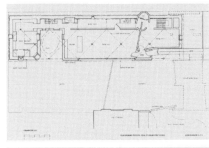

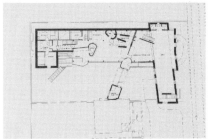

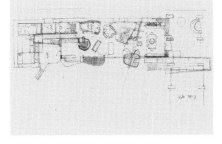

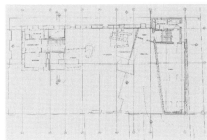

9 October 1997

Islington Gazette: 'It's the dream house that sounds like a NIGHTMARE. When the builders have finished, number 9 Stock Orchard Street off Caledonian Road will be... a pile of straw.'

■ JEREMY Till and Sarah Wrigglesworth: planning the ultimate environmentally friendly home.
Picture **Tony Ga...**

Dreaming of a house of straw

IT'S the dream home that sounds like a nightmare. When the builders have finished, number 9 Stock Orchard Street off Caledonian Road will be a....pile of straw.

By CHRIS GOODALL

But for Islington architects Sarah Wrigglesworth and Jeremy Till, the three-bedroom house will be a dream come true.

It will be cheap, cosy, trendy and sustainable and probably the only place in Britain where you can grow strawberries on the roof.

"It's not a gimmick," said Mr Till, who lives and works with Sarah in Fairbridge Road, Archway. "It's an absolutely serious project. Straw houses are unusual but they are beginning to take off in America. There's been one in Nebraska for 100 years.

"Straw is an excellent insulator. It's quick to build and it's incredibly green. We're out to show that low energy buildings don't have to be boring."

About 700 bales of straw will be needed to build the house which will provide both a home and working environment for Sarah and Jeremy. They will be specially treated so that they are no more of a fire hazard than more conventional building materials. One wall will be built out of sandbags to reduce noise from the railway next door.

In keeping with the eco-friendly aim, the smallest room in the house will feature a "composting" lavatory. The couple plan to grow strawberries on the roof which will also be made of straw.

The cost of the project is expected to be around £220,000. Naturally they went to the Ecology Building Society for a mortgage.

Fears that Islington Council planners might raise their eyebrows at the sight of plans for a house of straw were unfounded.

"They were excellent," said Mr Till. "We had absolutely no problems."

Islington Gazette

10.00 am 9 October 1997

Phone call from Interbuild, the largest building trade exhibition in Europe. They offer us a place on their show stand 'Façades of the Future'. This will involve building a full-size prototype. The show opens in four weeks. We ask for time to consider the feasibility; we haven't even *designed* the wall yet.

12.30 pm 9 October 1997

Ring back Interbuild and confirm that we are willing to go ahead, on the condition that we are placed next to the Future Systems' prototype of the Lord's Media Centre, which is described as seven metres long and shiny.

11 October 1997

In normal practice, straw bales are rendered inside and outside. However, for both technical reasons (it will ventilate the outside face of the bales) and aesthetic reasons (we will be able to see the bales) we are developing a system of rain screen cladding. We telephone a large polycarbonate manufacturer to get sponsorship for Interbuild. He is circumspect when we tell him about the straw bales. 'We do not want our product associated with a marginal application – I'm afraid we cannot help,' he states, and puts the phone down.

9.30 am 13 October 1997

The sizing of the window is first on the critical path for the Interbuild exhibit. To get it delivered on time we need to give its size to the manufacturer today, but then we need the size of the timber box surround, which depends on the spacing of the timber ladders, which depends on the size of the straw bales. What is the size of a straw bale?

11.30 am 13 October 1997

The internet may appear a strange place to look for straw bales, but the electronic Yellow Pages yields a huge list of fodder merchants. Farmers contacted are not used to such exacting questions about dimensions of their bales ('It's a natural thing, you know, they are sized to fit the back of my Land Rover') and remain cautious about our request that they should all be the same size ('The horses don't usually mind,' they say).

12 noon 13 October 1997

We have tracked down a centralised straw bale merchant. He calls the bales commodities, which slightly dampens our romantic ideal of buying direct from the land, but at least commodities can be sized and delivered on time at a more competitive price.

5 November 1997

The joiner with whom we have placed the order for the window surround phones. He announces that he now cannot make it. This is serious, since we could never find someone else to make it in the given time. I get tough:

'We have a contract.'

'But it's taking up all our time,' he says.

'What's the problem? You told Gillian that it would be fine.'

'There are too many numbers,' he says, 'they're all over the drawing.'

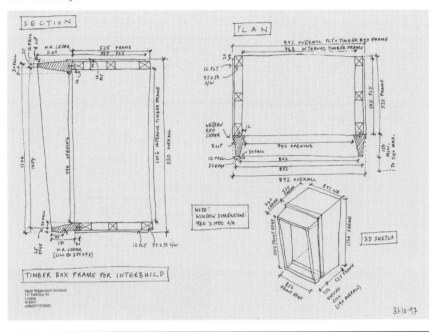

6 November 1997

Gillian goes round with a new drawing with hardly any numbers on it. Everything is OK.

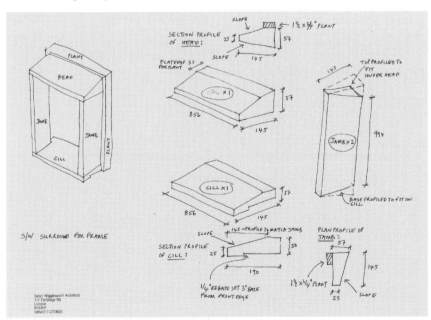

10 November 1997

Meet Railtrack on site with our engineers, Price & Myers. Railtrack back off a bit. It appears that it may be possible to build the office as long as we first erect a structural scaffolding fully clad to withstand the impact of anything or anyone falling off the building.

11 November 1997

Timber ladders for Interbuild arrive. They are a proprietary Swedish system called Masonite, which champions its green credentials. The huge truck in which they are delivered has travelled 250 miles, completely empty but for our six beams.

8.20 am 17 November 1997

Arrive at the National Exhibition Centre, a vast hall full of articulated lorries. Our van looks tiny.

9.00 am 17 November 1997

Set out our pitch. A month's work suddenly feels extraordinarily small.

10.00 am 17 November 1997

Lay out base blocks and perforated metal rodent screen. It is apparent that Sarah and Gillian are the only women working in the hall.

11.30 am 17 November 1997
The timber ladders go up on schedule. A thick-bellied, crack-arsed man comes and stands over Sarah and Gillian, shaking his head. He raises his eyebrows conspiratorially at Jeremy.

12 noon 17 November 1997
A wonderful moment when the bales arrive, filling the hall with colour and smell against the stick-on brick walls, plastic bathrooms and ironmongery displays.

1.00 pm 17 November 1997
Fire Officer arrives. He says we must stop building immediately.

1.30 pm 17 November 1997
Fire Brigade arrive. They inform us that:
- straw is unsafe
- it will spontaneously combust
- we have to stop construction and go home with the bales.
As a demonstration of his knowledge, the FO usefully takes a single piece of straw and sets it alight. 'See what I mean?' he says. The Interbuild representatives go white.

1.35 pm 17 November 1997
We respond that:
- compacted bales do not burn because oxygen cannot get to them and they have fire certificates in Canada and the USA
- it is hay that spontaneously combusts and not straw
- we must keep working.

1.40 pm 17 November 1997
'Young man,' he says, 'you are looking at over thirty-five years of fire-fighting experience, do not tell me what burns.' Having exerted his credentials, however, he seems satisfied. We compromise on agreeing to spray every single bale inside and out with some kind of fire retardant. It looks completely useless, but for the Fire Brigade it is reassuringly expensive.

2.00 pm 17 November 1997
An Interbuild electrician comes over.
'I have seen a lot of things in my life but never a hairy wall. Are you lot at university, then?' he asks.
'No,' we respond.
'But you must once have been at university to do this.'

8.00 pm 17 November 1997
Twelve hours after starting and the majority of the bales are up.

2.00 pm 19 November 1997
The Future Systems exhibit arrives by post. It has shrunk from the promised seven metres and now looks a little sad marooned on the carpet.

8.30 pm 19 November 1997
After three long days, the exhibit is finished. The hall around us has filled up. We leave a stack of postcards emblazoned with our slogan 'THE FUTURE IS HAIRY'.

10.00 am 24 November 1997
Return to Interbuild the day after the opening of the exhibition. Sit on the spare bales and wait for the comments to come.

11.00 am 24 November 1997
Man into mobile phone: 'I am standing in front of a fooking haystack and they are calling it the future.'

12.30 pm 24 November 1997
By lunchtime we have had a constant stream of visitors, most of whom are at least interested, many of them actually supportive. Some have also asked whether this is a system which we are marketing.

5.00 pm 24 November 1997
By the end of the first day our only bite is a man who wants us to advise him on how to make straw coffins.

11.00 am 25 November 1997
Man in suit: 'We are surveyors. We make money out of people like you whose buildings fail.'

1.00 pm 25 November 1997
Man asks us if we have patented the system and when we reply that we can't, he spends the next half hour copying our details and measuring the wall.

5.00 pm 25 November 1997
We know that we have conquered Middle England when the magazine *Plastics Today* presents our polycarbonate supplier with the award for Advertiser of the Month in front of our exhibit.

22 January 1998
First meeting with our cost consultants. We agree a budget price of £750 per square metre and leave them with a full set of drawings and specification.

2 February 1998
The backlash starts early. In the eco-fundamentalist magazine, *Building for a Future*, Tony Currivan writes: 'Equally innovative but daft [at Interbuild] was a straw bale wall construction by Jeremy Till and Sarah Wigglesworth.'

10.00 am 4 February 1998
Our cost consultants fax their estimate. We rip the paper off the machine in some trepidation. The message on the first page is blunt. 'Please find attached our preliminary budget estimate in the sum of £1,354,000 which equates to £3,270 per square metre.' This latter rate is underlined, as if they have taken some curious kind of pride in pushing the price so high.

7.00 pm 4 February 1998
Jeremy drowns his sorrows at a party full of architects. He asks everyone what their most expensive job has been and can find no one to match the £3,270, except for one, but that was for a fully equipped operating theatre.

6 March 1998
Relieve our cost consultants of their duties, despite their having completely re-priced the job and coming up with a new sum of £1,600 per square metre. Having already lost our services engineer we wonder if this professional fallout is typical of all jobs in which the architect is also the client.

12 March 1998
Martin, who we have taken on as project manager, prices the job on exactly the same information at £1,100 per square metre. This is mainly achieved by cutting out any middlemen. The price is still 30 per cent too much and we must embark on a series of cuts.

18 March 1998
Immediate 10 per cent saving achieved by placing plans on photocopier and pushing the 95 per cent button. Never having worshipped at the altar of hidden proportions this is surprisingly unpainful. Less easy to bear is the loss of the entrance ramp and sliding guestroom.

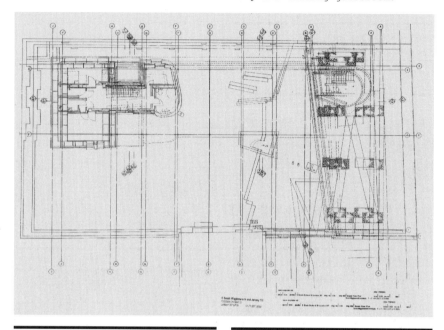

22 April 1998
Redesign plan for the nth time in an effort to reduce costs. In its final resolution we realise that we no longer have a front door to the house. Enjoy this enforced abandonment of social and architectural convention.

5 May 1998
Submission for Building Regulations approval. The explanatory document runs to over twenty pages. Most paragraphs begin with: 'Due to the fact that this aspect is not covered under existing legislation, we refer the District Surveyor to the following:...'

15 May 1998
Revised estimate down to near our budget price. Instruct Martin to arrange for a contract start on 28 June.

18 June 1998
Finally agree contract with Talkback, the television production company who are to make a fifty-minute programme on the building of the house as part of a new series for Channel 4 entitled *Grand Designs*.

24 June 1998
First meeting with the District Surveyor on our Building Regulations application. Starts with embarrassed mentions of the composting toilet: shit and regulatory authorities do not mix. We find the way that they have prioritised the countless anomalies plays into our hands. We give way on things that are important to them (drainage runs, escape doors) but sacrificial to us. Straw bales are low on their list.

28 June 1998
Still nowhere near a start on site. Costs have risen as more accurate quotations come in. We embark on a summer of revisions, negotiations, refinements. Martin attempts to console us by stating that buildings generally get better when they are refined for costs. We are not so sure.

1 July 1998
Conditional Building Regulations approval received. The conditions run to twenty-five points.

6 August 1998
Following an alarming silence on the costs, Martin confirms that the contract sum appears to be drifting upward again. Feel that we are chasing a target that moves away from us each time we take a step closer.

8 August 1998
Arrange to go down to the Cotswolds to see the field in which the barley for our straw is growing. We want evidence of an attachment to the earth.

12 August 1998
On our return from a short holiday there are four messages from Talkback. They are extremely concerned about whether we are ever going to start. TV deadlines and building contracts are an explosive combination.

13 August 1998
The only heatwave of the year. Farmer rings to say that he has had to harvest the barley.

14 August 1998
Meeting with the District Surveyor. List of twenty-five points is reduced down to two substantive issues.

15 August 1998
Down in the Cotswolds, our bales are safely stacked; we see our house for the first time. We measure them, nervously, since the whole building has been dimensioned to an agreed bale size. However, we are fortunate in that Frank, the farmer, is also an inventor and has taken out a patent on a series of baling devices that ensure regular dimensions.

1 September 1998
Stock market collapse. Steelwork prices spiralling. The target moves still further away.

16 September 1998
Martin confirms the final cost. It is still 15 per cent over our budget. We start to cut for the last time, but instruct a start on site despite the fact that we have no agreed contract sum or main contractor. It will be procured through a series of subcontracts and we will build until there is no more money.

21 September 1998
It transpires that the District Surveyor is working off an outdated edition of the Building Regulations. We are down to one major point of contention.

9.00 am 12 October 1998
Work starts with demolitions. Talkback are there to record the first blow. We suspect they are more relieved than we are that the job is finally under way.

10.00 am 12 October 1998
The first visit to the site kicks in the adrenaline. At £1,000 a day it is an expensive habit, but what other drug can deliver such a heady mixture of fear and exhilaration?

10.30 am 12 October 1998
Tom gently bounces the roof of the old forge with his JCB. Jeremy goes white as a section of it lurches alarmingly over the neighbour's garden. 'Don't worry,' says John, 'our man Tom can open a can of coke with that thing,' and sure enough, with a gentle tap, the roof comes back to our side again.

10.00 am 13 October 1998
Talkback are on site again. At this rate they will see more of the contract than we do.

4.00 pm 13 October 1998
Tom complains that with so many television cameras and photographers around he can hardly go for a piss without being filmed.

10.00 am 14 October 1998
Steve goes to retrieve a tree branch that has fallen on to the side of the railway tracks. As he does so, a train emerges from the tunnel. It stops.

12.30 pm 14 October 1998
Visit from Railtrack supervisors. They place an injunction, which shuts the site down until further notice.

Ordinariness and perfection

Sarah Wigglesworth

The desiring genre in architectural photography stages a fantasy of orderliness and control. It presents a setting empty of people, where space, light, clear geometries, fresh colours, shiny surfaces, glamorous furniture and clean, new materials come together with a minimal number of props to offer a vision unadulterated by the grunge of everyday life. Glass balustrades are free of fingerprints; possessions are few in number and those not stored out of sight are arranged in an orderly fashion. The 'rogue elements' of domestic clutter (clothes, toys, bags, keys, hastily discarded shoes, waste-paper, post, food, stains) have vanished. Daily life, time, dirt and comfortable chaos are erased in the pursuit of the timeless, the clean and the disciplined. In these representations, architecture is no longer the backdrop to life: it is an object of desire in its own right. Such photos speak of universals, of timelessness. Space and surface are fetishes masking the life to which buildings play host. They celebrate the power of the designer to transcend ordinariness and enable the construction of a work of art.

Although we know this image is a fiction, the power of the myth is enduring. This aesthetic hopes to suppress the reality of lived experience which is the basis for architecture. However, in my view, and particularly in domestic buildings, it is important to acknowledge the casual, unselfconscious possibility of 'home' that escapes the intrusive eye of the lens.

Most architects want to believe this image of timeless perfection. After all, the image is one thing that is possible for them to control. Yet the suppression of the real leads to a rejection – almost a pathological hatred – of reality, and of clients and users. Clients impede the direct route from creative idea to faithful realisation. Users are those that destroy the myth and challenge the architect's creative authority. Real life misuses the work, leaving marks and scars, the stains of ageing and the need for maintenance. Photographs of new buildings speak to the moment of their pristine emergence into the world, a virgin state

The dining/conference room

of grace which will never be regained. Immediately the client takes possession there is a fall. Reality reminds us that the act of handing over a new building is an inevitable act of partition, a relinquishing of authority. Users appropriate, amend, change, add, remove, repaint, replace and reorganise without asking the architect's permission. Photographs are the lingering memory of a lost moment, a virginal fantasy, forever fictionalised as a perfect product.

The aesthetic behind this form of representation rejects lived experience. It dismisses the reality of everyday tasks and denies the celebratory rituals of life: cooking, socialising, playing, caring, child-rearing. Change, time, dirt, wear, patina, discolouration, staining and weathering are refused acknowledgement. In maintenance of the fiction, in regaining what is lost through the wear and tear of real life, we do not recognise the humble (and mostly women's) work of cleaning and tidying up that hopes to return a building to its pre-lapsarian state. The work of the female is forgotten in an attempt to maintain the fictional perfection.

9/10 Stock Orchard Street aims to rediscover the presence of the (female) body. It shuns the fantasy of the perfect product. As designers interested in what buildings bring to life, we see buildings as a setting, a stage for action and events. We want our architecture to return the female to centre stage, for our buildings to embrace the social, to accommodate mess, to acknowledge time and dirt, to age gracefully and to wear well because they are the inevitable and meaningful scars of the business of living. We celebrate life with all its complications, roughness, provisionality, ambiguity and compromise, and we want our architecture to embrace it. We want occupants to take possession of our architecture and see it as a provocation to creative inhabitation. We do not prescribe fixed rules or proscribe particular forms of behaviour. We want women to see buildings, especially their homes, not as places of drudgery, entrapment and oppression but as sensual playthings.

If the photograph of a completed building represents an ideal condition after the event, drawings show architectural intentions prior to construction. To capture something as large as a building on the size of a piece of paper, architects work to a reduced scale, using symbols and codes to represent the world. When we were designing 9/10 Stock Orchard Street we were trying to find a way to capture the idea of creative occupation. How could one use the conventions of architectural drawing to describe space as a lived experience rather than a static or predictable moment of perfection?

The dining table as symbol of creative occupation
The dining table, along with the room it sits in, has an iconic status in the design of the house/office complex. A sequence of four drawings entitled 'Table Manners' explains how a plan can overcome the absence of time and use, making them the wellspring for the design of a home. Using conventional architectural representation, the drawings attempt to extend the possibilities of orthogonal representation. By subverting its codes they aim to critique the drawing's own limitations.

Drawing 1 – place settings

This drawing shows the plan of the table top set with the requisite tools for a dinner for eight people. The drawing looks quite normal, easily comprehensible to the architect. What does the drawing tell us? On a flat, clean, white sheet of paper there is a set of black lines all of the same thinness. Thin lines are good as they pretend not really to be there. We know it is only an outline and, representing an edge – the edge of the table top is not really a line at all – the thin line denotes the fact that the line does not really want to exist. A thin line is also good, as it demonstrates the skill of the author to other architects. Drawn using an old-fashioned Rotring pen 1.3mm thick, these notoriously temperamental nibs are prone to give trouble and need to be treated with respect. So the control over the line quality is a symbol of the control of the designer in representing the world in the conventional manner of the architect.

The frame outline is the extent of the table top. On the table top are eight place settings consisting of knives, forks and spoons, a side plate, glasses and a folded napkin, all in place ready for the meal. There are three along each long side and one at each end. Chairs are drawn up to each place. The rituals of dining – order of service, our cultural codes for handling food, the customary location of the required implements – all suggest an understanding of how the meal will proceed, what is going to happen and in what sequence. These are received codes of behaviour so well ingrained in our cultural understanding that they need no explanation.

The drawing shows a frozen moment of perfection. It is the controlled anticipation of an acquired ritual that confidently purports to know how a meal takes place. The clean sheet of paper, the flatness, the accuracy of line, the thinness and the ordering of all implements speak of the pristine world of architectural and social myth. As with the architectural photograph, so this architectural drawing aims to describe the world as a fiction of order and perfection.

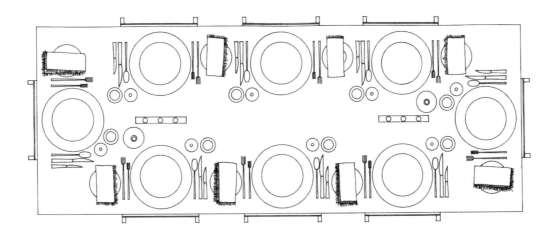

Drawing 2 – the meal takes place

The drawing shows events unfolding in time as the dinner takes place. Using the same graphic style the outlines of objects are recorded at intervals on the surface of the paper as the events they depict shift in space and time. The jumble of lines that form bare outlines of the objects demonstrates the difficulty this method of drawing has in representing things in time. These images share with conventional drawings the character of describing precise relationships between objects in space, but not in time. Notwithstanding, the action can be made out, and a sense of the eventful chaos of the dinner is expressed, contrasting with the static predictability conveyed by the previous drawing.

The contrast between the first and the second drawing illustrates the difference between static space and lived-in place-time. It also reveals the difficulty that conventional architectural drawings have in expressing time with its shifting social intercourse and unpredictable outcomes. How, then, is it possible to capture something of this lived action which seems to defy the limitations of time and of the pen?

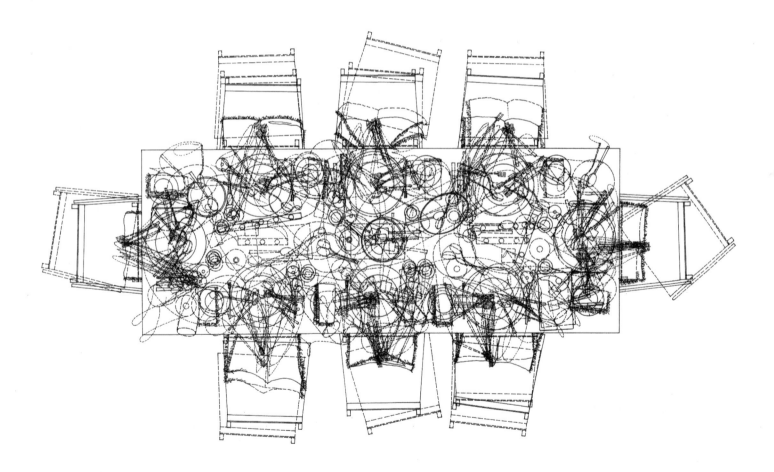

Drawing 3 – after the meal

This drawing shows the dining table once the meal has finished. The table cloth is marked with the stains of the food and drink that were served. Equipment lies haphazardly, chairs are pulled out, and serving dishes remain on the table where someone left them. The traces echo the events that unfolded and form a record of the experience of the dinner. Mess, chance, arguments, likes, dislikes, friendships, (dis)agreements, desires are all inferred in the position of objects on the table top. Memory is inscribed, as every feature of the meal's remains tells a story of how it came to be there. The drawing reminds us that the orderliness we expected in the first drawing is just a desire we have to shape the world as an ideal.

How, then, can the architect begin to capture the unpredictability of life suggested by the dining table? How do we reconcile the fact that drawing conventions obstruct our ability to see architecture as anything other than a predictable set of occurrences?

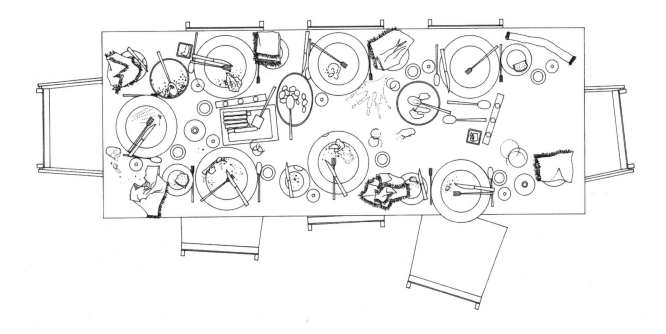

Drawing 4 – the plan

The drawing shows the same frame, and objects on its surface, in locations that are similar to the previous image. Yet something is different. This table top is the plan of the house, and the outline is now the floor plate. The lines here mean different things. They are edges but they now represent the boundaries of walls or zones. The scale has changed and what were formerly serving dishes have become rooms. But their disposition in relation to each other recalls the haphazard traces of the meal recorded in the previous image, and it reminds us that life itself is unpredictable and chaotic. Why not, then, inscribe this 'disorder' in the plan of the building?

The sequence of drawings shows the limitations of conventional forms of representation in acknowledging the chaotic and unpredictable nature of life. It also demonstrates how easy it is for drawings to delude architects into believing the myth of order and perfection in the world they create and in the everyday life around them. A drawing's form, content and making are the cause of many misapprehensions. The dining table series asks: 'How can we make representations that embrace the unpredictability of lived experience in time?' It prompts us to find ways of celebrating change and time, allowing them to enter architectural consciousness. It asks that we find new ways of describing the world around us, to question the pervasive requirement to define, confine and refine. It asks us to accept approximation, to expect no perfection, to embrace change, to befriend time and decay, and above all, to remain sceptical about the meaning of the lines we draw.

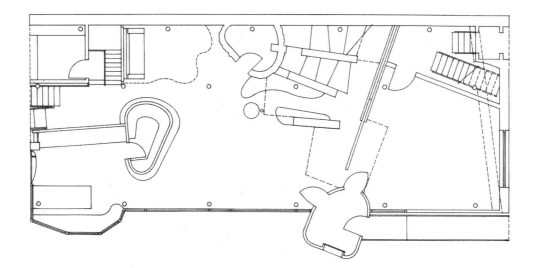

The dining room

9/10 Stock Orchard Street is not simply a house: there is also the office. At the crux of its two buildings, the dining room represents the confusion and coming together of its living and working components. Not only is the dining room itself at its physical centre, it is also a space with a dual function around which the programme for the building revolves. The room itself contains a dining table and eight chairs, recalling the dining table in the drawings. It is the final space in the open-plan sequence of the house and is bounded by three solid walls and a fourth, glazed side. The first wall divides the dining room from the remainder of the house, but both spaces are reunited when a wide sliding door is drawn back. The second wall separates the dining room from a lobby reached from a half landing on the office staircase. The third is the wall shared with the office. During the day the dining room is used as a conference and meeting room. At all other times the lobby door can be locked shut, the sliding wall drawn back and the space now becomes the formal dining room in the house. To give added flexibility the dining table can expand and reduce in size according to need.

You are aware that this space is out of scale. It is deliberately pompous. At its highest the ceiling is six metres tall. At first-floor level there is a balcony (a minstrel's gallery) that connects to the mezzanine in the house through three folding doors. A huge square window addresses the street beyond. It frames the view up the gently sloping Stock Orchard Street and, because the room is at the same level as Caledonian Road, it makes a connection to the wider city. Like a television screen, the window acts as a form of proscenium where, from outside in the street, small figures can be seen performing the rituals of daily life and of architectural practice. It reminds the occupants that they are participating in a game of role play. The suggestion of artifice and performance suffuses the space.

But so does the atmosphere of domesticity. When professionals enter the room there is a moment of adjustment as the expectation of characterless meeting rooms is retuned. The dining room is other. In this room one is aware of the extending relationships with the other parts of the building, layering memory, image and surface one upon another. The wide expanses of wall accommodate large paintings and photographs, references to other built environments. They are personal artefacts collected by us, the owners, though their large scale is unusual in a domestic setting and allies the room with the reception foyer adorned with corporate art. The table is clearly not an impersonal, corporate, conference table; it is domestic in scale, in appearance and in construction. These clues create doubts concerning the room's precise character, prompting questions and evoking feelings of slight insecurity. By destabilising expected categories we are reminded that identities are themselves unstable, and that work and home are non-exclusive sides of our humanity.

Live/work

The dining room is the site that condenses the programme for the buildings. Its dual function sustains a twenty-four-hour cycle of occupation: as a daytime meeting room and as a dining room during evenings, weekends and holidays. In addition, the room's double identity encompasses a broader agenda behind the meaning of the buildings. Because the project is based around an exploration of living and working in the same place, the confusion inherent in this room's identity is a theme developed through the spatial, scalar and material languages of the design.

It is only since the development of capitalism that the separation of living and working space has become commonplace. From the time of mass industrialisation men's work usually took place at a site away from home, such as in a factory or an office. Women's work involved caring for the house and household. For the distant worker the house was a place for his relaxation and leisure and it was expected that the housekeeper would service this arrangement. The endless round of 'women's work' – cleaning, caring, cooking, gardening, shopping and washing – meant that work never ceased. Yet, because this work was unpaid, the housekeeper was financially dependent. Her only personal money consisted of hand-outs or what she managed to save from the housekeeping budget.

Traditionally, an idle woman was an adornment to the domestic sphere, which was regarded as a place of innocence and purity, fit for raising children and located at a safe distance from the city, regarded as a place of coarseness and dubious morals. A woman at home meant that the family was well-off, having sufficient money to live free of work, often with servants and other comforts. Women cultivated interests such as sewing, drawing and playing the piano, adornments that reflected their husbands' career achievements on social occasions.

Middle-class women were encouraged to become voracious shoppers, consuming the products of factories far and near, and ostentatiously demonstrating their husbands' wealth.

As women have entered the workplace and have won financial independence, so now some men keep house. Nonetheless, the home is still a place of mixed meaning, where (house)work needs doing in order to keep everything in order. Computer technology has assisted work to take place in the domestic setting, enabling remote working as well as self-employment. This has had an important impact on women who can perhaps more easily (or secretively) combine the traditional duties of caring with paid employment. Many a female architect who has set up shop in her kitchen can operate effectively and confidently from remote locations thanks to information and computer technology.

Equally, those at work do not suddenly cease being human immediately they set foot inside the workplace. Although an appropriate level of application is needed to perform one's work, shopping still needs to be done, children need to be collected from school and taken home if they are ill, the elderly need help, meals need preparing. Not all work is the same, and some is quite social in itself: networking, creative work, debate, learning and teamwork are all social activities carried out in the workplace. Amidst the list of (other) activities that take place at work, electronic social networking and e-buying accumulate on thoughts of loved ones, planning holidays and birthdays, organising a social life. All these activities can and do take place during, within and around office hours. Life, therefore, invades work in the same way that work invades life.

In the context of women's lives there is little distinction between home and workplace: they are both sites of production. In addition, since computers are mobile and broadband is becoming commonplace, work and leisure occupy the same physical space. Equally, as the country that works the longest hours in Europe, Britons apparently take pleasure in their occupation and many (especially architects with their long-hours working culture) develop a social life around their work. The distinction between work and leisure is becoming erased, and questions arise as to the meaning of 'work' in the context of home and the meaning of 'down time' in the context of work.

9/10 Stock Orchard Street asks questions about what settings we make for living and working. For a female architect running her own practice the question is especially apposite. The majority of my work is social, involving collaborating closely with colleagues, networking, designing, team building and motivating. Other parts need quiet contemplation and solitary space. In creative work the scenario requires a combination of engagement (grappling with a problem, working over solutions and trying out ideas) with retreat. It demands gathering and analysing information in combination with taking inventive leaps in the direction of different solutions. Design comes about at the intersection of ideas with raw data – site, programme, social context, money. It is not a linear or a wholly rational process, forming networks across a variety of issues and looping in time, revisiting assumptions and critically questioning material. Proposals do not necessarily fall out straight away; indeed, more questions may be raised than are answered. A period of reflection is equally important as a face-to-face encounter with the issues. Sometimes this can happen when doing a drawing, sometimes when discussing something with a colleague or client, but often it can happen in the most unlikely of places at the most unexpected times. For me, washing up, ironing and gardening are particularly productive moments for a new idea to appear. Cycling is another activity that gives rise to creative thoughts.

In the environment at 9/10 Stock Orchard Street it is possible, during working hours, to pop into the house to raid my library for sources of inspiration. Hanging up the washing at lunchtime, shopping locally for groceries or even collecting the hens' eggs are good mental breaks that allow the mind to drift. I often work at home during evenings and weekends, finding the change of scene productive to different forms of concentration. Work comes in many guises and is stimulated by many different settings, activities and social contexts. The artificiality of the majority of 'work' places, the expectation of what goes on there and the settings that make these things happen are limited and unresponsive to our needs. The organisation of 9/10 Stock Orchard Street offers an alternative way of thinking about this issue.

9/10 Stock Orchard Street consciously builds on the relationship between the worlds of work and of leisure, asking 'Where does work take place?', 'Where is the place for leisure and relaxation?' and 'Where are we genuinely most productive?' Sometimes an eight-hour shift in the office can leave me without a sense of achievement, but a chance conversation over dinner can spark a new idea; equally, I can google at home as part of my leisure time in exactly the same way as I can search the internet for building products – it's the same activity just taking place in a different setting. At home there are myriad tasks to be performed that are more work than leisure (shopping, cleaning, gardening, mucking out the hens, mending the fence, raking the gravel). Likewise, the office has a social aspect to it that is important when spending eight hours a day together: office lunches, meetings, drinks, events, CPD. We enjoy this collaboration, and the social cohesion and supportive environment of the office is as important as the skills base we have. Equally, we choose our consultants in the same way we choose our friends: because they empathise and think the way we do.

The buildings at 9/10 Stock Orchard Street recognise and celebrate these ideas. This happens in three ways: spatial, material and technical. An inversion of binaries is used to develop the idea, turning the logic of each in on itself to question the assumptions inherent within it.

Spatial

In the first, the spatial typologies of house and office are exchanged. Accordingly, the house adopts the spatial organisation of the office, and specifically *Bürolandschaft* or office landscape, a scenario in which wide, open-plan space is subdivided casually into departments in such a way as to optimise social encounters between associated colleagues. So the house occupies a space 7m deep and 11m long, uninterrupted by columns and with the 'departments' of daily life distributed across its floor plate, accommodating an element of fluidity in adjacencies and activities. At the same time, the office adopts the spatial typology of the domestic setting because it is conceived as a lateral conversion through a terrace of houses. The scale of domestic space is expressed in the supporting cross-walls, of which the typical 'second-class house' of the nineteenth-century developer comprises a unit with party walls at 16.5ft (5m) apart. This dimension became the spacing for the gabion walls. The consequence of the exchange of spatial typologies is that the house is larger than the office. Approaching the building from the street, the domestic scale of the office building echoes the adjacent houses.

The entire ensemble is placed in a setting comprising a hard landscaped *court d'honneur* and a garden that is both ornamental and productive. So while it provides a place where dinner can be harvested a few minutes before it is cooked it is also a place where you can sit outside and eat a meal in a garden setting. This is an unusual juxtaposition for an office environment but a beautiful and well-appreciated one.

Material

Under the material theme the idea was to invert the expectations of material iconography by cladding each building in its anticipated 'other'. Accordingly, the house adopts the appearance of a factory, using corrugated iron and polycarbonate to clad the walls. Meanwhile the office building is finished in a padded quilt, recalling upholstery and referring to domestic settings. While used only at first-floor level for practical reasons, the appearance of the quilt on the street façade is designed to provoke interest and questions.

Finally, in selecting an appropriate material language for the building we made judgements based on their efficacy to do the task required, whether so-called 'high' or 'low' technologies. The gate is an example of how this plays out, combining both steelwork and willow wattle hurdle in the same component. Traditional materials such as lime render and wood wool were chosen along with state-of-the-art glazing components and ecological plant wherever they were most appropriate, regardless of ideology.

These concerns play themselves out further in the landscape at 9/10 Stock Orchard Street. Once fields, then market gardens, then domestic gardens, then railway sidings, then forge, the site has once again returned to its origins. Recognising this, the site cross-categorises, combining both productive and ornamental species in the one plot. Order (in the rectangular beds) is set up only to be overturned in the haphazard habit of the planting which spills over and self-seeds wherever it wants. The colour scheme moves from dark purple at the east end to white at the west, but this spectrum is not rigidly imposed, and as time has gone on, hybridisation has occurred in several species. Hens share the undercroft with cycles and tools. We found birds nesting in the gabions this year, as they have done in previous years in pockets in the retaining wall. Frogs have bred in the pond. Foxes have been seen playing tag in the dawn light among the flower beds. Tulip bulbs are a feast for the squirrels. The grass roof has become a meadow, barely cared for but accepting whatever is blown up there. Opportunism and co-existence characterise the site in its every aspect.

Technical

In deciding how to construct the building we were looking for techniques without a history. We arrived at bale building by accident, through a chance encounter with a friend. We liked it for the very reason that it had only recently come to notice in the UK so it was not associated with any orthodox construction methodology (or so we thought). Assimilating masses of information on bale building very quickly, we were struck by the open, fluid and inventive voyage of discovery that accompanied earlier US experiments in bale building, so unlike the paternalistic and admonitory diktats of the building construction books we were urged to read in architecture school: patriarchal command handed down through generations of architects. I particularly wanted to challenge the alleged authority of the 'master' builder that I had encountered on site in my early career, where patronising dismissals based on historical precedent were so often used as the reason to ignore my earnestly expressed instructions.

Furthermore, as a self-build project, we wanted to lead by example, to embolden the amateur builder with the confidence to widen the range of construction techniques beyond the conventional field. To bring this about we recognised that it was important to use simple ways of doing that were easy to learn. So we began to compile a range of products and techniques such as bales and gabions based on straightforward details and craft-based techniques. The sandbags arose from the desire to craft things on site easily and cheaply, no matter how rough their appearance. Finally we tried hard to keep details and construction unfussy, so that our builders could develop the techniques with us in an efficient way.

Architecture's concerns with the minimal, the refinement of detail and the visible suppression of the fixing were aspects of building craft that did not interest us. Moreover this concern is fetishistic, diverting the architect's attention into the small but irrelevant things that can be manipulated, in order to compensate for our inability to address larger social and political issues that lie beyond our control. So we delighted in using cheap and readily available materials that could be fitted with a minimum of mastery, knowledge and craft. Call it a modern vernacular. Call it a mess. Call it the everyday.

Laying out the rituals of the everyday

The design for 9/10 Stock Orchard Street aims to resist objectification and fetishisation by using conventional techniques, images and drawings against themselves. Working from a critique of existing ways of knowing and doing we sought to create a place that was capable of being both consciously designed but also open to change. We aimed to embrace the inevitable effect of time, event, wear and use that sweeps through a building in occupation and to find a way of accommodating the incompleteness, provisionality and absence of control that is the reality of life and living. What is an architecture of the everyday? One that resists expertise, is informal, is able to change and is accepting of difference?

In *Architectural Design: The Everyday and Architecture* we acknowledged that the architect who tries consciously to incorporate the informality of the quotidian is doomed to fail, because design is by definition a process of selection and ordering. 9/10 Stock Orchard Street attempts to probe how far this process can go and to what degree this experiment can be successful across a wide range of forms of representation – drawing, programme (brief), construction and detail. To raise this issue is not a question of success or failure: photographers continue to photograph the project in the format of conventional publicity; the drawings rely on orthographic representation as the basis of their ordering; and, although obviously designed, one grand, elderly architect described the building as 'crafted' (and this was not intended as a compliment). As we see it, the value of this exercise is in exploring how far, under current modes of communication and material culture, one can take the dialogue that posits a different way of thinking about space, time and architecture.

Washing line, May 2008

Design drawings

Sketch plan, February 1997

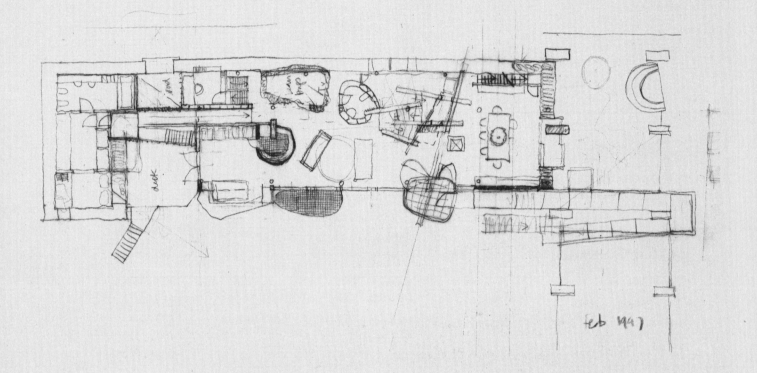

'Blue' Series: short and long sections, 1998

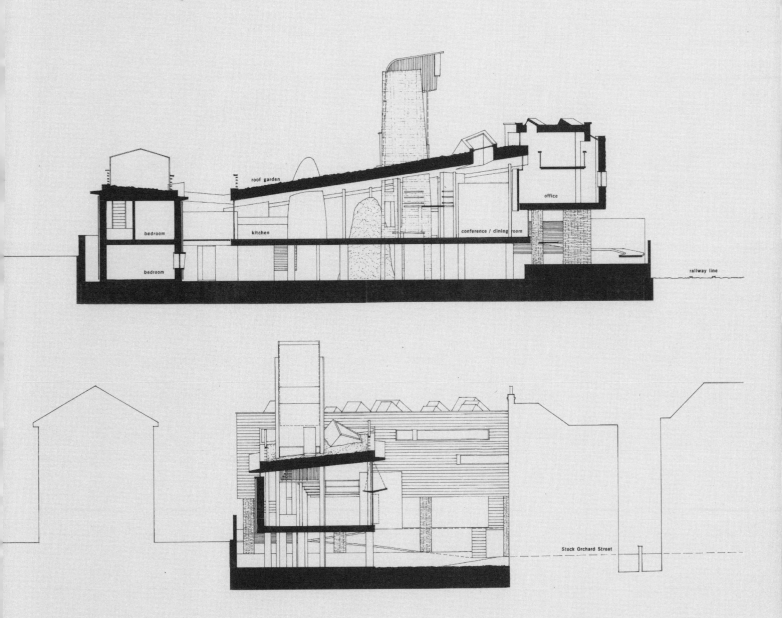

'Blue' Series: ground floor plan, 1998

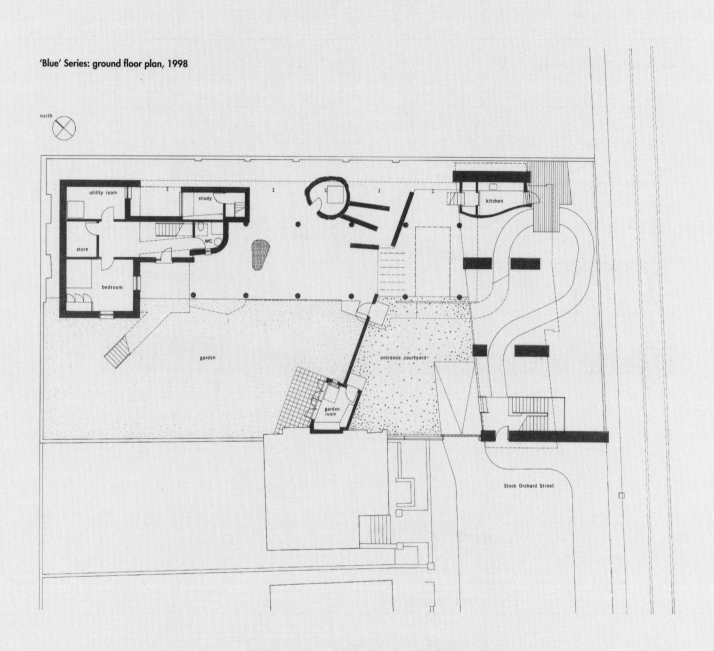

north

utility room
study
store
WC
bedroom
garden
garden room
kitchen
entrance courtyard
Stock Orchard Street

'Blue' Series: first floor plan, 1998

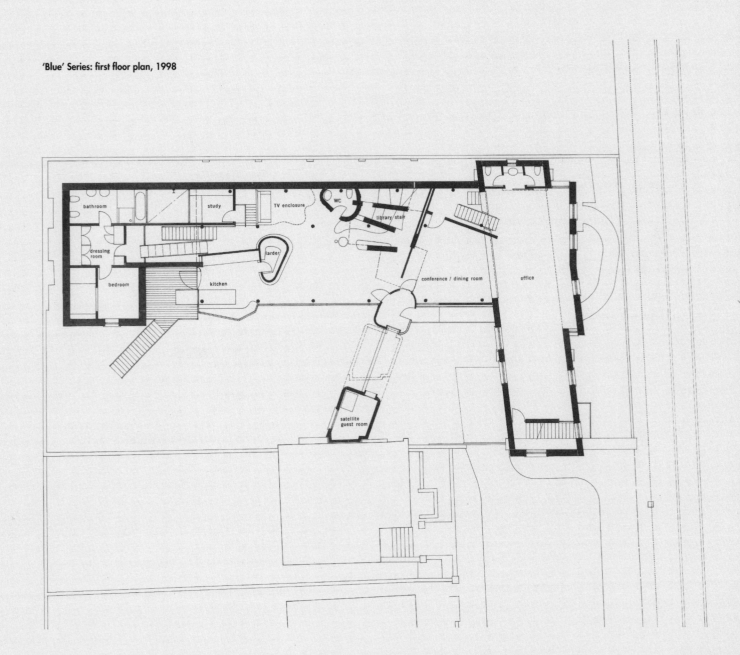

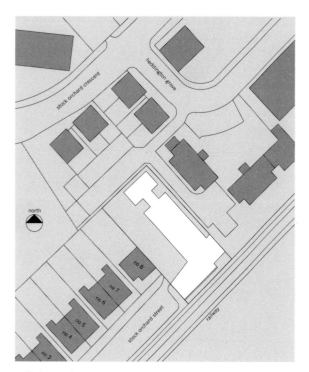

As-built: site plan

As-built: ground floor plan

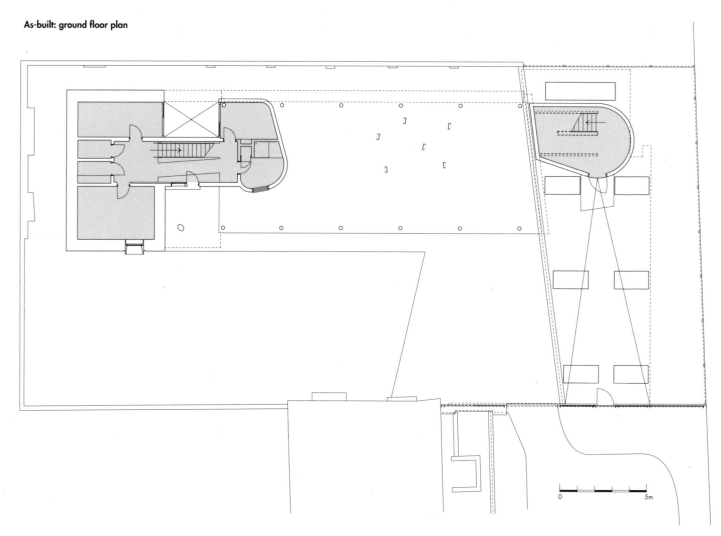

As-built: first floor plan

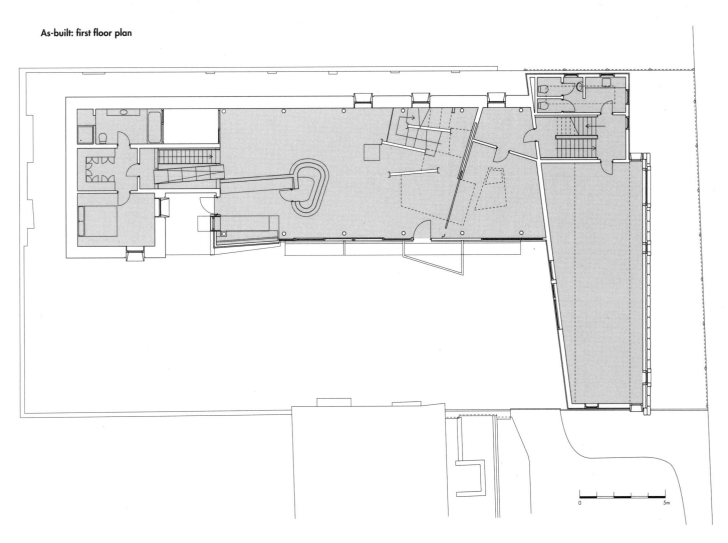

0   5m

As-built: long section

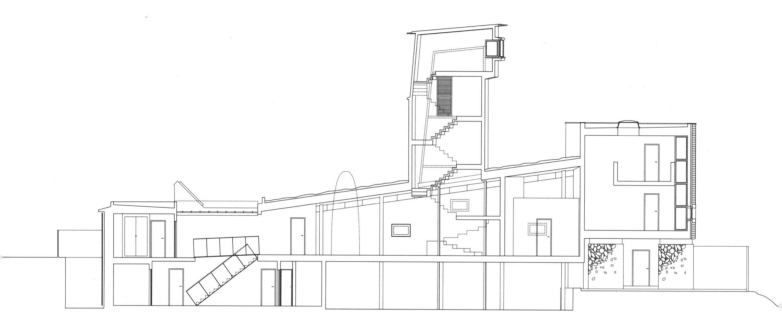

As-built: short section

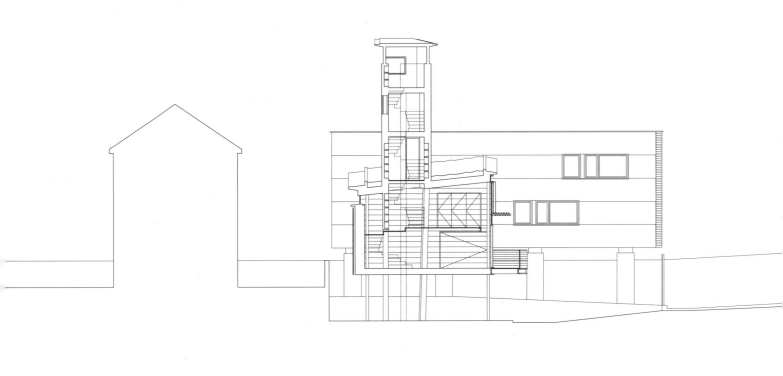

0   5m

As-built: south-west elevation

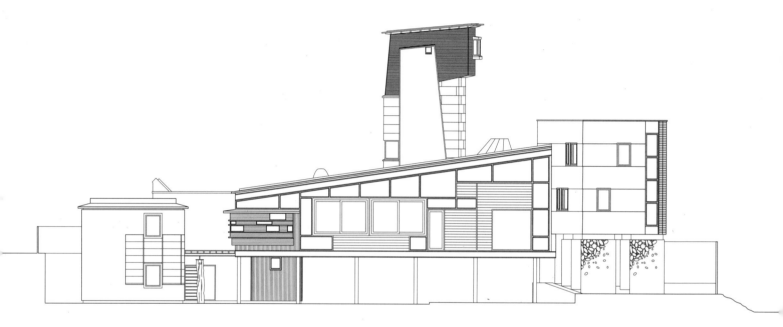

0   5m

As-built: north-east elevation

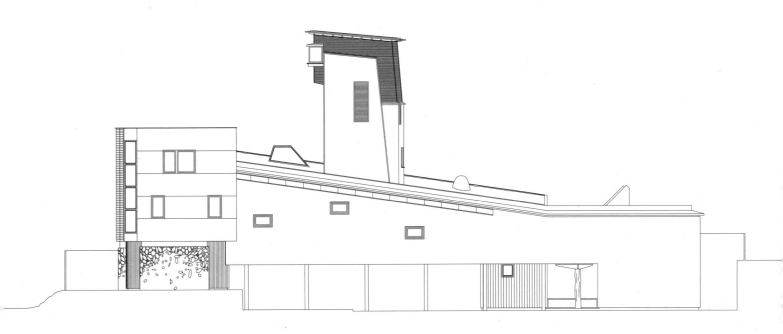

0   5m

Part 2

House with associated office?

Frances Holliss

The Wigglesworth/Till building at 9/10 Stock Orchard Street is generally referred to as a 'house with associated office'. But it is more than that. Chemistry occurs when the functions of dwelling and workplace are combined in a single building that results in a different building type. Such dual-use buildings have existed for hundreds if not thousands of years, in every country and culture across the world. Neither house nor office, nor even hybrid, the Straw Bale House belongs to this tradition.

This is an old but little written-about building type. It was in almost universal use before the Industrial Revolution, when people didn't differentiate between their productive work and the domestic aspects of their lives, so its history can readily be traced. The buildings are all familiar, but we are not used to thinking of them as a specific type. The medieval longhouse was a single-storey open-plan home and workplace for rural peasants who shared their space with their animals. Proto-industrial craft-workers' houses had large upper-floor windows that lit weaving or watchmaking workshops [Fig 1], while nineteenth-century artists' studio houses often quirkily combined large-volume, highly glazed studios with conventional domestic spaces [Fig 2].[1] Pubs and corner shops with proprietors living above are so common that we no longer notice them. And increasingly, in the context of a globalised economy and advanced telecommunications and information technologies, people work at home at the kitchen table,

in a spare bedroom or in a shed at the bottom of the garden [Fig 3, 4, 5]. Or even, occasionally, in purpose-built 'live/work', or 'work/live', units inspired by the imaginative inhabitation of disused light-industrial New York lofts by artists [Fig 6, 7].

Although it exists all around us, knowledge about this building type is fragmented and hidden away in publications about houses or workshops, particular architects' oeuvres, historical periods or geographical regions. It seems to have resisted collection and categorisation. Carl Linnaeus, the eighteenth-century botanist whose classification system for the biological sciences is still in use today, said: 'Without a name, the knowledge of an object is lost.'[2] This may be key. This building type became nameless when the term 'house' shifted from referring to dual-use buildings (with subsets of 'bakehouse', 'bath house', 'alehouse', etc) to purely residential buildings in the twentieth century. While the term 'live/work' is increasingly used to refer to buildings that combine dwelling and workplace, it remains closely associated with the loft-style apartment it was coined to promote and market. As a result the wide range of other dual-use buildings tends to be ignored, and the knowledge of this overall building type has been lost. Or maybe just never collected together. In order to get around this, a new generic term, 'workhome', has been coined. In the same way that the term 'dwelling' refers to all the buildings we live in and 'workplace' to all the

1

2

3

4

5

6

7

Fig 1 Nineteenth-century silk weavers' workhomes in Queen Street, Coventry, photograph 1950–1959

Fig 2 Artists' workhomes at St Paul's Studios, Talgarth Road, London, 1890, Frederick Wheeler, photograph 2010

Fig 3 Home-based worker at kitchen table, photograph 2004

Fig 4 Home-based worker in spare bedroom, photograph 2004

Fig 5 Home-based studio in shed at bottom of garden, photograph 2004

Fig 6 Live/work units at King's Wharf, Hackney, London, 2001, Stephen Davy Peter Smith Architects

Fig 7 Work/live units in Orsman Road, Hackney, London, 2001, Robert Barnes Architects

[1] See Prest, J M. *The Industrial Revolution in Coventry*, pp. xi. 152. pl. 5. London: Oxford University Press, 1960, and Walkley, Giles. *Artists' Houses in London 1764–1914*. Aldershot: Scolar Press, 1994.

[2] Linne, Carl von, and Stephen Freer (eds). *Linnaeus' Philosophia Botanica*. 1st English edn. Oxford: Oxford University Press, 2003.

buildings we work in, the term 'workhome' refers to all the buildings, combining dwelling and workplace, in which people both live and work.

Once we have a name for this building type, life becomes easier: 9/10 Stock Orchard Street is a workhome. As such we can locate it in a tradition that stretches back thousands of years and includes not only vernacular buildings but architectural gems by many of the great designers of the twentieth century. Chareau and Bijvoet's Maison de Verre (doctor's surgery/family home), Corbusier's Atelier for Ozenfant (artist's studio and gallery/home), both in Paris, and Ray and Charles Eames' Case Study House for themselves at Pacific Palisades, LA (design studio/family home), represent three radically different approaches to the design of the workhome. Yet they are rarely, if ever, discussed in these terms. Similarly, this aspect of Wigglesworth and Till's building in Stock Orchard Street is usually dismissed in a sentence in favour of lengthy expositions on the material, constructional and environmental aspects of the project. On reflection, this is extraordinary because in each of these four cases the dual use is central to the design ideas behind the building.

Workhomes come in all shapes and sizes. A spectrum can be identified, which ranges from the largest and most opulent (such as the White House or Buckingham Palace) to the most humble (for example, the council flat of the piece-worker making cardboard boxes on the sofa). They can all, however, be classified according to their dominant function, either as a home where the inhabitant also works, a workplace where the occupant also lives, or something else altogether, that gives the two functions equal status. Stock Orchard Street falls into the third category. Neither predominately dwelling nor workplace, it is an L-shaped building, raised on piloti, with (straw bale) home in one arm and (quilted) office in the other [Fig 8, 9]. From the street its functions are difficult to read, but the single gate gives dwelling and workplace elements equal status [Fig 10]. Its double doorbell is reminiscent of that of the Maison de Verre, a similarly indecipherable workhome, where family home was combined with gynaecologist's consulting rooms, and

8

9

10

Fig 8 Straw Bale House
Fig 9 Quilted office
Fig 10 Gate gives equal status to house and office on to the street

three bells (for 'doctor', 'visitors' and 'tradesmen') made different sounds to enable the right person to answer the front door that served both dwelling and workplace elements of the building [*Fig 11, 12*].

Stock Orchard Street, like many workhomes, combines an intensely public function with a very private one. To achieve this, Wigglesworth and Till have created a degree of spatial separation between the two functions by giving them separate, and quite different, entrances. Once inside the street gate, the (public) office door is immediately visible, on axis, reached via a formal colonnade created by the structure of the office above. Crunchy gravel makes one selfconscious about one's approach [*Fig 13*]. On leaving, it becomes apparent that the volume hovering above the gate, facing the street, is the office, the public workplace for an architectural practice with a dozen employees. Reaching the concealed (private) house entrance, by contrast, involves taking a meandering route through the vegetable garden, past chickens and bicycles [*Fig 14*]. It is a path taken only by those who know it is there. A similar strategy

was employed at the Eames House where the street-front studio, presenting the public face of the Eames' partnership, shielded the privacy of the dwelling element behind. The Maison de Verre, on the other hand, combined doctor's surgery with family home within a single volume that, albeit beautifully screened to prevent stray patients from wandering up into the first-floor living room, provided no acoustic separation between the two functions. Family life can be noisy; it is difficult to imagine how the impact of this upon the elegant and restrained private consulting rooms below was managed.

Both the Eames House and Straw Bale House are workhomes designed and inhabited by people whose identity was/is closely tied up with their profession. Acting as living, breathing business cards, they demonstrate the expertise and skill of their respective designers, helping to generate commissions and put their designers 'on the map'. A parallel may be drawn with the vast and elaborate studio houses built by aspiring nineteenth-century artists from wealthy backgrounds as

11

12

13

Fig 11 Double front doorbell at 9/10 Stock Orchard Street, Islington, London, 2010
Fig 12 Triple front door bell at the Maison de Verre (image from *La Maison de Verre, Pierre Chareau's Modernist Masterwork*, 2007 Dominique Vellay, Thames & Hudson
Fig 13 Colonnade to office front door, across crunchy gravel
Fig 14 Meandering route past chickens and bicycles to home front door

14

a way of asserting themselves in the art world and impressing their clientele with their apparent financial success. These workhomes were often idiosyncratic in terms of their form and their elevations, the architecture reflecting their dual functions. Usually characterised by vast expanses of glazing, large-volume working spaces were juxtaposed with conventionally scaled living spaces, often on the public face of the building [*Fig 15*]. Smudging the boundary between 'work' and 'home', social gatherings in these buildings doubled up as events where work could be exhibited and potential clients cultivated. Le Corbusier's workhome for Amedée Ozenfant in Paris was in the same tradition. Incorporating a small gallery space as well as a home and studio, Ozenfant ran a painting academy from the building for many years. The top-floor double-height studio, fully glazed on both street elevations and with saw-toothed north-facing roof lights and domestic-scale floors below, was both a practical response to the artist's unconventional lifestyle and an advertisement for his business [*Fig 16*].

Unlike the nineteenth-century studio houses or Ozenfant's Atelier, Stock Orchard Street is neither prominently placed nor very legible in terms of its dual function. But its form is certainly idiosyncratic and, despite being a comparatively small building hidden away at the bottom of a cul-de-sac and backing on to a railway line, it seems to have fulfilled the same purpose as the nineteenth-century artists' studio houses. Published, apparently, in more than twenty countries and described by Deyan Sudjic as Wigglesworth and Till's 'architectural manifesto', it has provided an effective platform for the pair as architects and intellectuals, largely on account of its innovative and sustainable approach to materials and construction. Its importance as a workhome, however, has been overlooked.

The relationship between dwelling and workplace functions is fundamental to this building type. Stock Orchard Street has an inherent affiliation with the 'living above the shop', or 'live-adjacent', type of workhome. The dwelling and workplace elements of the building are contained in distinct but adjacent compartments, with

15

Fig 15 Leighton House, Holland Park Road, London, 1865–1881, workhome of the artist, Lord Frederic Leighton, photograph 1880
Fig 16 Atelier Ozenfant, Paris, 1924, Le Corbusier, architect

16

separate entrances. The office could, at a future date, be rented out; Wigglesworth refers to it as her 'pension'. Like many traditional shops in which the shopkeeper lives upstairs, there is an internal connection linking the two compartments and a space, between dwelling and workplace, which is dual use. This degree of spatial separation lies somewhere between the other two types, 'live-with', where both functions are contained in a single compartment with a single entrance (as exemplified by the 'working in the bedroom' or 'double-height space with mezzanine' models, and the Maison de Verre), and 'live-nearby', where the two functions are contained in separate structures a small distance apart (as exemplified by the 'mews' or 'shed at the bottom of the garden' models, and the Eames House).

The character of the dwelling and workplace parts of the Wigglesworth/Till building is different. Free-flowing living space is organised around a beehive-shaped cool-room, an eco-fridge that uses no power, highly insulated from the heat of the house and allowing a chimney of cold air to be drawn from below the house and expelled through the roof. Personal spaces designed around the needs of each of the inhabitants include Wigglesworth's tiny history-filled study [*Fig 17*] and the treetop perch where Till writes his books [*Fig 18*]. The bedroom is as far from the office as possible, half a level below and at the opposite end of the workhome. The kitchen/diner is surprisingly modest, considering the overall size and scale of the building [*Fig 19*]. The workplace element, the office, is by contrast a rational, businesslike, rectangular box, a single open-plan space with a central island of workstations and restricted views [*Fig 20*]. An upper level, connected by section, can be rented out separately when necessary.

A double-height formal meeting room, described by Wigglesworth as a 'pompous space', forms a pivot-point between home and office. Devoid of personal possessions, it separates the open-plan kitchen/dining/living space from the office wing [*Fig 21*]. A sliding wall, kept shut during the working day, slides open at night, allowing this intermediary space, which doubles as a dining room when incorporated into the 'home', to form an internal

17

18

19

20

Fig 17 Wigglesworth's tiny history-filled study
Fig 18 Treetop perch where Till writes his books
Fig 19 Modest kitchen-diner
Fig 20 Rational, businesslike rectangular office

89

21

22

route between living and working spaces [*Fig 22*]. The table sits, regally, on axis with the street. A large square window frames the view of the street for participants during meetings [*Fig 23*]. By day reflections maintain the privacy of the inhabitants, but at night the arrangement takes on an exhibitionist quality. Riotous dinners, one imagines, take place in full view of the neighbourhood. There seems to be a touch of the modern manor house here: the elegant dining room of the big house overlooking the street of humble railway cottages below. But, of course, even a railway cottage in Islington is now worth more than half a million pounds.

Most discussions of Stock Orchard Street, like the Eames House, have focused on its innovative approach to materials and construction. While Ray and Charles Eames adopted the 'live-nearby' approach to designing their workhome, with home and studio components separated by a small courtyard, the fact that it was conceived as a single building is underlined by the use of the same construction and materials in both elements [*Fig 24*]. Each consists of a double-height space with a

mezzanine, constructed from a lightweight steel framing system, with a regular structural grid and similar cladding components. This lack of differentiation corresponds to the lack of differentiation between 'work' and domesticity in the Eames' lives. All parts of the building were actually used indistinguishably as both home and workplace.

A different approach has been taken at Stock Orchard Street, where separate dwelling and workplace components are contained in a single building. They are, however, carefully articulated in terms of their spatial character, their construction and materiality. From the street, the flat-roofed rationality of the office wing is emphasised by the order and (almost) formality of its plain 'quilted' façade on to the street, with just a glimpse of the butch sandbagged railway elevation peeping around the corner. The few windows are sparse and rectilinear, giving restricted views. By contrast the mono-pitched dwelling element of the building is a bit bonkers. A patchwork of different materials and elements collide in apparently (almost) random high-spiritedness.

23

Fig 21 Formal meeting room, sliding wall closed
Fig 22 Dining room, sliding wall open
Fig 23 Meeting room window framing the view of the street
Fig 24 House and studio elements of the Eames House use the same technology

24

This perhaps recalls Alvar Aalto's summerhouse at Muuratsalo, Finland, with its experimental masonry, described as 'a living architectural sketch-pad', an echo of the description of Stock Orchard Street as an architectural manifesto. Timber and glass dominate the Straw Bale House's south-west-facing elevation, inviting the vegetable garden and chickens into the home.

Comparable workhomes for nineteenth-century manu-facturers incorporated the employer's home and space for a dozen or more employees in a radically different way. Workshops were hidden, either attached to the back of what appeared from the street to be an imposing house, or banished to its top floor [*Fig 25, 26*]. Out of sight. Valued customers would be entertained in the ground-floor parlour, possibly un-aware of the work being carried on behind the scenes. Separate rear entrances and stairs, shared by household servants and workers, ensured minimal contact with family or customers. A stout locked door separated dwelling and workshop; employees were paid through a small hatch.

The contrast with Stock Orchard Street is striking. Whereas the master-manufacturer's workhome char-acterised the workers as untrustworthy thieves, domestic privacy and security in the Straw Bale House is maintained through trust. There appears to be a mutual understanding of, and respect for, the boundary between home and office. Forty-four millimetres of sliding plywood divide meeting room from the main living space, which itself separates the workspace (and therefore workforce) from the most intimate domestic space, the bedroom. Wigglesworth keeps this sliding door locked during the working day, mainly so she can feel secure about the large numbers of visitors to the office, but her employees are very respectful of the boundary between home and workplace. The separate office entrance is crucial to this; the workforce never enters the domestic zone unless specifically invited. In another architecturally celebrated workhome, designed by Prewett Bizley for their own use in 2005, a shared entrance and stair to dwelling and workplace leads employees (and sometimes clients) past private kitchen, bathroom, bedroom (and drying laundry imaginatively hung above the stair) on

25

26

27

Fig 25 Nineteenth-century silk weavers' workhomes in Fournier Street, Spitalfields, London, with upper-storey workshops
Fig 26 Nineteenth-century master watchmaker's workhome, Allesley Road, Coventry, photograph 1954
Fig 27 Architect's workhome, Newington Green, London, 2005, Prewett Bizley, photograph 2010

the way up to the second-floor studio [*Fig 27*]. The architect has worries that this compromises his professionalism, and his wife has a niggling uncertainty about employees' boundaries: do they poke about in private spaces when their boss is out?

The three iconic Modernist workhomes display three radically different approaches to this central issue of public/private. The Maison de Verre had a clearly defined ground-floor workspace; members of the public never entered the first-floor home. Dr Dalsace's first-floor study, which had a soundproofed telephone booth so he could talk to his patients in private, was linked to his consulting rooms by a tiny dedicated staircase. If one ignores the acoustic issues, work and home, public and private were kept fairly separate. Ray and Charles Eames used a completely different spatial strategy to control the extent to which public and private functions overlapped: the studio element of their workhome fronted on to the street, shielding the domestic spaces behind from unwelcome public intrusion. Amedée Ozenfant, on the other hand, painted and taught in his studio, but also used it as his main living space. Clients, pupils, friends and family all entered the building by the same front door and climbed the same stairs to the same space, passing gallery and bedroom *en route*. Perhaps his persona as an obsessive artist swept concerns about privacy to one side.

Of course, this analysis of Stock Orchard Street is paradoxical because, in many occupations, 'work' in the twenty-first century is no longer an activity restricted to a particular space or geographical location. The Industrial Revolution may be defined, spatially, as separating dwelling and workplace both at the building and at the urban scale. Industrialised manufacturing processes led to the development of collective workplaces such as the factory and mill. Having engaged in home-based work for generations, people's lives were transformed when they started to leave their homes to 'go out to work' in these new buildings. Social reformers elided the problems of overcrowding and poor sanitation with a negative attitude to home-based work. Intent on improving both the physical living conditions and the morals of the working classes, they replaced slums with so-called 'model' dwellings in which home-based work was initially discouraged and ultimately prohibited. At the same time, Ebenezer Howard's vision of the garden city introduced functional zoning to urban planning, separating housing, industry and commerce into distinct areas of the city. Home-based work continued throughout the Industrial Revolution and, indeed, the twentieth century, but it was gradually marginalised. The built environment was designed around the dominant social form which involved the male 'head of the family' going out to work, while the wife stayed at home, managing the domestic side of their life and looking after the children and elders.

This is still, generally, how we conceptualise the city. Contemporary structures of government, involving separate 'silos' for 'trade and industry', 'work and pensions' and 'housing' at both central and local government level, are organised around an unquestioning separation of work and home. Mono-functional building classification systems, such as the planning 'Use Class Order', perpetuate apparently rigid 'residential' and 'employment' zones within the city.

However, in a globalised economy with advanced telecommunications and information technologies, people in a wide range of occupations no longer need to gather in collective workplaces in order to work. With Wifi and a laptop, all sorts of spaces can now function as workplace, including train and car, café and bar, and, of course, the home. Where the Industrial Revolution separated home from workplace, the information economy is bringing these two spheres back together. Thus while we can analyse Stock Orchard Street as a building that combines dwelling and workplace in two separate zones with a dual-use area in between, we can also approach it from a different angle. Jeremy Till, though he has a full-time job and a designated office space elsewhere, also 'works' in Stock Orchard Street, but not in the 'work' zone of the building. Describing himself as a 'nomad who likes to settle', he tends to write in the space at the top of the book tower. And in bed. And at the kitchen table. And on the sofa. And thinks quite a lot about what he is going to write in the bath. Sarah Wigglesworth, by contrast, does most of her work in the designated office. Or so one might think. But out of hours she too can be found at her laptop on the sofa, or jumping out of the shower to jot down an idea. Neither has a nine-to-five approach to their work, nor confines their work to its designated space.

It is possible to design a workhome around the spatial requirements of a particular occupation and working situation, but the patterns of use depend very much on the personality, family context and working practices of the individual home-based worker. A social policy researcher with a large family and several employees would obviously require a very different set of spaces to a solitary obsessive artist making vast sculptures out of welded steel. But, less obviously, another pair of architects might inhabit the spaces of Stock Orchard Street completely differently to Wigglesworth and Till.

The potentially conflicting programmes of private dwelling and public workplace for a dozen employees are elegantly resolved in this building. Yet although, in its own terms, Stock Orchard Street is an exemplary workhome, it also has to be said that this building does not offer a useful template to roll out in a more generalised way. This is an elitist project, spacious beyond belief. With a floor area of 240m², the house element is big enough, according to the space standards (considered generous by some) specified in the Mayor of London's emerging *Housing Design Guide*, for twelve people to live in. The office, at 175m², provides twice the area needed by Sarah Wigglesworth's practice, so the upper floor is rented out, providing a no doubt welcome additional income. This project is comparable with the other elitist workhomes discussed in this chapter. Truly great projects, they illustrate some of the principles involved in designing buildings that combine dwelling and workplace, but are of limited interest at the broader level.

There is a substantial, and rapidly growing, home-based workforce in the UK. It is difficult to know exactly how big it is, because there is no consistently accepted definition of what a home-based worker is, and no effective system of collecting data. It is estimated, however, that at least a quarter of the overall UK workforce either live at their workplace or work at home for at least one day a week, which is the point at which it is considered to be spatially significant.[3] The number of people who admitted to 'working mainly at home' doubled between the 1991 and 2001 censuses in England and Wales.

This is a popular, family-friendly, environmentally sustainable working practice. Research shows that people dislike commuting and enjoy home-based work because, no matter what their occupation, they gain more control over their lives. It makes life easier for people combining paid employment with caring responsibilities, and enables disabled, sick and elderly people to remain economically active. It is also good for the economy, at both the macro

and the micro scale. It increases the profitability of major corporations: BT save £5,000 p.a. in overheads for each of their home-based employees. They are 30 per cent more efficient and take one-third less time off than their office-based colleagues. Home-based work also helps people with limited resources out of worklessness; most start-up and micro businesses are carried out from home. This working practice is also good for the city, town and village, as it contributes to the creation of busier, and therefore livelier and safer neighbourhoods. Workhomes are likely to be inhabited through twenty-four hours, reducing the tendency for residential areas to be deserted during the day and commercial or industrial areas to be empty at night and over the weekend. Because people working from home tend to use local services, this encourages the development of local social networks and boosts the local economy. But perhaps its most important characteristic, in the context of a global environmental crisis, is that it reduces commuting and therefore carbon emissions. Research shows that 30 per cent of current surface carbon emissions are created in journeys to and from, and in, work.[4] When they switch to home-based work, people radically reduce their annual car miles, often getting rid of a second car, walking their children to school and shopping locally instead of driving between workplace and home, school and shops.

So why is it that we rarely design for this working practice at either the urban or the building scale? It is likely that our villages, towns and cities would take a radically different form if they were organised around people working in their homes and living in their workplaces, rather than the idea that they are all 'going out to work'. Why doesn't the housing being built today consider the needs of the home-working resident, whether child-minder or IT worker, architect or furniture-maker? Because if one scratches the surface of the city it becomes clear that so-called residential areas are full of people working in their homes. These 'homes' are also workplaces, and a large number of people may be found living at their workplaces. 'Industrial' and 'commercial' buildings also emerge as homes. What is going on? Why isn't this a hot topic, driving the 'housing' of the future?

Stock Orchard Street can give us some clues here. First, despite being a high-profile and exemplary workhome, it has not, until now, been discussed in these terms in any depth. Perhaps because they have been name-less, these dual-use buildings seem to be invisible, their importance to contemporary society overlooked. Second, if we look at the apparently boring details of the governance of this building, a strange reality comes to light. In the UK, governance of the built environment assumes the dominant spatiality of the Industrial Revolution, separating dwelling from workplace. Organised around mono-functional zoning and building classifications systems, it has difficulty accommodating dual-use buildings. As a result there is a lot of confusion about what one is, and is not, allowed to do. From a governance point of view, Stock Orchard Street is dealt with as if it were two buildings: a house and an office. Each part has a different planning permission and is taxed differently, despite the fact that it is clearly a single building. Most people working in their homes (or living at their workplaces) today do so covertly, however, either because they are anxious that they may be breaking some regulation or other, or because they actually *are* breaking some regulation or other. In particular, many believe that they would not be granted planning approval for a workplace in a residential area or to live in a commercial/industrial zone. They also often want to avoid an economic penalty, imposed through the simultaneous application of business rates and council tax, on buildings assessed as combining dwelling and workplace.

The emergence of the 'live/work' genre appears, perversely, to have done a disservice to the cause of designing for home-based work. It was marketed as an exciting new building type in the 1980s and 1990s, but nothing could have been further from the truth. This building type, and lifestyle, has been around for a very long time. In retrospect 'live/work' was primarily a highly successful branding exercise for loft-style apartments. It has, however, led to a tendency for the wide range of other buildings that combine dwelling and workplace to be ignored. In addition, and more seriously, many planners are now against it because unscrupulous developers used it as a means to achieve virtually residential prices on light-industrial land. Many home-working inhabitants of 'live/work' developments are now applying to have their spaces reassessed as residential, to reduce the amount they have to pay in property tax.

Home-based work is likely to become increasingly common over the next few decades. The profound ignorance of contemporary practice that leads many professionals to think that the 'spare bedroom' or 'kitchen table' approach is an acceptable spatial solution is likely to be replaced by a more sophisticated understanding of the field. At some point in the near future we will start to think seriously about how this transformation in working practice impacts upon the buildings we inhabit and our villages, towns and cities. Our ideas about home and workplace, neighbourhood and city are likely to be transformed. Buildings like Stock Orchard Street, intelligently addressing some of the issues raised by combining dwelling and workplace in a single building, make a valuable contribution to this emerging conversation. By reinserting employment, with all its comings and goings, into a residential street, Stock Orchard Street helps us to imagine a city without zoning, where home and work can be interwoven in terms of both individual lives and the fabric of the city. By rejecting carbon-wasting commuting in favour of an integrated lifestyle, this building, tucked away in a hidden corner of the city, is a clear pointer towards a more sustainable future.

[3] Holliss, F. 'The Workhome... A New Building Type?' Ph.D., London Metropolitan University, 2007.
[4] Barrett, M. 'Road Transport, Energy and the Environment'. UCL Energy Institute, 2008.

Getting it built

Martin Hughes

The building of Stock Orchard Street required a large amount of design research and innovation. While the design of the building did not change dramatically after the start on site, most of the detailing and construction decisions were taken during the construction phase. As a test bed for a range of different construction techniques it was a unique project, which occasionally felt more like a Bruce Goff house in the American Midwest than the site of an old glass bottle factory next to the railway in N7.

But somehow it also had to be built, and this chapter looks at the techniques that were used to do this. Ten years on, it also considers their relevance today.

Cost

We were initially approached to see if we could reduce the cost of the building – the first client QS's estimate was over £1 million.

Unusual designs attract a premium from contractors owing to the risk element – fear of the unknown. If it is impossible to contain the full scope of works within traditional work packages and pass the risk on to others, the contractor must build in this risk. If time is the determining factor, the contractor will price in the cost of possible delays. If the project is relatively small, say, under £1 million, the contractors tendering may not have sufficient management skills to mesh the individual work packages together.

It is possible to model the costs of a building from sketch scheme onward. It is rarely done, but when budgets are tight, it avoids the need for redesigns if tenders come back too high. Since the cost of change increases exponentially during the course of a project, it is best to make changes at the beginning when it's cheap.

Over six months, the scheme design was cost planned three times, with adjustments made at each stage.

The shape of a building can easily be adjusted at sketch scheme stage to maximise volume. (In our case the volume was reduced by 5 per cent.) The cost of wall, floor and roof elements can be reduced by cutting back the number of layers and/or components. The complexity of construction can be reduced by lowering the number of processes or trades involved in any one element. The straw in the straw bale walls cost £5/m², and was installed by volunteers. However, the wall still cost £115/m² to build. Compare this to the lime-rendered Heraklith walls with Warmcel insulation (£9/m²) which cost £112/m². The latter contained fewer layers of construction, and the overall labour content was less.

At the end of the pre-construction design process, the price target set was £498,000 or £1,130/m².

The cost plan followed a traditional NBS layout, but the spreadsheet database function was used to extract both the cost of work packages and the cost of individual construction elements (like the different types of wall mentioned above). Variations were monitored section by section, so that it was possible to see where we were over- or underspending.

During construction, the ground works increased by 24 per cent, with foundations increasing by 31 per cent; the superstructure increased by 20 per cent, with external walls increasing by 21 per cent; the mechanical and electrical services increased by 3 per cent and the preliminaries by 33 per cent (the programme increased from sixteen to twenty-eight months). The final account was £601,000 (£1,370/m²), an increase of 21 per cent.

Ten years on we continue to model the costs of designs in much the same way. We now have a large database of information and this allows us to pinpoint if individual elements of the construction are higher than the industry average. Similarly we can compare the cost and payback times of alternative mechanical and electrical installations. We can also argue for the need for both an integrated control system and a realistic energy storage strategy – but more on that later.

Programme

Programming software has improved dramatically over the past ten years, as have the ways of sharing information among the project team. However, the principles of programming have not changed that much and the effectiveness of a programme still depends on willingness of all stakeholders in the project to buy into it.

We have worked on a complex infrastructure scheme recently, where multiple projects are taking place simultaneously on the same site, each project having its own team of consultants and contractors. Management costs can be as high as 40 per cent of construction

cost. Everyone relies on a master programme, but a failure in communication or changing requirement is often enough to make progress unclear, and for costs to escalate. Sometimes the technology itself changes too fast or is hard to coordinate.

Historically the industry has attempted to control projects by finding the most efficient way of managing time and cost with little emphasis on the importance of quality. On Stock Orchard Street the problem was different. Cost and quality were paramount, and time had frequently to give way. We had to find ways of making sure that delays didn't dramatically increase costs or result in claims. The contract between KOYA and Sarah and Jeremy was specifically written to make it clear that risk was shared between the two parties.

For the programme we concentrated on a network (or PERT) chart [Fig 1] to show the inter-task dependencies rather than a timeline (or Gantt) chart that displays sequences. A network chart can show why activities might take much longer than the timeline chart implies.

Pinch points tend to occur where there are multiple dependencies between tasks. On this project, the major pinch points were:

– the setting out of the steel frame on to springs at ground-floor level (house) and on top of the gabions (office)
– the junction between the steel frame and the already built timber-framed bedroom wing
– waterproofing the roof of the steel-framed part of the house – junctions with the larder, tower and bedroom wing movement joint
– the galvanised steel cladding to the straw bales that wraps around both the bedroom wing and the rear of the steel-framed living area
– the glazed south-west elevation of the living area
– plastering.

The programme was divided into three parts: substructure, office and house. But the house itself was divided into two different types of construction: the timber-framed bedroom wing and the steel-framed, spring-loaded living area. This created a movement joint fault line between the two, which was difficult to deal with as the mono-pitched roofs all drained towards it.

In practice the bedroom wing and office were completed first – the two opposite ends of the building. The living area was completed last and most of the pinch points listed above relate to this area.

A network analysis of the south-west elevation shows that there were twenty-one processes involving ten trades. Some of these processes could be carried out in parallel, but most relied on the completion of the previous task. On a timber-framed house we recently completed, we found that the rear elevation required twenty-seven processes and thirteen trades, and on a large office fit-out, we found that the ceilings required thirty-one processes and fifteen trades. Often this density of

dependencies does not show on timeline programmes, and it's a mystery to all concerned why the programme is so delayed.

If these areas are highlighted early enough in the design process, an attempt can be made to reduce complexity – i.e. reduce the number of materials or components required (the product design approach) or prefabricate and reduce site work to fixing large elements containing multiple parts (the packaged plumbing unit approach). The latter option is not usually viable on small projects; the former option often is.

Other activities in the programme had fewer successor dependencies, which meant that even if they were complex in themselves, their completion didn't impact upon the critical path. Examples were the sandbag cladding and

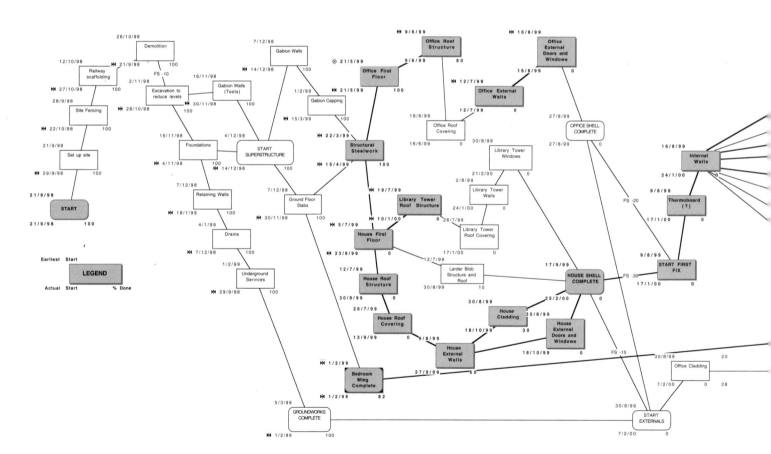

Fig 1 Stock Orchard Street PERT Chart, June 1999: KOYA Construction

fabric cladding – since the building was already watertight, their completion only controlled when the scaffold could be struck. The scaffold was hired on a lump-sum basis, so extended hire periods were not a major concern.

The programme was also used to check lead times – do long lead times impact upon the critical path and, if not, how much slack is built in? It is usually the frame or the windows that destroy a programme – in our case both. The steel frame was probably the biggest technical achievement, but it was also the major delay. As a result the building was started from opposite ends, and the steelwork when it arrived had to joint the two ends together – a case of 'I wouldn't start from here'.

Procurement

The method of procurement adopted at Stock Orchard Street was developed from a model used at the CUE building, part of the Horniman Museum. CUE was a prefabricated long span timber-framed building with a natural passive ventilation system built into the structure. The building itself attempted to stimulate curiosity in green building design.

It was tendered traditionally, and the lowest tender came back 67 per cent higher than the cost plan. The preliminaries were 249 per cent higher and the mechanical and electrical (M&E) services were 324 per cent higher.

The project was eventually built by dividing it into thirteen work packages which were directly supervised by the design team.

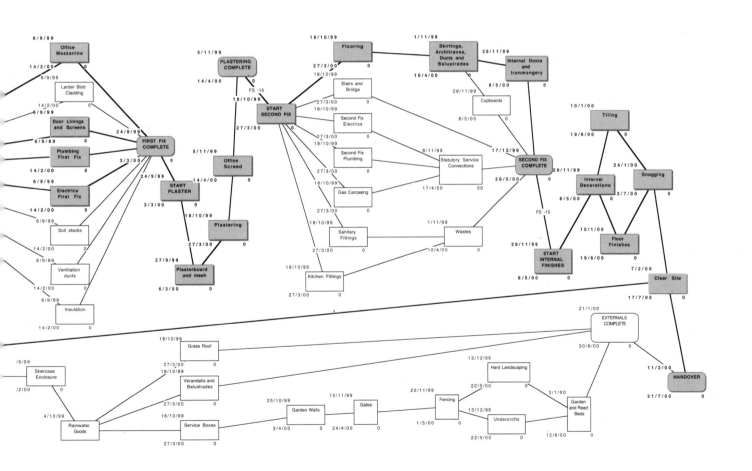

A contractor was employed to manage the site – they also undertook three of the work packages. This model meant that the management layer between designers and constructors was very slim. In addition, the on-site team were able to continually solve problems (typically builders' work requirements) between the various work package contractors. The client had less cost certainty, since any dispute could involve several parties, but cost and time savings were worth it.

The final account was only 27 per cent higher than the cost plan and the building was erected in eight weeks. The M&E Services were still 79 per cent higher, but preliminaries were 11 per cent *lower*!

On Stock Orchard Street, there were forty-six work packages and KOYA took on a far higher proportion (twenty-seven), because materials prototyping made them hard to let. Seventeen were subcontracted and two omitted. We tried to reduce the complexity of the tender packages by tailoring the information, sometimes adding additional general arrangement drawings and schematics, and omitting information that was not required. This is rarely done in subcontractor tendering, owing to the risk of leaving out information that could later form part of a subcontractor claim. As a result the tender package needs to be carefully checked, but the advantage is less perceived risk for the subcontractor and therefore lower tenders.

Taking on so many packages meant that we had to keep a larger team employed than is optimal (seven or eight). Every time there were delays, our non-productive costs escalated. Other concurrent projects were taken on to solve this problem, including a timber-framed house nearby, but the downside was that it was hard to maintain momentum which is a key to progress. This is usually achieved by one team chasing another (e.g. tackers fixing plasterboard force electricians and plumbers to complete their first fix). By taking on so many of the packages ourselves, the strength of this mechanism was diluted.

The only dispute on the project was with the single membrane roofing contractor. It dragged

Fig 2 building the gabions: time lapse photograph, 1999

on for several months, but had to be solved due to warranty requirements.

During the ten years since this project, we have concentrated on collaborating with large contractors, and using their resources on a flexible basis, rather than increasing our own workforce. This has allowed us to reduce construction times while still being able to deal with delays without claims. Shorter contract periods mean that high cost options such as temporary roofs and tower cranes become economically viable.

But the fundamental priority is to keep the management layer slim, and avoid the duplication of tasks. Diffuse potential disputes quickly, and maintain a small team mentality, even when the project is large and complex.

Techniques

Technology is the knowledge of techniques. This knowledge is passed on by the manufacture and use of products and artefacts. The development of this body of knowledge often appears wild and chaotic. Rarely linear, it is full of dead-ends, repetition and the reinvention of previous solutions.

The design of objects attempts to produce a solution from all the relevant constraints – price, size, strength, materials, time and so on. Each problem has its own particular list. Product design proceeds typically by framing and reframing the problem and objectives. Alternatives are created and the best alternative intuitively chosen. Products are prototyped early and often – either digitally or through physical models.

Good design pares away at all the unnecessary elements of a product, but again the process is rarely strictly linear or even a revolving wheel of iterations. Design thinking harnesses the designer's innate knowledge rather than the explicit knowledge of logically expressed thoughts. This is the reason why design education relies on a project-based approach, learning by doing.

This design approach applies to many of the components of a building, but less so to the overall building design. Architectural detailing tends to be additive rather than reductive. This is often determined by the way the various trades and specialist subcontractors come together to assemble the building. Although this also happens in the car industry, in this case the volume of production allows for the development of high-value components and reduction in the number of parts.

In construction, prefabrication of elements of construction (the frame, roofing system, cladding system, mechanical services) is common, but volumetric prefabrication is always subject to the vagaries of the economic cycle.

Stock Orchard Street was unusual in this respect. While the three-dimensional design was largely complete before we were appointed (compare the model with the completed building), the construction and detailing were developed during construction.

The straw bale wall was prototyped by Jeremy and Sarah before we were appointed, but the design was adapted during construction and the galvanised steel cladding was developed after an early case of vandalism led to worries about fire resistance. The detailed design of the following projects were all developed on site:

- gabions with concealed reinforced concrete columns and cappings
- installation and setting out of spring boxes
- sandbag cladding
- fabric cladding
- brick larder
- south-west glazed elevation including the kitchen.

These mini-projects would typically involve full-size mock-ups. Batch production techniques would then be devised to make the mock-ups buildable. Giving these projects nicknames (e.g. beehive, nappy) was interestingly an important communication tool and helped to simplify the often complex interfaces between work packages.

How has the body of knowledge generated by the project been passed on? On one level publications disseminate the information; on another the people involved rework ideas on future projects. But this process is genuinely chaotic. The Segal self-build movement would

pass on tips and techniques through publications and social contact, and the architects involved would update specifications over time, but on a series of projects in the 1990s I was struck by how random this process is. We built three timber-framed public buildings in succession, all with similar but evolving detailing. Two were let to the same contractor. It became clear on their second project that they hadn't retained any of the staff from the previous building, and the whole timber frame learning curve had to be repeated.

Ten years later
What's different? Workflows have changed out of all recognition and information can be tracked down at the press of a button (sorry, tap of a screen). I regularly attend meetings with a laptop that contains the cost plans, drawings, specifications and photographs of all the projects we have undertaken over the past ten years. Project information is stored online and is accessible by all. We are already living in an age of ubiquitous networked devices.

This doesn't mean that design and project management is of a higher quality – that still depends on the skill of practitioners and dynamics of project teams – but the tools are there to be used.

And the buildings themselves? We are moving towards a state in which information is potentially available wherever we need it, and it is beginning to have a significant and meaningful impact upon the way we live our lives. It is as if the web is detaching itself from the desktop, and turning up everywhere.

There is a logic of convergence as tools and services are all expressed digitally. Everything connects. The sensors, tags, chipsets and routers that make this network possible are cheap and plentiful, as are the data centres where this information is stored.

Our commercial projects reflect these changes, with all services monitored, controlled and optimised by a networked building management system (BMS), which in turn can be monitored off site. However, the software that runs these systems remains primitive and proprietary – a throw-back to the operating systems of the 1980s and early 1990s. Controls are only 'smart' to a limited extent and buildings are controlled by IT specialists who guard their secrets well.

Of course this will change, and open standards[1] like Modbus and XML will take over while GUIs[2] will gradually catch up. But when will this impact upon housing?

On one level there has been barely any change over the past ten years. We completed a highly insulated timber-framed house three years ago, with heat pump, photo-voltaics, solar thermal panels and rainwater recycling. A data network was installed so that energy usage could be monitored. But the software that interprets this information remains backward and non-intuitive.

Clearly a revolution is about to take place. The market for the digital home will be its own driving force. At present this is limited to ambient lighting systems and networked HiFi; but like it or not, in a few years' time your fridge will be texting you to say it's short of milk, and your front door will be tweeting that it needs a new coat of paint.

Other changes? Volumetric or modular prefabrication was expected to become a large segment of the market, but industrialisation of the construction industry is still in its infancy. We are not like the car industry, moving from production-line efficiency to 'just-in-time' forms of manufacturing. We are moving from craft-based, bespoke operations to a more industrialised model. We are not shaving seconds off production times – we are working in minutes, hours and days. Framed structures are still common and, combined with cladding systems, have brought a degree of prefabrication to the private house building market and speeded up construction times. But investment in fabrication plants still suffers from the vagaries of boom and bust in the industry.

Insulation standards have continued to increase and specifications requiring sustainably sourced materials have become the norm. Ventilation design continues to lag behind.

The long British tradition of leaky buildings has come to an end. Airtightness requirements mean that framed buildings require careful detailing, and high standards of site work. This adds some interesting complexity to construction – such as on a current project to refurbish a Segal timber-framed house, a building type that was based on the leaky building principle. Similarly we have undertaken other projects to remove rot from timber-framed buildings where condensation has been trapped within the construction.

The recycling and disposal of waste has become a major cost; so has the transport of goods and services from site. The management and implementation of site safety has dramatically changed. The production of building log-books and manuals has been integrated into the construction process.

Micro-energy generation has become the norm, and we now install as standard a combination of heat pumps, solar panels and wind turbines. As a counter to this, there are arguments for passive design and for the centralisation of renewable energy generation in larger, more efficient installations. Energy storage, like BMS software, is still at a backward stage, with few designers incorporating the space for heat stores or even understanding the need for them.

The ideas behind the construction of the Stock Orchard Street building are still current, and building sites do not look dramatically different today. But the sum total of changes over the past ten years is significant, and it feels as if we are close to a tipping point.

[1] Although there is no single definition, an open standard of software is generally one that is publicly available and has various rights to use associated with it.
[2] Graphic user interface, an interface that allows users to interact with software. A GUI makes use of visual indicators and graphical icons as opposed to text based interfaces.

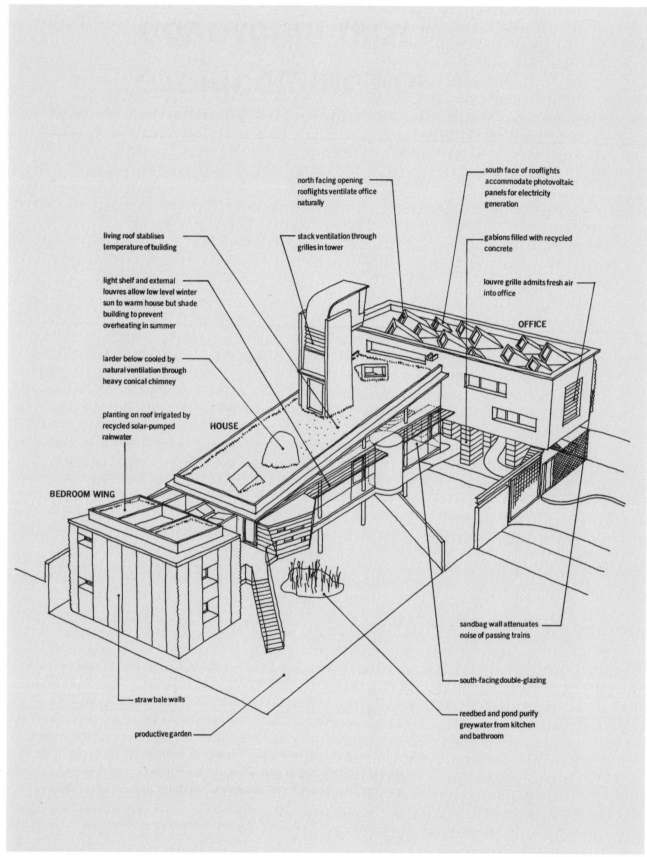

north facing opening rooflights ventilate office naturally

south face of rooflights accommodate photovoltaic panels for electricity generation

living roof stablises temperature of building

stack ventilation through grilles in tower

gabions filled with recycled concrete

light shelf and external louvres allow low level winter sun to warm house but shade building to prevent overheating in summer

louvre grille admits fresh air into office

OFFICE

larder below cooled by natural ventilation through heavy conical chimney

planting on roof irrigated by recycled solar-pumped rainwater

HOUSE

BEDROOM WING

sandbag wall attenuates noise of passing trains

south-facing double-glazing

straw bale walls

reedbed and pond purify greywater from kitchen and bathroom

productive garden

9/10 Stock Orchard Street: early study of sustainable features

From innovation to commonplace

Trevor Butler

It is 2009, and, in the midst of global financial crisis, we are once again asking ourselves: What is a sustainable model for living? In a life-cycle assessment of our buildings, the main impact – believed to be upward of 70 per cent – occurs during the period when a building is in use. Therefore, even the greenest buildings will only get us so far. Rather, what is needed is a shift in our behaviour that compels us to better understand and manage our buildings and make lifestyle choices consistent with an environmental awareness. For some it will mean trying to fly less or getting a smaller car, while others will look at buying local food or finding ways to reduce their utility bills.

Providing a green building cannot in itself guarantee a greener lifestyle; indeed, carbon-neutral buildings are only carbon neutral if the occupants use energy within the capacity the building has to create energy by itself. You would need approximately 20m^2 of photovoltaic panels to enjoy the use of a single forty-inch plasma TV in a carbon-neutral environment. Stewardship of resources is a key non-negotiable. Yet we still live in a society where we are required to design as if we have not accepted this principle. As a result the buildings we produce are forced to compensate for the increasing energy demands that we create. In the twenty-first century the global problem that we face regarding our planet's finite environmental capacity and the socio-economic stresses of modern life cannot be addressed through green building design alone; we need to accept that we must change the way we live. But we can use green buildings to help us do this.

While it is clear that providing a green building is not enough, in and of itself, to make our lives truly sustainable, the places in which we live and work have significant environmental impact; in helping to bring about change by altering our living patterns, building ecologically can make a major contribution to reducing its effects. In our homes and workplaces we must do all we can to make these day-to-day activities as green and affordable as possible.

Despite the current economic slowdown, the design and construction industries have responded to the challenge of climate change by embracing and exploiting a new market in green consultancy and sustainable products ranging from the sublime to the ridiculous. These include 'eco-concrete' with zero environmental impact and 'passive ventilation' that breaks Newton's Second Law of Physics due to supposed 'enhancements' in thermo-dynamics such as we have seen at some 'leading environmental' developments in the UK.

It is against this background that I would like to investigate how 9/10 Stock Orchard Street demonstrates a step change in green design that can benefit the wider market and, at the same time, identify what refinements or improvements are needed to serve a larger audience.

In the context of an expanding definition of what sustainability means, how do we characterise the green credentials embodied within 9/10 Stock Orchard Street? Experimental buildings such as Alex Pike's Autarkic House (1971 to 1979), the Autonomous House (Brenda and Robert Vale, 1993), Hockerton Housing Project (Brenda and Robert Vale, completed in 1998) and Sue Roaf's Oxford Ecohouse of 1995 helped research and develop our understanding of how green buildings work and the potential that exists to service them by harnessing the natural environment. Much of this work was related to building systems, and as a systems engineer I have found their work inspiring because it stakes out what can be achieved by considering building design holistically, when delivered through an integrated design approach.

The process of holistic building design with environ-mental considerations as the prime driver is generally not 'business as usual' in the construction industry. The first step is to establish a clear passive strategy that identifies the environmental benefits of the site's microclimate in relation to the functional needs of the building. Factors considered should include seasonal climatic data such as sun-path, prevailing wind, noise and air quality. These factors may be used advantageously to gain free natural ventilation and daylight through the way that the building form is orientated and planned. The building

should also mitigate against overheating by the sun through careful siting of window openings, window sizes and shading. The materials that are used in construction can also play a part in the passive design strategy. For example, thermal mass maintains steady internal temperature, reducing the need for resource-based heating or cooling systems. The user interface with environmental control such as temperature, lighting, shading, and ventilation should be as simple and fail-safe as possible. There is a growing trend in building design to place reliance upon complex technology to produce a so-called 'intelligent building'. It is my view that buildings should be designed to operate by their own built-in, passive survivability, in the event of power or technology failure. Therefore simple intuitive control is the most resilient in the majority of building types. The embodied energy – arising from extraction, processing, manu-facture, delivery, installation and maintenance – of all materials also needs to be considered through a life-cycle perspective.

9/10 Stock Orchard Street embodies many of the lessons explored by its predecessors, while simultaneously dealing with the constraints associated with a dense urban context. I am referring here to the site constraints (the railway, the orientation, the access) that demand compromises on ideal conditions. The development also has two distinct programme uses – the house and the commercial office space – each with their own unique environmental issues to resolve. In commenting on the innovations, I propose to follow a rationale aligned to the design process, highlighting the key decisions and considerations made. These will range from site matters and building location to building materials and systems.

The site and the buildings

The site had been previously occupied by heavy industry, and its buildings were in a poor condition prior to commencement of works, though the site was not contaminated. The building programme was intended to provide spaces for living and working within the same development. The two different elements each have their own occupancy patterns on a daily, seasonal and annual basis. Site access was relatively restricted and the proximity to the main east coast railway lines from King's Cross was one of the main drivers in the layout and zoning of the site.

In plan arrangement the buildings take the form of an inverted L with the office structure parallel to the railway, shielding the house that extends at a right-angle behind it. The building is located to the north-east (house) and south-east (office) of the plot, allowing for a sunny south-west-facing garden. The majority of the building is at first-floor level on columns, but one small part of the house stands on the ground, providing a form of 'basement' at garden level. Raising the principal occupied levels up to first-floor level allows cooler air to enter the building from the shaded areas below while also permitting easy access to the composting toilet in the 'basement'. The building's windows are orientated chiefly towards sunlight while the tower's louvres are sited away from prevailing winds.

Acoustic and vibration issues associated with trains, as well as privacy, led to the living area being located deeper within the site footprint and the bedrooms being located furthest away from the railway. This reduced the available sunshine to the dwelling where it is closest to the office, while at the same time exposing the office space to the potential of higher solar gain.

The buildings align with the orientation of the site, which is south-east–north-west. The walls to the north are heavily insulated and the south-west-facing façade of the house has relatively higher proportions of glazing in order to allow greater insolation (i.e. the heating effects of the sun's rays falling on glazed surfaces).

The building was constructed in an era when the architectural design community was debating the relative benefits of lightweight versus heavyweight construction, and in the case of 9/10 Stock Orchard Street the two buildings showcase two different approaches. The architects chose to make use of thermal mass in the office because of its exposure to sunlight (south-east-facing) and due to the office's occupation patterns, i.e. eight to ten-hour days continuously throughout the year. The office is a hybrid construction combining lightweight walls lined in Gyproc plasterboard and heavy construction (floors and ceilings). The house, by contrast, is entirely lightweight, reflecting the shorter and more flexible occupation patterns characteristic of that zone. At the design stage, the architects were advised that the house would benefit from thermal mass, but it had already been decided that the structure of the house would be Masonite joists, chosen for their low embodied energy. Structural limitations meant it was unwise to apply a topping screed, but because of the house's exposure to south-westerly sun, this may have proved a short-sighted decision. My view is that as climate change becomes more of a central concern of the mainstream than it was ten years ago, these factors will become increasingly relevant.

In addition, the external envelope of both the house and office are detailed as breathing walls (including, it is

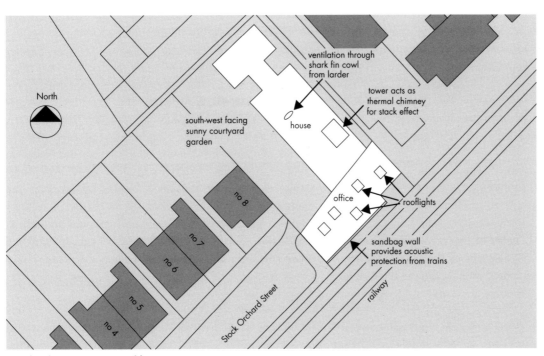

Site plan showing environmental features

assumed, the bale walls), following the Walter Segal method of construction.

The office

Compared to the living space, the office has significantly higher incumbent heat gains due to its orientation (south-west–north-east), density of occupation, equipment loads and lighting standards. The potential problem that the additional solar gain could have caused to the office was mitigated largely through the smaller windows that face south-east on to the railway lines. The problem of train noise and vibration was addressed by providing an envelope to the railway line (the cement bag wall) that contained mass to reduce noise ingress; the smaller windows are also a key part of this strategy, together with a heavyweight floor and ceiling. Cooling is provided naturally through windows on both sides of the office. In addition to this, vents in the floor allow cool air to be drawn from the shaded undercroft at garden level and exhausted at high level through fans in the cheeks of the roof lights. At the time of writing these floor vents have yet to be realised, and it is expected that they will become operational in the near future if warmer summers (from climate change) and a growing office population threaten to strain internal comfort levels.

Noise and vibration are causes of psychological stress. Dealing with these problems can be expensive and, from a design point of view, dull. The railway wall achieves its performance through the use of sand, lime and cement-filled sandbags stacked on top of each other. Openings are framed with reused railway sleepers found on the site. Now, ten years on from construction, most of the netting is fraying as intended, yet the sand cement content remains solid. The sectional buildup of the railway wall has the sandbags on the outside facing the tracks, an air gap of 50mm, then a breather membrane on 9mm Panelvent, recycled newspaper insulation between 150mm-deep softwood studs and 15mm Gyproc Duplex (foil-backed) plasterboard forming the internal skin. The method of employing mass to the railway wall to reduce noise demonstrates a simple solution that is as technically effective as it is economical, and is achieved through a design that is fun and highly original. This is an important yet commonly overlooked point when considering green design, something that has too often led to inferior design quality.

Other strong visual aspects of the office architecture are the gabion column surrounds and the north-west-facing quilted wall. The quilted wall is well selected. It provides an impervious barrier against the strong northerly winds that the site experiences in the heating season. The air permeability is likely to be significantly lower with this construction than with a traditional wall. This is again a new innovation that has yet to be taken up further by mainstream design.

The gabions make use of waste concrete salvaged from other building sites, which was coarsely crushed and filled into wire cages. This is consistent with the building's material selection aimed at employing recycled and waste materials. The aesthetic aspects of reused or recycled materials should be seen as great opportunities for innovating in design and not shied away from as many architects continue to do. The design of 9/10 Stock Orchard Street has demonstrated some of the opportunities available for reusing materials, including straw, and has made excellent use of them throughout the construction.

The house

Although straw bale construction is not a new technology – some such houses in France and the USA are over 200 years old – it serves as a powerful reminder of what is achievable with this natural building method. In London, this places it on the world stage, and communicates that alternatives to man-made materials are technically viable as well as ecologically the right thing to do. Fear associated with off-gassing of chemically derived building materials is another reason why materials such as straw should be given serious consideration.

Ten years on, the straw bales are still in excellent condition thanks to the meticulous construction detailing that was developed by the designers. The aesthetic of the building seeks to raise awareness of 'green' by extending the language of ecological buildings to embrace recycled and non-standard materials, something already noted in relation to the gabion columns. Because of this the ecological building practices employed within the building have been widely publicised and the technology has been transferred for use on other projects, such as Modcell panels; this in itself is admirable in an age when intellectual property rights dominate many areas of our industry.

The thermal properties of straw are extremely favourable, with U-values of $0.12W/m^2K$. Straw has limited thermal mass, yet, when straw is compressed tightly in the bale construction, the increased density improves its thermal properties. This effect is further enhanced through the application of lime/sand render that is between 25 and 70mm thick. The next step of design development could be to use the straw bale as insulation that encloses a heavyweight interior to absorb the heat in summer time.

It is also worth noting that daylight quality can be reduced due to the thickness of the walls when straw bales are used. Window placement and size are key considerations to embrace as bale wall design develops. However, in 9/10 Stock Orchard Street the straw has been used in the north walls (and bedrooms) where window sizes are deliberately kept small. The insulation is most appropriate where the majority of heat is lost. Where non-load-bearing straw construction is employed, such as here, sizes of openings can be made to suit.

The house was occupied before certain features could be afforded, and living in it has revealed where some modifications would improve liveability or comfort. It was always expected that the living room would require solar shading and indeed the main modification was the installation of timber slats to provide shade to this area. In the conference/dining room heat and sun is tolerable when this space is used for living or dining but in the office mode, when used for business meetings and presentations, it has proved more problematic. Heat buildup during the hottest of summer days and strong high-level sunshine made screens invisible and drawings glare. The incorporation of vertical louvres at clerestorey level has helped resolve this and the space is now flexible for use in a variety of settings.

One of the most architecturally prominent features of the house is the five-storey tower that accommodates a library, study and guest accommodation. The tower also provides an excellent means of natural ventilation through stack effect. On the ground floor of the house, manually operated vents allow air to be drawn through the living areas from the shaded undercroft, and the

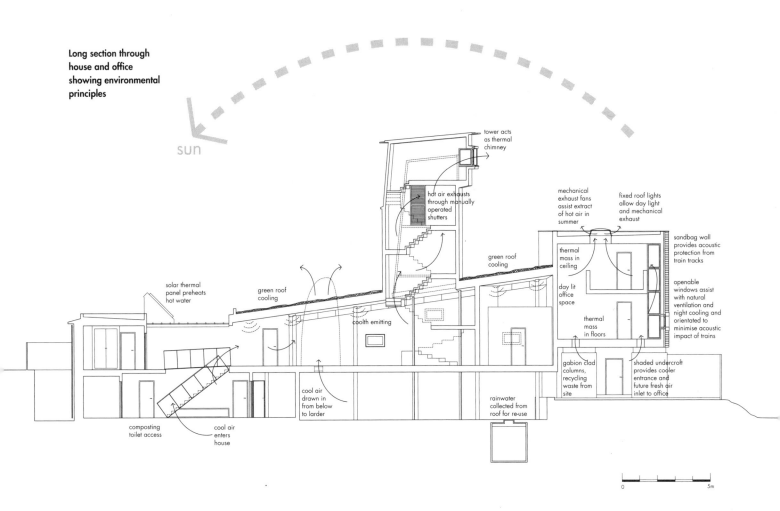

Long section through house and office showing environmental principles

sun

tower acts as thermal chimney

hot air exhausts through manually operated shutters

mechanical exhaust fans assist extract of hot air in summer

fixed roof lights allow day light and mechanical exhaust

thermal mass in ceiling

sandbag wall provides acoustic protection from train tracks

green roof cooling

day lit office space

openable windows assist with natural ventilation and night cooling and orientated to minimise acoustic impact of trains

solar thermal panel preheats hot water

green roof cooling

coolth emitting

thermal mass in floors

gabion clad columns, recycling and waste from site

shaded undercroft provides cooler entrance and future fresh air inlet to office

cool air drawn in from below to larder

rainwater collected from roof for re-use

composting toilet access

cool air enters house

0   5m

tower acts like a huge chimney to exhaust the stale air through similar manually operated shutters. While this is good for cooling the house in summer, it would be very inefficient to throw away heat during winter. At this time of year, the vents are kept firmly closed and the well-sealed door to the tower prevents hot air from drifting up from the living areas.

The kitchen larder also uses stack effect to keep its contents cool throughout the year. Fresh air is drawn directly from the shaded undercroft through the floor of the larder (which is concrete) by a controllable vent and is then exhausted through the top of the larder through side vents in its projecting tip. The larder works effectively through the year, especially at mid-season.

The house also incorporates a green roof over the entire expanse of the living area (not the bedrooms). Ten years ago it was a radical proposal for an urban house to have vegetation on the roof but the majority were manicured lawns requiring high maintenance. Since then there has been a major shift in European countries such as Switzerland and Germany, where it is now policy to install green roofs on all urban buildings. Thanks to the work of advocates like Dusty Gedge of LivingRoofs, we are now seeing the Greater London Authority adopt this as a strategy for planning development throughout London. The benefits of green roofs are a reduction of storm-water flow, a lowering of the urban heat island effect and enhancing biodiversity in addition to protecting the waterproofing layer from harmful ultraviolet light. On recent inspection the roof meadow is flourishing. A self-sustaining ecology of native wild plants has established itself. In an era when green roof manufacturers balk over guarantees and servicing contracts it is heartening to observe that the waterproofing is still functioning well, the drains still work and there is no need for constant maintenance. 9/10 Stock Orchard Street shows that roofs can survive as natural habitats with very little maintenance.

Building systems

The building systems demonstrate a good mix of the innovative coupled with the conventional, which is still a sensible approach today. The innovations included the use of solar thermal collectors to supplement the domestic hot water to the house; whole house ventilation and heat recovery; rainwater harvesting; and composting toilets. As the basis of the building design was to follow passive approaches to design using the fabric of the building to do the majority of the work, the use of systems has been minimised. Despite their simplicity, the designers had problems with the functioning of both of these systems. The solar panels took five years to work properly, with no help provided by the manufacturer/supplier in the Netherlands, and a dearth of spare parts emerged when the model specified for 9/10 Stock Orchard Street was replaced with a newer version. The rainwater recycling pump began leaking and needed replacing. The composting toilet took some time to understand fully, and trial and error have been the making of this technology. Over time these systems have become much more reliable and have moved from cutting edge to mainstream with many technical glitches resolved.

The solar thermal collectors were installed while this technology was beginning to gain popularity in the UK. The system uses flat plate collectors, which are still the standard panel used for most projects. However, the evacuated tube solar thermal systems have improved efficiency by around 30 per cent since then. They are especially suited to the UK due to their ability to work in overcast conditions; flat plate will not perform so well.

The heat recovery ventilation system for the whole house was introduced into the UK for the residential market ten years ago. During this time we have seen these systems becoming more extensively used and more significant as building envelopes become tighter. We used to be able to rely on leakage for background ventilation but tighter building envelopes mean less accidental air leakage. The consequence has been that the health issues associated with good air quality in houses are now serious and whole house heat recovery systems are becoming more important.

In the original heat recovery system stale air was extracted from the bathrooms and composting toilet unit, and the waste heat was used to pre-warm the incoming fresh air. At the time of construction the technology of the heat exchanger was not adequate to prevent cross-contamination: odours were transferred as well as heat. In response, the composting toilet receptacle was disconnected from the heat reclaim system and given its own dedicated extract fan. Ten years on, my view is that the technology is still not of suitable standard to use the heat from composting toilets as an exchange for fresh air. There are some vents that need to be separate, and waste is one of them.

However, this did not mean that the composting toilet installation was a failure. The designers used the best system on the market – the Clivus multrum – and in doing so bought twenty years of tried-and-tested development from the company, mitigating risks associated with such a radical step. This was an extremely important decision and has led to the successful operation of composting human waste on site in a safe and hygienic manner for over ten years. The outputs of the multrum are inert compost and liquid fertiliser, both of which are used in the garden or on the green roof. The UK building codes still insist on providing at least one flushable toilet, but this project shows that alternatives are clearly viable when set up and managed correctly. Since around 40 per cent of domestic mains water consumption is used for flushing the toilet, this will become more important as water shortages increase.

The designers are able to avoid using mains water for flushing office WCs by using rainwater collected from the office roof. This was achieved using simple technology comprising a storage tank, filter and small pump. The relative benefits of not putting waste products into the water supply and of using composted waste in growing things need to be weighed up against the non-benefits of making a vessel out of recycled plastic in addition to the transportational energy from factory to retailer to site.

A wood-burning stove is used in the coolest months to supplement the gas-fired central heating system. The fuel is collected from waste, and stored to dry in the undercroft throughout the year. Wood-burning stoves evoke a sense of cosiness in the room, and when in use reduce the thermal load upon the fossil fuel-based natural gas central heating system. While running on non-renewable fossil fuels, the central heating system is powered by one of the most efficient condensing boilers available. The Viessmann systems were among the first 'complete' energy-efficient solutions dedicated to residential properties. Ten years ago, the owners were buying the best that they could get, and even now the boiler's performance is still credible.

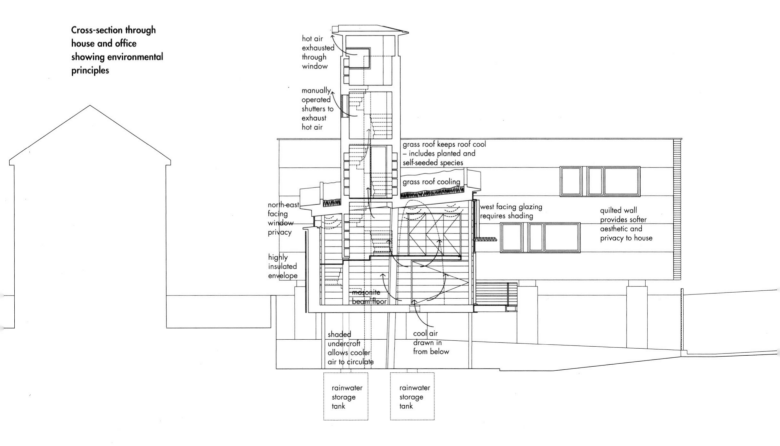

Cross-section through house and office showing environmental principles

hot air exhausted through window

manually operated shutters to exhaust hot air

grass roof keeps roof cool – includes planted and self-seeded species

grass roof cooling

north-east facing window privacy

west facing glazing requires shading

quilted wall provides softer aesthetic and privacy to house

highly insulated envelope

masonite beam floor

shaded undercroft allows cooler air to circulate

cool air drawn in from below

rainwater storage tank

rainwater storage tank

Summary

When 9/10 Stock Orchard Street was conceived and built ten years ago, it pushed the boundaries of green urban design through its building materials, passive design strategies and low resource-consuming building systems. In that time it has been a beacon for demonstrating what green building solutions can mean in urban settings, and it has helped to facilitate a change in lifestyle, and hence empower users to operate in a more sustainable manner. This has benefits for sustainability and urban design around the world. The lessons learned from the impact of living with innovative systems have been shown to be much simpler than we might imagine. The key steps to innovation are to know the risks and to take steps to mitigate these through selection of low maintenance systems that work simply and that the users can control by themselves.

As a tribute to its forebears, Pike, Vale, Broome and Roaf, the house at 9/10 Stock Orchard Street has sought to build on earlier approaches, yet it has extended its response into the urban context and into the design of office environments. It does not claim to be an autonomous house; rather it acknowledges that it is part of a much larger city metabolism with infrastructure and site constraints, yet it makes the best possible use of what is available for free.

Moreover, where previous pioneers tended to focus on systems and their aesthetic desire was to look acceptably 'normal', it is its material use that sets 9/10 Stock Orchard Street apart as the next generation in green architecture. In particular, I believe that in the future we will see more use of natural materials produced from our traditional waste streams such as straw, crushed concrete, recycled timber and metals, reused brick, and green and brown roofs. Until the construction industry begins to exploit the value of existing materials and abandons the use of natural resources and materials made from virgin stock, this is likely to be a medium-term goal. We may have to wait some time until we realise that we are in extreme resource crisis, forcing us to look for alternative products; simultaneously, we may have to reconsider some of our restrictive regulations. Those such as the British Board of Agrément will need reorientating to approve the use of alternative materials in construction.

What will the next ten years hold for 9/10 Stock Orchard Street? It will still be working passively as intended, and its materials will weather some more, but its design approach, including its combination of flexible live/work situations, will stand strong as an example of green design that continues to inspire and lead the way forward. In order for society to function in a more sustainable manner, we will need more than green buildings; we will need to shift how we choose to live. The role that experiments in green architecture such as 9/10 Stock Orchard Street play is to provoke debate, demonstrate alternatives, convince those currently sceptical about green design and catalyse some of this change. This change will be felt across our homes and our workplaces – and 9/10 Stock Orchard Street is playing its part in driving this process forward.

Steel frame erection, May 1999. Note spring box on gabion cap in foreground.

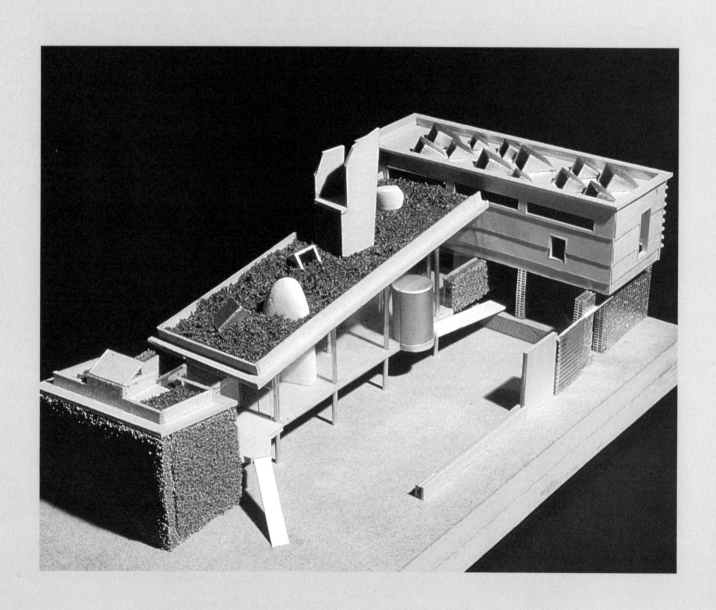

The model: deconstructed

Jan-Carlos Kucharek

To be honest, I don't think Sarah and Jeremy were that sure what Stock Orchard Street would really look like when they came to see us, but I don't remember that bothering them. They had ideas for sure; metaphors, materials and methodologies of construction, but perhaps not a clear sense of what all these, once brought together, would realise. So the next step, after concept sketches and scaled drawings, seemed to be to pull it together in three dimensions. For Steve and myself, who had spent a year wandering lost through the wide open landscapes of Jeremy's diploma unit at The Bartlett, it was an opportunity to get a handle on whatever it was that he had been banging on about all year: suburban obsessions, the significance of programmes, justifications of materiality and the conscious layering of meaning behind the drawn image. Our job, sitting around the kitchen table for a few evenings armed with their drawings and our scalpels, was to create a real model of that imagined thing. Or an imagined version of a real thing. Perhaps both were real. Or both imagined. Maybe one could never truly represent the other and any efforts would just be a form of artifice. Either way, from paper

sketches, materials and time itself, some*thing* was craving to be realised – the straw bale house needed to be brought in from the damp, ergot-riddled threat of thinking.

In a sense, their hand had been forced into making the decision to build the model. The cold, 'objectified' nature of the planning process demands that not only the volume and material of the design, but its philosophies and intangible aspects be distilled to drawn lines. But I think they felt that by actually modelling the house, they were entering dangerous territory – an ultimatum to concretise the gestating, nebulous thoughts that they had probably lived with for years. There was a feeling that in their minds it was already an occupied space, lending a spatial edge to their personal politics, informing their critical responses and academic papers; expanding and pushing away by tiny degrees like some diaphanous inflatable at the lath and plaster walls of their idyllic north London Victorian terrace. I loved their old home, but with hindsight I see a lovely poetry in thinking that they never really did.

According to the modern dictionary definition, a model can

have a number of interpretations. It can be example for imitation or comparison to show the construction or appearance of something, or a person or thing that serves as a subject for an artist, or a simplified representation of a system or hypothesis. But the word 'modello' actually originated in Italy in the sixteenth century and coincided with the Renaissance. This, as it turns out, was no coincidence. Before this time, building had no need for models. Its codes were locked in the minds of the master masons, and passed on on-site and through an oral tradition. What need was there for a model when you were building the real thing? But with the rediscovery of classical architecture all that changed. 'Design' emerged as a distinct intellectual discipline, whose new interpretations of its ancient orders and proportions were based on the scaled drawings of 'architects'. Architecture went into schism. You were either the intellectual rendering the building on paper, or you were the craftsman building it – and the 'modello' was the progeny of a necessary liaison. Historically then, the model was doomed to be a subordinate tool – a banal and descriptive representation of a pre-ordained drawn concept. Yet this was the last thing that Sarah and Jeremy wanted. For them, to 'model' meant absorbing all the definitions of the word simultaneously to create an experiment in generating the 'speculative space' of research for designing and building. We were not being asked so much to 'build a model' as to 'model a building'. This being the case, the unresolved nature of the initial sketches was prerequisite – their ambiguity allowed us, as it did them, the space for invention and surprise.

Investigation is easy when all the clues are in place. The house was, by its nature, intended to encapsulate aspects of the found and the ready-made, an assemblage of components; reused bricks from the site, straw bales, gabions, earth, bags of cement whose contents would never see the light of day; and it was in this spirit that we chose to approach the model's design. The ensuing visit to the craft shop, I recall, proved to be a strangely anodyne experience, with an emptiness in the representational nature of its scaled materials with their 'mini-me' reality. It is with regret that I bought the metal sheet for the gabions – for some reason we had preferred, but

shied away from, the hairiness of wire wool. Foam was used as a default material, to give form to amorphous volumes that were themselves of as yet undefined materiality. But beyond that, the late hours constructing it dictated the use of ingenuity and locally sourced materials. The base was made of the sanded leftover pieces of a hand-made mattress base left in the attic by a former tenant. Its cement wall was a cardboard box stripped down to its structural corrugations. Fill for the gabions were drunkenly formed from obsessively sliced corks of the numerous bottles of wine consumed while building. The circular 'transfer pod' to the guestroom, originally supposed to hang off the flank wall of the neighbour end-of-terrace (sadly, never executed) was a sawn-off aluminium pencil holder, and the final materiality of the straw bale wall and grass roof ensured that my housemates were left hopelessly searching the house for scouring pads weeks later. I felt that when the completed model finally left the kitchen table, it had, by a process of inadvertent osmosis, absorbed something of the domestic history of our own home.

Imbuing ideas with a new level

of reality, models can be dangerous things, and like the heresy of a Galilean orrery, sometimes they are best left out of sight. There, complete, in its thick matted green and *blueness*: even its designers could not deny Stock Orchard Street's 'otherness'. It became blindingly obvious that as a way of explaining the project to the planners, the model was more likely to confound the realisation of the real thing – it seemed to make the strength of the drawn idea too *material*. Its physicality became something even its architects couldn't handle, and, concerned by its possible ramifications, another was conceived. Safely homogenised, the model the planners finally saw was a palimpsest of milky-white card.

Yet that sense of 'otherness' made manifest in the original remains one of the defining characteristics of Stock Orchard Street – an idea of a home, not slave to style, where sustainability rubs up against almost outrageous decadence, a place of political complexity and spatial incident. The odd thing is that not being born of a preconceived agenda, the built reality defies categorisation. Despite its lectern-like library

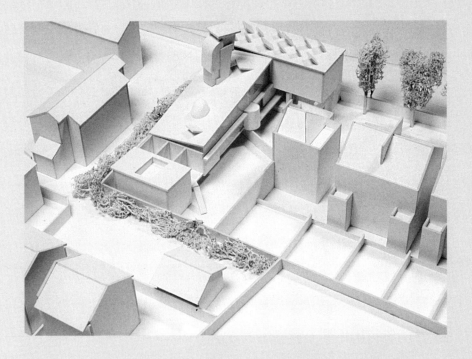

tower, it does not preach, but sits benignly at the dead-end of a street, so part of its place and of itself that it almost eschews discovery. I feel to this day that the model generated concepts and materiality that the drawings alone could never have foreseen. Arising from the methodologies that inspired the design of the building, the model, in the end, could not deny its nature.

One day, after the house was nearly finished and while the owners were out, some youths broke in via the utility room – at the only point where the house proper makes contact with the ground plane. But this was no mere breaking and entering or mindless trashing; in fact, evidence points to the building being occupied by the uninvited guests for some time. Bizarrely, holes were bored through books in the library with the owners' own drill and then replaced on the shelves, and are still, on occasion, discovered even now. The composting toilet obviously intrigued, with various household objects thrown down the WC pan, only to be sluiced out and discovered at a later date. The miscreants, it appears, made themselves at home in the straw

bedroom downstairs, at the time being used as a living room – a natural deduction, given the empty bottles of claret left rolling around when Sarah and Jeremy returned; but apart from this, nothing was really touched. Except for one further curious discovery in the room. Both models of the house – not untouched however, but meticulously taken apart piece by piece, the elevations and floor plates peeled away – were laid out and arranged on the floor, its three dimensions returning to two.

One would assume this to be an act of random vandalism, but I would like to think not. Perhaps, for the intruders, it was a literal attempt to comprehend for themselves the strange alien space that they too had chosen to occupy. In doing what they did, the model deconstructed was to become a metaphor for the design of the house itself. A normally blindly accepted method of architectural representation challenged and forced back into two dimensions; an iterative, chance occurrence when the drawing became a model, only to become a drawing again. Perhaps this explains why Sarah and Jeremy were so sanguine in the face of the break-in – for

ultimately it reinforced their aesthetic approach. Dismantled within the walls of the built reality, both the model's value and redundancy in the design process was laid bare. Like a champagne bottle smashed against the slowly sliding side of a ship's hull, this was the straw bale house's cathartic moment of end and beginning. Its conscious creation marked by conscious destruction.

And it seems that it's full steam ahead. In an empty space between its steel piloti, on the portside of the utility room window, Sarah's inkling is that they'll fit a sauna.

The excessive materiality of Stock Orchard Street: towards a feminist material practice

Katie Lloyd Thomas

'Is it possible to actively strive to produce an architecture of excess, in which the "more" is not cast off but made central, in which expenditure is sought out, in which instability, fluidity, the return of space to the bodies whose morphologies it upholds and conforms, in which the monstrous and the extrafunctional, consumption as much as production, act as powerful forces? Is this the same as or linked to the question of the feminine in architecture?' Elizabeth Grosz[1]

In her short essay 'Architectures of Excess', the feminist philosopher Elizabeth Grosz uses the figure of excess to make connections between different feminist approaches which have dominated the past forty years. First, excess describes all groups, including women, who are marginalised as 'other' in society. Second, excess refers to those aspects of life and culture which disrupt conventional categories and are banished to the outside, which of course include and can be understood in relation to the feminine. Third, and less explicitly in this essay than in Grosz's more recent writing, excess also seems to stand in for the proliferation of possibilities, for the opening of new processes and ways of living, that would not be built on principles of equality, nor by promoting the supposed feminine over the masculine, but instead by moving out of existing structures and logics towards the unknown conditions of the future.

Trying to define what this future excess might be like, at least for architecture, Grosz draws on a number of figures of the feminine which emerged in particular from French feminist theory, psychoanalysis and deconstruction. These include the monstrous rather than the ordered and harmonious, the superfluous rather than the necessary, the unstable rather than the security of the fixed and immutable. Each of these figures brings to mind aspects of the excessive architecture of Stock Orchard Street; its 'hairy' straw bale walls and its 'fat' gabions:

[1] Elizabeth Grosz, 'Architectures of Excess' in *Architecture from the Outside*, Cambridge, Mass.: MIT Press, 2001, p.163. First published in Cynthia Davidson (ed.), *Anymore*, Cambridge, Mass.: MIT Press, 2000.

0171 732 3307 15/4/99 2:16pm 1/1

KOYA

Construction
and Project Management
84 Furley Road London SE15 1UG
Tel 0171 639 6255
Fax 0171 277 7918

DATE: Thu, Apr 15, 1999

TO: Andy Heyne, Price & Myers Fax 0171 436 4905
cc Gillian, SWA.

FROM: Martin Hughes
Tel 0171 732 9817 Fax 0171 732 3307
e-mail: Treharris@compuserve.com

NUMBER OF SHEETS INCLUDING THIS ONE: 1

Re 9 STOCK ORCHARD ST N7

Andy,

We noticed that the spring nearest to B3 (ie the smallest one on the Gabions) could be manually deflected, and that it made a hissing sound (air escaping) when it was being deflected. The other springs are much stiffer. Does this sound okay or should we check this with Gerb?

Also we released the nuts which we presumed were for tightening the springs for transport, but left the studs in place.

Martin

Fig 1 fax dated Thursday, 15 April 1999 from Martin Hughes to Andy Heyne, structural engineer

'Why should engineering always be about the minimal? Why not an economy of excess?'[2]

the 'crude' superfluous bags and quilts which wrap the office building; the tiny hi-tech springs in smart green boxes on which it perches whose hissing and leaking is an ongoing worry to clients, builders and engineers:

'We noticed that the spring nearest to B3 (i.e. the smallest one on the Gabions) could be manually deflected, and that it made a hissing sound (air escaping) when it was being deflected. The other springs are much stiffer. Does this sound okay or should we check this with GERB?'[3] [Fig 1]

and, moreover, the proliferation of material and structural solutions which each retain individual identities rather than being subsumed into a unified whole:

'Too many ideas.' 'Too much going on.' 'Inconsistent.'[4],

'Less is more: Mies, Less is a bore: Venturi, Mess is the Law: Till.'[5]

There is just 'more' in general at Stock Orchard Street. Each of these figures might, at least in Grosz's terms, be linked to the question of the feminine. In troubling the boundaries of architecture's orthodoxies, what has been cast out – the excess – enters in.

Sarah and Jeremy are unusual among architects in that they are happy to ally their practice with feminism, and move beyond the comfortable discourse around equal representation that is exemplified by *Building Design*'s 50/50 campaign.[6] In their own writing around Stock Orchard Street the question of gender often emerges. They are alert to women's marginalisation in the building industry:

'Five weeks later we arrive, three amateurs (two of them women) in a self-drive van at a hall full of trucks and big skilled men.'[7]

Professional expertise, so keenly defended by architects and so determining of practice and architectural principles, is the subject of ongoing critique[8] and is specifically referred to as 'patriarchal' in an unpublished version of 'The Future is Hairy'.[9] They play with many of the binaries which underpin architectural and social structures and conventions:

'straw = hairy = handholding = female = amateur = crude = non-rational'[10]

At Stock Orchard Street it is notions of domesticity in particular that are worked into the design for the office in order to confuse the conventional distinctions between home and work:

'The office is usually seen as a place set apart from the home and architecturally assumes an identity of decorum and order. There is a gender thing going on here, in the separation of the wilful domestic from the ordered office and the identification of the female with the former and the male with the latter.'[11]

2 Jeremy Till and Sarah Wigglesworth, 'The Future is Hairy' in Jonathan Hill (ed.) *Architecture: The Subject is Matter*, London: Routledge, 2001, p. 20.

3 Fax from Martin Hughes, project manager, KOYA Construction to Andy Heyne, structural engineer, Price & Myers, 15 April 1999.

4 Till and Wigglesworth, 'The Future is Hairy', p. 27.

5 Jeremy Till, *Architecture Depends*, Cambridge, Mass.: The MIT Press, 2009, pxi.

6 See www.bdonline.co.uk/hybrid.asp?typeCode=204&subTypeCode=12737&pubcode=60, accessed 9 April 2009.

7 Till and Wigglesworth, 'The Future is Hairy', p. 13.

8 See in particular Till and Wigglesworth, 'The Future is Hairy', Till, *Architecture Depends*, and Sarah Wigglesworth, 'A Fitting Fetish: The Interior of Maison de Verre' in Iain Borden and Jane Rendell (eds) *Intersections: Architectural Histories and Critical Theories*, London: Routledge, pp. 91–108.

9 Sarah Wigglesworth and Jeremy Till, 'It's Just a House', unpublished lecture given in November 1998, p. 10.

10 Till and Wigglesworth, 'The Future is Hairy', p. 14.

11 Ibid., p. 24.

By introducing Grosz's notion of 'excess' I want both to explore these terms and to extend a feminist reading of Stock Orchard Street beyond them. I map out an excess that is here achieved primarily through the material register, as opposed to the formal (an excess which was to become rampant in the intervening years between the realisation of the house and today). Because Sarah and Jeremy provide such detailed and critically incisive accounts of the building of Stock Orchard Street, we are able to see what processes and resistances are mobilised in realising an architecture of excess – aspects that are necessarily overlooked by Grosz because hers is figuration, a description of a feminine imaginary. As such, I want to suggest that Stock Orchard Street provokes us to move beyond the limitations of working with masculine/feminine binaries towards the possibilities of processes of building that might exceed existing practices and could perhaps be described as feminist material practice.

Material excess and the feminine

It could be argued, paradoxically, that the material is already excessive to architecture proper. Alberto Pérez-Gómez has shown how the discipline of architecture founded its separation from mere construction on its use of descriptive geometry, an ideal system of representation which relied precisely on the exclusion of the material and enabled the literal separation of architecture from building.[12] More recently Peter Eisenman has argued that formal manipulation should be regarded as the 'interiority' of architecture.[13] Robert McAnulty has called for the inclusion of 'matter' within the design process which would be different to a preoccupation with building materials that are already embedded in the dirty world of capital and commodification.[14] If building materials are understood as outside architecture, they are the very point where the supposed non-architectural inevitably enters in.

For the feminist theorist Catherine Ingraham, whose work has influenced my own, the denial of the material occurs because architecture is burdened with 'linearity' and relates to a repression of the material register which was also being explored in other areas of feminist theory. Grosz had made corporeality central to her feminism in the mid 1990s, arguing that to omit the question of the body in order to avoid the problems of essentialism was simply to return to an old Cartesian idealism which held little hope for new figurations in the feminine.[15] Julia Kristeva had argued that Lacanian psychoanalysis overplayed the 'symbolic' aspects of language in socialisation and that feminist theory needed to explore the ways in which the 'semiotic' or bodily registers also structured the subject's entry into culture – and continued to trouble notions of fixed meaning and identity, through non-signifying aspects of poetic language or the non-geometric aspects of painting such as colour.[16]

Ingraham took up these ideas and suggested that for architecture it was in the geometric line that there was a repressed materiality. The geometric line is defined as extension without breadth and denies 'its own thickness and fleshiness'.[17] As such it is an element of an ideal system which always resists 'animality, impropriety, disease, and contamination'. Furthermore, Ingraham identified the 'space of the line' with the wall and its counter-geometric life with sexuality:

[12] Alberto Pérez-Gómez, *Architecture and the Crisis of Modern Science*, Cambridge, Mass.: MIT Press, 1983.

[13] See, for example, Peter Eisenman, *Eisenman Inside Out: Selected Writings*, New Haven, Conn.: Yale University Press, 2004.

[14] Robert McAnulty, 'What's the Matter with Material?' in *Log 5*, Spring/Summer 2005, pp. 87–92.

[15] See Elizabeth Grosz, *Space, Time and Perversion; Essays on the Politics of Bodies*, New York: Routledge, 1995, and *Volatile Bodies: Toward a Corporeal Feminism*, Bloomington, Ind.: Indiana University Press, 1994.

[16] See Julia Kristeva, *Revolution in Poetic Language*, New York: Columbia University Press, 1984, and *Desire in Language*, Oxford: Blackwell, 1984.

[17] Catherine Ingraham, 'Lines and Linearity; Problems in Architectural Theory' in Andrea Kahn (ed.) *Drawing/Building/Text: Essays in Architectural Theory*, New York: Princeton Architectural Press, 1991, p. 72.

Fig 2 column poking through gabion stones

Fig 3 upholstered wall being fixed

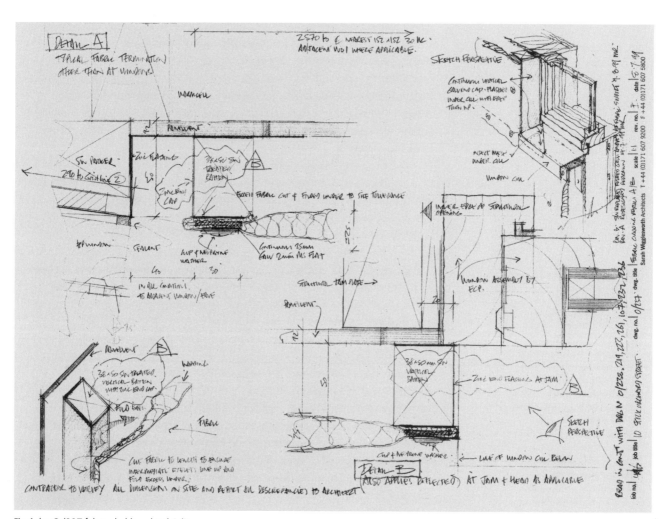

Fig 4 drg O/237 fabric cladding detail A/B

'This wall which always dreams of itself as the sexless geometric line, is where the differences of sexuality begin to be homologized as material differences, albeit in complex ways... The cool geometric line in architecture in fact harbours a hot materiality.'[18]

Thus in Ingraham's account there is a repressed materiality both in the space of the lines describing the wall, and in the conceptualisation of the wall itself. In Katherine Shonfield's wonderful essay, 'Why Does Your Flat Leak?' the cavity wall is shown to exemplify this. While outwardly the concrete brutalist wall appears to conform with the demand for structural honesty, inwardly, she explains, the solution to the 1973 oil crisis 'was to cram the interior with insulation' and then to avoid the ingress of water with '"plastic weepholes", waterproof linings, high specification cavity trays, cavity wall "bats", shiny plastic discs. All is protected from the slightest contamination drop.'[19]

In the installation which Shonfield made with Frank O'Sullivan, presented at the end of her essay, the interior walls of an underground public lavatory were covered with white feathers. Although this is described as the inclusion of dirt and contamination, it also appears to be a defiant move against the hidden world of the cavity in which the insulation 'dragged into the outside air... could be an alternative future for building construction: of invention, fun and decoration'.[20]

At Stock Orchard Street the exposure of what might usually be interior to the wall is a frequent motif. A transparent polycarbonate skin allows a view into the interior of the straw bale wall – 'the secret life of the building' – and reveals potential contaminants such as rot, condensation, insects and rodents. In the gabion walls a concrete column hides inside the mass of fill [*Fig 2*]. And where a soft, shiny quilt has been wrapped around the office building, Sarah and Jeremy recall how both their fathers thought this must be an internal layer still awaiting the final cladding [*Fig 3*]. The quilt is not, however, included in the calculation of the wall's thermal resistance; it is in fact mounted on to battens fixed in turn to an inner wall built up with conventional insulation [*Fig 4*]. The quilting is, to use Grosz's term, 'extrafunctional'. It is intended to signify domesticity by alluding to the conventional feminine sphere. 'We want it to feel like domestic upholstery, puckered and buttoned, deflating any corporate pretensions. There is a gender thing going on here as well.'[21]

It is used as decoration – an excess that Jennifer Bloomer has associated with the feminine: 'The ornamental has come to be associated with dishonesty, impurity (ordure), the improper, and excessiveness or exorbitance, characteristics that the Symbolic order has deemed feminine.'[22]

The use of the quilt remains representational. Its meanings are effective because they disrupt existing structures (the separation of work and home, associations of softness with domesticity and the feminine and so on). Although the quilting employs techniques that are usually associated with women and domestic work – pattern cutting, stitching and upholstery – its manufacture is in fact highly prescribed by the architects [*Fig 5*]. The quilting makes a point but, like so many of the alternatives proposed by feminist theorists working with masculine/feminine binaries, its critical power relies on relationships with existing discourses and practices, rather than opening up alternatives to existing structures. What else might the excessive materiality of Stock Orchard Street make possible?

[18] Catherine Ingraham, 'Initial Properties: Architecture and the Space of the Line' in Beatriz Colomina (ed.) *Sexuality and Space*, New York: Princeton University Press, 1992, p. 266.

[19] 'Why Does Your Flat Leak?' in Katherine Shonfield, *Walls Have Feelings*, London: Routledge, 2000, p. 45.

[20] Ibid., pp. 32–52.

[21] Till and Wigglesworth, 'The Future is Hairy', p. 24.

[22] Jennifer Bloomer, 'D'or' in Colomina (ed.), *Sexuality and Space*, p. 168.

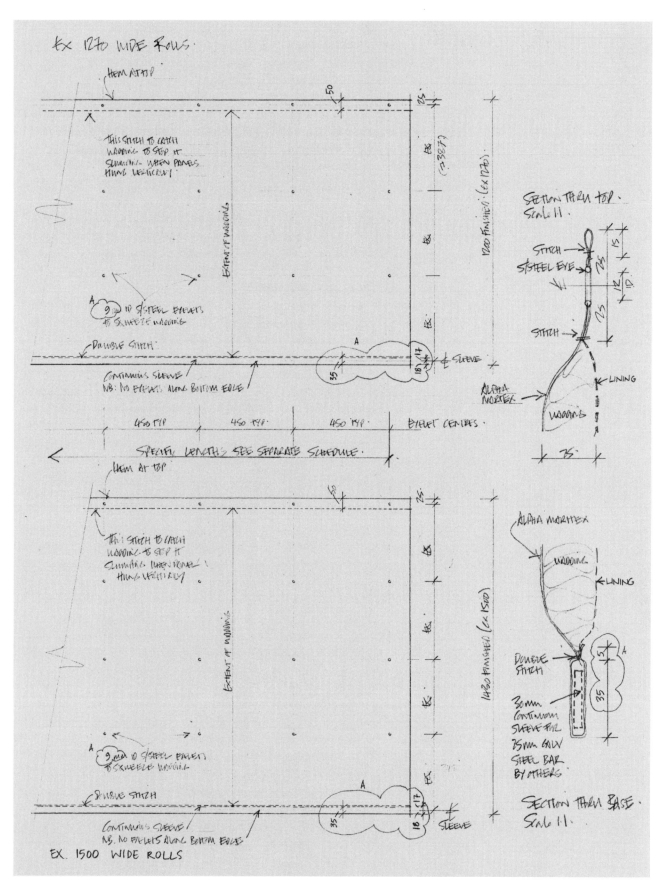

Fig 5 drg O/240 fabric wall details

Exceeding the limits of proper materials

Item 29 of the schedule was part of the conditional Building Regulations approval for Stock Orchard Street [*Fig 6*]. As with so many of the materials and construction techniques used at Stock Orchard Street, the quilted wall falls outside the category of 'proper materials' as defined by the Building Regulations. Its 'extrafunctional' status is not just determined by the architects' choice to use it symbolically. As a one-off walling material, a bespoke invention designed and produced for this specific condition, it bears none of the appropriate marks which permit its inclusion within existing regimes of approval and has not been tested to demonstrate its conformity with required standards. As such – untested, unmeasured, unapproved – it cannot be counted in the functioning buildup of the wall.

Similarly, the sandbags which clad the wall to the railway are 'extrafunctional' in terms of the Building Regulations, even though they dampen the sound and vibration caused by passing trains. Their use is inspired, Sarah and Jeremy tell us, by a photograph of a London coffee house during the Blitz, and not in explicitly critical terms. The sandbag wall is also carefully detailed [*Fig 7*]. Stitching patterns, dimensions and special window frames are worked out with precision; bags that will appear at the end of the wall have hidden seams. But the realisation of the wall allows for deviations in construction and for the exigencies of time and weathering. Drawing no. O/243 [*Fig 8*] shows a fully developed design for a 'sandbag filling rig' complete with

29.

Building Regulations – Regulation 7

Any building work shall be carried out:

(a)   with proper materials which are appropriate for the circumstances in which they are used; and

(b)   in a workmanlike manner.

"Proper materials" shall include materials which:

(a)   bear an appropriate EC mark in accordance with the Construction Products Directive; or

(b)   conform to an appropriate harmonized standard or European technical approval; or

(c)   conform to an appropriate British Standard or British Board of Agrement certificate; or

(d)   conform to some other national technical specification of any member state which provides, in use, an equivalent level of protection and performance with respect to the relevant requirements of the Building Regulations, as an appropriate British Standard or British Board of Agrement certificate.

is this likely to be a problem?

Fig 6 Item 29 of schedule attached to London Borough of Islington Control approval, in respect of 9/10 Stock Orchard Street, 1 July 1998

125

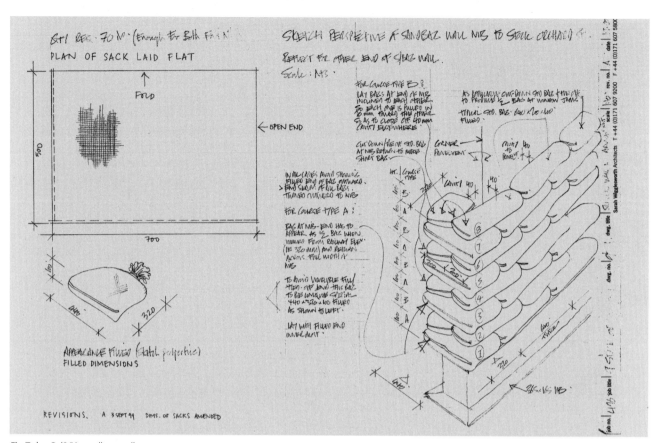

Fig 7 drg O/251 sandbag wall arrangement

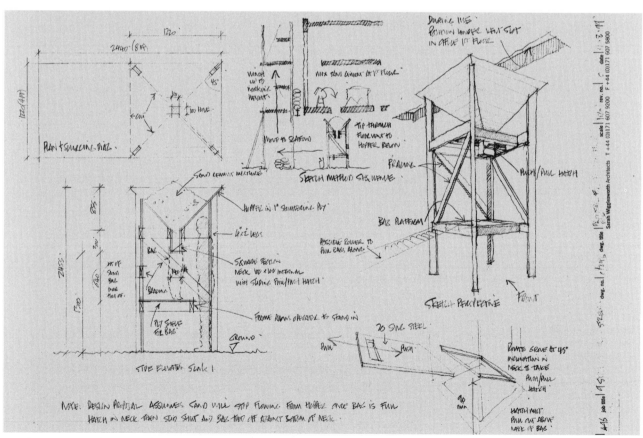

Fig 8 drg O/243 proposal for sandbag filling rig

Fig 9 ad hoc filling funnel

dimensions, 'push/pull hatch' and directions for utilising parts of the existing building structure for winching, mixing and filling, but is in the end replaced by the builders' own invention, using items already on site such as plastic piping [*Fig 9*]:

'*In their making of the building, the builders have suspended their initial belief in the project and have claimed the various unknown technologies as their own.*'[23]

The polypropylene sacks are intended to decay and peel away, and fingers are crossed that shedding fragments do not end up on the track. Here the use of a material outside 'the world of the proper, the system, form, regulated production'[24] sets up a condition in which productive forces exceeding those prescribed by the architects become part of the wall's realisation.

It is in the design and realisation of the straw bale wall that these issues come most to the fore. In their descriptions of building a prototype wall at the Interbuild Exhibition Sarah and Jeremy describe how a number of conventions are transgressed. For example, the use of polycarbonate cladding – a 'proper' building material – in conjunction with 'hairy' straw scuppered the chance of any sponsorship for the exhibit:

'*We telephone a large polycarbonate manufacturer to get sponsorship to Interbuild. He is circumspect when we tell him of the straw bales. "We do not want our product associated with a marginal application – I am afraid we cannot help," he states, and puts the phone down.*'[25]

Gillian, Sarah and Jeremy built the wall. Professional architects became amateurs and improvisers. Women did the 'man's work' of building, and a hybrid that fitted the expectations of neither mainstream nor ecological building was produced:

'*The eco-people are offended by the polycarbonate (plastics are not wholesome). The technocrats are confused by the natural stuff.*'[26]

When the straw bales are used in the building of the house they are included as part of the performing construction and are not only 'extrafunctional'. As such they provoke a series of negotiations and contestations which begin in the public space of Interbuild when the Fire Officer insists that the bales are fire protected even though they are not in fact combustible:

'*1.00: Fire Officer arrives. He says we must stop building immediately
1.30: Fire Brigade come. They inform us that
a) straw is unsafe
b) it will spontaneously combust
c) we have to stop construction and go home with the bales.*'[27]

At the house, Building Control decides that there is insufficient evidence to allow the bales to be used structurally (they must remain 'extra-structural' – a kind of relegation to secondary status in conventional architectural terms) and to avoid their outright rejection the architects design a vertical timber

23 Till and Wigglesworth,
   'The Future is Hairy', p. 16.
24 Grosz, 'Architectures of Excess',
   p. 153.
25 Wigglesworth and Till,
   'It's Just a House', p. 11.
26 Ibid., p. 14.
27 Ibid., p. 12.

truss which can have the official, demonstrable role of taking the loads'
[*Fig 10*]:

'*The argument is that the wind loads are transferred via the cladding ladders and therefore the bales do not enter into the structural argument because they are being treated as non-structural infill material.*' [*Fig 11*][28]

When Building Control ask Sarah to produce an Agrément Certificate for the straw bales Jeremy gives them an enormous stack of documentation compiled from straw bale builders' handbooks, internet sites and informal advice. Building Control can no longer simply rely on the standardised mechanisms of inclusion and exclusion. Instead, what authorises the use of a material is opened up to negotiation in which non-professional voices play a part, and the capacities of all to draw on their specific knowledge and experience are mobilised. The unquestioned certainties (outside most architects' knowledge even when they depend upon them) which statutory approval and professional authority usually lend to building are destabilised. These processes reveal and produce anxieties: around rodents, fire, structural soundness, even Jeremy's concerns about the final arrangement of the façade, but they may also extend the ownership of the building process by opening it up to contestation and involvement.

[28] Notes of a meeting between Mr Seyon and Mr Andrews from London Borough of Islington Building Control and SW and JT, 24 June 1998.

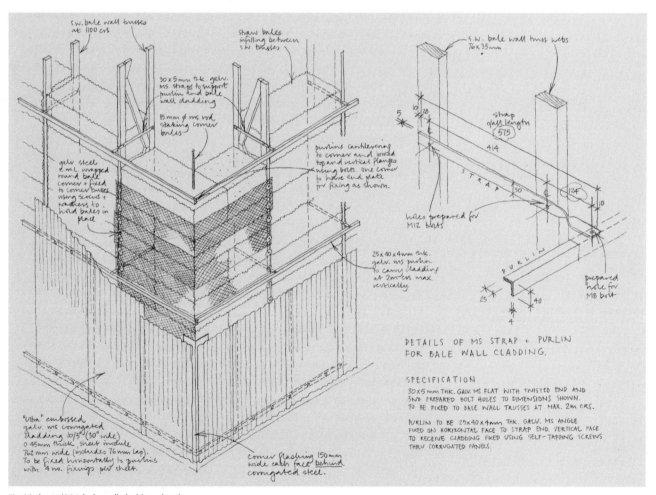

Fig 10 drg H/231 bale wall cladding details

Fig 11 straw bale wall
showing ladders

Fig 12 the junction
between cloth cladding
and sandbags

Where the use of materials exceeds the limits of what is already defined in regulatory and construction conventions, it can also lead to openings, contestations and invention within otherwise prescribed processes. These openings do not necessarily lead to unconventional outcomes, since those involved in the building process are perhaps as steeped in aesthetic conventions as architects. Sarah has described, for example, how the builders took the decision to use only the grey pieces of broken concrete in the gabion columns and filtered out the coloured pieces, or how the render to the interior of the irregular straw bale wall was made perfectly flat by the plasterer without reference to the architects' preferences. Where there are openings and opportunities for others to take part in the invention and design of the building, it is not so much the realised outcomes that are significant as the processes of design, negotiation and building.

Towards a feminist material practice

Stock Orchard Street involves many of the kinds of excess elaborated by Grosz in her essay. Amateur builders and women – groups often marginalised in architectural production – are involved in the processes of building. A number of architectural conventions are disrupted: separations between domesticity and work are confused materially and spatially, detailing is 'maximal' rather than minimal, materials are left in unstable states where they might vibrate, sag or decay. Assumed hierarchies are undermined: the interior of the wall – usually hidden – becomes part of the architectural expression while structural elements disappear from view, and there is a proliferation of 'extrafunctional' elements, so often considered as mere decoration and extraneous. As Grosz notes, following Georges Bataille, 'a radically antifunctional architecture' can also be 'anti-authoritarian and antibureaucratic'. 'The ornament, the detail, the redundant, and the unnecessary,' she continues, 'may prove provisional elements of any architectures of excess.'[29]

If Grosz proposes some provisional strategies for an architecture of excess, Stock Orchard Street gives us an opportunity to track the processes and negotiations which may be necessary for such an architecture to be realised. It becomes apparent that, to some extent, it is the same bureaucratic and authoritative structures which already determine what is understood as excessive. The 'extrafunctionality' of the sandbag wall or the upholstered cladding is not a physical characteristic of the materials or simply a result of their cultural meaning [*Fig 12*]. These materials become redundant or decorative at Stock Orchard Street precisely because their performance cannot be quantified or approved as satisfying statutory requirements. The logic of excess is itself determined by the same system which it is intended to exceed, a problem which occurs also when the 'feminine' is celebrated or the tenets of modernist architecture are reversed.

However, Grosz offers some speculations about the kinds of possibilities 'excess' might open up, including altered understandings of space and time, the making of spaces where 'women can live' and the provision of 'some of the necessary conditions for experiments in future living'[30] which might find places for other marginalised or excluded groups, as well as an architecture of superabundance, generosity and gift. Here, excess is not understood as what is cast out or marginalised, but as productive potential: 'An

---

[29] Grosz, 'Architectures of Excess', p. 154.
[30] Ibid., pp. 165–166.

31 Ibid., p. 164.

32 Elizabeth Grosz, *Chaos, Territory, Art: Deleuze and the Framing of the Earth*, New York: Columbia University Press, 2008, p. 7.

33 Ibid., p. 9.

34 See in particular Stacy Alaimo and Susan Hekman (eds) *Material Feminisms*, Bloomington, Ind.: Indiana University Press, 2008.

35 For the significance of this term see in particular the work of Bruno Latour, *Pandora's Hope*, Cambridge, Mass.: Harvard University Press, 1999, and 'Mixing Humans and Nonhumans Together' in William Braham and Jonathan Hale (eds) *Rethinking Technology: A Reader in Architectural Theory*, London: Routledge, 2007, pp. 309–324.

36 See Judith Butler, *Gender Trouble; Feminism and the Subversion of Identity*, London: Routledge, 1990, and *Bodies That Matter: On the Discursive Limits of Sex*, London: Routledge, 1993.

37 Mariam Fraser, 'What is the Matter of Feminist Criticism' in *Economy and Society*, Vol. 31, No 4, November 2002, p. 614.

38 See, for example, Donna Haraway, *Modest_Witness@Second_Millennium.FemaleMan©_Meets_OncoMouse™*, New York: Routledge, 1997, and Isabelle Stengers, *Power and Invention: Situating Science*, Minneapolis, Minn: University of Minnesota Press, 1997, and, with Bernadette Bensaude-Vincent, her wonderful *History of Chemistry*, Cambridge, Mass.: Harvard University Press, 1996.

39 Karen Barad, 'Posthumanist Performativity: Toward an Understanding of How Matter Comes to Matter' in Alaimo and Hekman (eds) *Material Feminisms*, p. 124.

architecture of excess must aim not to satisfy present needs but to produce future desires.'[31]

What may be more potent about the excesses of Stock Orchard Street is that to begin to test architecture at the level of material excess is not only to play with notions of the feminine, even sexual difference itself; it is also to trouble the material conditions of architectural production. In their careful analysis of the building process at Stock Orchard Street Sarah and Jeremy reveal the fixity of the boundaries drawn around the material and the difficulty of loosening the knot of industrial, economic, legislative and disciplinary forces which constitute the material in architecture. What is suggested in terms of the future are some of the productive possibilities of dialogue, contestation, contingency and invention which a critical materiality might open up.

In a more recent essay Grosz develops her notion of superabundance in terms of Irigaray's notion of irreducible sexual difference, giving the examples of 'the haunting beauty of birdsong, the provocative performance of erotic display in primates, the attraction of insects to the perfume of plants' as 'in excess of mere survival'.[32] She relates this 'excessive and useless production… production for the sake of profusion and differentiation'[33] to art (where she locates architecture) with its capacity for the proliferation of sensations. But it is not enough to consider material excess only in terms of its aesthetic effect or insofar as it is part of artistic production since, as Stock Orchard Street shows us, material excess is also necessarily constituted within the specific industrial and disciplinary practices of architecture.

What may be most productive about the attention Sarah and Jeremy pay to the altered material practices at Stock Orchard Street is that they go beyond the more general notions of the material invoked in feminist theory such as feminine 'matter', corporeality, or affect and sensation to give us an account of the *materialisation* of such excess. Recent discussions of ongoing feminist concerns with materiality[34] have also pointed out that the matter of bodies might not provide a starting point for thinking about other kinds of materialisations – whether of technologies or objects, or what is often referred to as the 'nonhuman'.[35] Mariam Fraser, for example, suggests that in Judith Butler's seminal work on the relationship of sex, bodies and matter:[36] 'The human realm is the only one in which matter for Butler really matters (or comes "to mean")'.[37]

The problems with applying feminist theories of matter developed in relation to corporeality may also undermine some of the ways in which feminist architectural theorists such as Bloomer and Ingraham have tried to understand the materiality of architecture and its representations in relation to the sexed matter of bodies.

For feminists working in science studies, however, it has been increasingly important to question the supposed boundary between human and nonhuman, to understand the capacities they might have in common and the productive possibilities for change and proliferation they might offer.[38] This also entails sustained attention to the ways in which different materialisations emerge within specific disciplines and practices. As Karen Barad, a feminist theorist and physicist, puts it, such a shift in feminist science studies would move from concerns with 'the nature and production of scientific knowledge' towards the 'study of the detailed dynamics of the actual practice of science'.[39] For Barad, we can take Butler's notion that the matter of bodies is not prior to discourse but is produced performatively and at the same time recognise that other kinds of matter are also enacted – 'matter is not... a thing but a doing'.[40] According to Barad we need to look in detail at the productive practices – which result in the materialisation of nonhuman as well as human bodies:

> 'What is needed is a robust account of the materialization of all bodies – "human" and "nonhuman" – and the material-discursive practices by which their differential constitutions are marked. This will require an understanding of the nature of the relationship between discursive practices and material phenomena, an accounting of "nonhuman" as well as "human" forms of agency, and an understanding of the precise causal nature of productive practices that takes account of the fullness of matter's implication in its ongoing historicity.'[41]

It seems to me that Sarah and Jeremy's detailed accounts of the realisation of Stock Orchard Street, and the shifts in 'material-discursive' practice entailed by working with materials which exceed the proper limits of architectural practice and regulation, provide some ways into thinking about the specific materialisation of architecture. If building materials are not inert, unchanging matter, resources to be mobilised at will, but are understood as 'nonhuman bodies' constituted through material-discursive practices (extraction, production, regulation, their specific designations in building and so on) then the selection and use of those materials has the potential to generate new material-discursive practices:

> 'I have detected visible signs of cracking along the central section of the building above this spring, indicating greater movement than was expected. In addition, the building in the region now vibrates much more than is desirable... Finally, the house spring on grid F3 is leaking fluid. Is this a bad sign and can anything be done about it?'[42]

It is these shifts – in the relationships between players including builders, architects, engineers, regulators, in the ways they found their expertise, in the negotiations between them, in the processes of design and construction, as well as in the appearance of new critical uses of materials – that I have tried to draw out in this account of the excessive materiality of Stock Orchard Street. It is this excess, this proliferation of possibilities for practice, of new ways of working and operating critically, even at the most intransigent, deeply embedded level of architecture's material production, that I want to claim as the legacy of Stock Orchard Street for a feminist material practice.

[40] Ibid., p. 146.
[41] Ibid., p. 128.
[42] Fax from SWA to Mr Hans-Georg Wagner, GERB, 7 March 2001.

Innovative but daft?

A prototype of 9/10 Stock Orchard Street's straw bale wall on display at construction trade fair Interbuild prompted the following opinion piece from journalist Tony Currivan. Writing in the eco-construction magazine *Building for a Future**, he challenged the architects to respond to his comments…

* Now entitled Green Building

Last writes
Tony Currivan sums up the past three months in the unfolding history of the construction industry et al.

Talking of building products, I and a couple of fellow AECB members dared to undertake one of the most challenging tasks in the construction industry – to visit Interbuild and come out alive and still talking! Like my visit to the Self Build Show earlier this year, it is as interesting to see what is not there. Perhaps the most striking aspect of the whole event was the absence of the many UK manufacturers. Indeed, it seems more and more to be a showcase for European and North American companies trying to gain a toe-hold in this notoriously conservative market.

While the increasing globalisation of the construction products market – I still cannot work out how Chinese roof slates can possibly be cheaper – continues apace there were a few beacons of more sustainable practice in evidence. Among the most interesting stands were Intermediate Technology with its low-tech, hand-made tiles, and Construction Resources, which offered an attractive and fascinating range of ecological products. Typically most of the latter were German and ranged from the thought provoking to the downright daft. Whatever one's

views of the ecological benefits, I still fail to see why an unfired clay brick has to be imported from Germany at a cost many times that of a standard brick.

Equally innovative but daft was the display on 'Building Materials of the Future' which featured straw bale construction – much to the bemusement of some brickies inspecting it at the same time as me. As you know, I am a bit of a fan of straw bale construction and I seem almost unable to write a column without mentioning it, so I am not arguing with the principle, but the application. The exhibit was a typical section of a proposed house and office by architects Sarah Wigglesworth and Jeremy Till, a project that has received considerable publicity, not least for its location in central London. As both are AECB members, I am reluctant to be too critical. However, first, the walls are non-load-bearing so that the bales provide purely insulation. Second, presumably to show off the fact that it is straw bale, they have clad the whole wall in polycarbonate sheeting. In so doing, they have needed a vented cavity space using large quantities of plastic and metal flashings and vents.

The whole assembly deflects from the original intentions of straw bale construction, namely a cheap and ecologically sound wall construction. Clearly what the

designers do with their own house is their affair, but what concerns me is that the publicity that they have deliberately attracted will now see straw bale as a fancy and expensive eco-tech material that cannot fit into any normal situation. Is this yet another example of the triumph of style over clear thinking? I am prepared to be told otherwise, and so challenge the designers to providing a response (or even an article). Who knows, we may even get a debate.

From time to time one comes across maxims that concisely but accurately condense a whole approach to a problem. The environmental field is no exception and a few remain true, such as 'long life, low energy, loose fit', even after being coined over two decades ago. Others continue to evolve, reflecting shifting ideas and priorities. One classic example is 'reuse, repair, recycle' which has been gradually expanded to include 'reduce' and 'reclaim (energy)'. I was amused to hear that it has recently been extended yet further, this time to acknowledge the importance of the production stage in the life cycle of the product. So the whole sequence now runs 'redesign, rethink, reduce, reuse, repair, recycle, reclaim' – still useful, but perhaps just a bit less catchy than the original.

Whose straw is it anyway?

Jeremy Till and Sarah Wigglesworth

Tony Currivan's critical comments ('Last writes', *BFF*, vol. 7 no. 4: 39) on our straw bale house project begged a response, both in terms of the project's intentions and the wider issues raised. We first need to address some of the specific points he raises. He accuses us of placing 'style over clear thinking' by choosing to clad the bales with a rainscreen instead of the usual practice of rendering the outside. In fact our solution is driven by clear technical consideration in an effort to avoid any problems of driving rain or interstitial condensation. While external render may be appropriate for the drier climes of the western United States (on which much bale precedent is set) it may encounter problems in our damper isles. Studies by the Canadian government on bale buildings in Quebec and Ontario (where the climate is as wet as ours) indicate that the rendering of the outside of the bales – even with so-called 'breathing' lime renders – may trap interstitial condensation within the straw leading to rot within the bales. The problem is made worse by the less-than-perfect detailing that many straw bale buildings have, particularly around openings at the top and bottom of the wall. It appears that a wave of enthusiasm for the technique has overlooked some of these fundamental building issues. Our solution to these potential problems is to ventilate the cavity between rainscreen and bales allowing any potential condensation within the bales to be dissipated. The rainscreen will also offer better protection to the straw than render in more exposed conditions. Second, Tony is misguided to accuse us of promoting an 'expensive and fancy' system. Considered as part of the overall building outlay, there is little difference in cost between load-bearing and non-load-bearing straw bale construction – and in fact the dry cladding system we have designed is (and was) built completely by amateurs whereas rendering requires an expert to be brought in. Most importantly, we are worried that a rash of bale buildings put up in optimistic but unconsidered fervour may be little more than expensive compost in twenty years' time. What price then the 'cheap and ecologically sound' system that Tony promotes? Evaluating the 'cost' of any building system in sustainable terms is notoriously difficult, since one has to take into account material cost, labour cost, embodied energy, energy-in-use, life-cycle cost and recyclability. Tony appears to be concentrating on only one of these elements at the expense of the other considerations – when in fact many argue that the prime ecological consideration is to limit heat loss, something we are obviously doing.

More contentiously we have chosen to make the cladding transparent (and thereby petrochemical) knowing that this would raise the type of comments made by Tony. Of course this cladding does not have the obvious eco credentials of lime render, but it may in the end be more ecologically conscious. The ability to 'show off the fact that it is straw bale' was indeed intentional – and one which we recognise is polemical. Our aim was to provoke debate on the use and benefits of materials such as straw by making them visible, and if that meant using some 'quantities of plastic and metal', then so be it. Judging by the overwhelmingly supportive response from the public at Interbuild, our polemical stance worked – if over 100,000 people see it and think about it then we would argue that this serves the ecological movement better than clinging to purist ideals. The point surely, as the name of our association suggests, is to be environmentally conscious rather than environmentally constrained. On what grounds therefore does Tony argue that our project 'deflects from the original intentions of straw bale construction, namely a cheap and ecologically sound wall construction'? Strange that such a young method – probably fewer than ten buildings in the UK thus far constructed – could be seen to have such originative claims. One of the many strengths of Steen, Steen and Bainbridge's book, *The Straw Bale House*, is a generosity in not making judgements as to how best to construct with bales and the freedom of invention encouraged by the authors – an openness based on actual experience that Tony would do well to follow. The worry is that his approach, and that of others following his dogma, will hijack straw bales into a vernacular cul-de-sac which may even be technically dubious. This is part of a wider problem which places ecological design firmly in the rural context when in fact the real crisis of sustainability which we should be all addressing is that of the urban. This is the route to eventual marginalisation – and depoliticisation – of the green movement, and it is a tragic route to follow given the vital importance of the issues at stake.

Although making no great claims, our aim has been to extend the use of straw bales beyond the limitations of the vernacular and to sensibly posit new ways of using them as inventive designers. There is often an underlying assumption that ecological design should 'look' green, leading to a certain type of traditional aesthetic. It has been our express aim as architects of our own home to explore spatial, material and formal solutions appropriate to the twenty-first century. We have also intentionally used them as positive propaganda for alternative materials. Interestingly our tactics have appeared to work. Far from 'deliberately attracting' publicity as Tony unnecessarily accuses us of, the mainstream press has come to us. This is the first time we have answered back – but perhaps that is because we believe that bales (and other methods) are too important to be constrained by misguided dogma. Whose straw is it anyway?

Construction drawings

House

H/206 steel frame spot heights

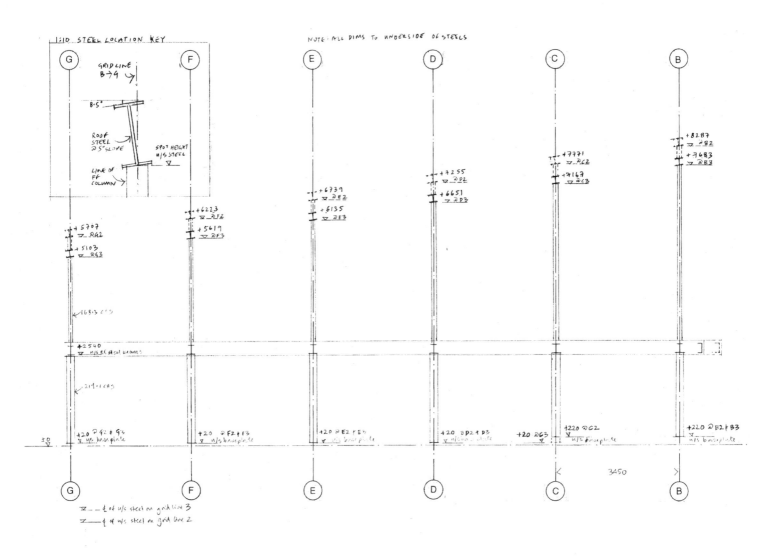

H/600 sketch setting-out of south-west elevation windows

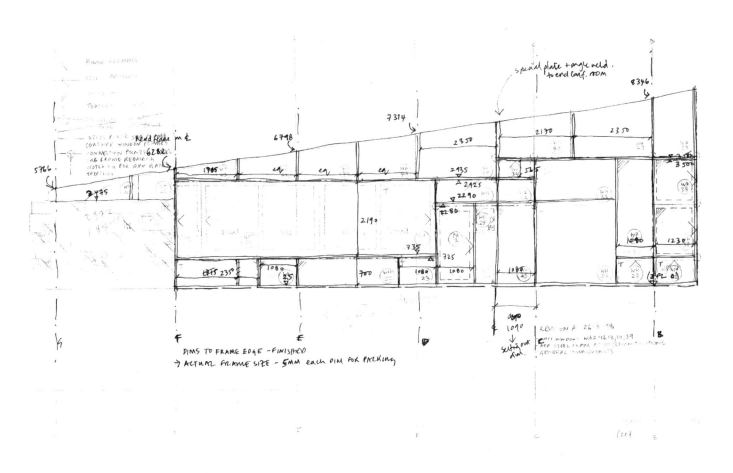

DIMS TO FRAME EDGE - FINISHED
→ ACTUAL FRAME SIZE - 5MM each DIM FOR PACKING

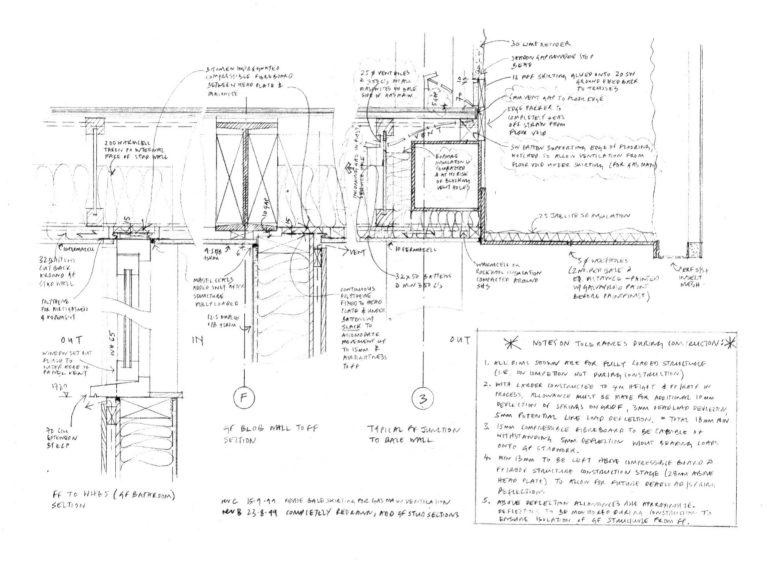

32 BATCHS
CUT BACK
AROUND OF
STUD WALL

POLYTHENE
FOR AIRTIGHTNESS
& MOVEMENT

200 WARMCELL
TAKEN TO INTERNAL
FACE OF STUD WALL

10 FERMACELL

BITUMEN IMPREGNATED
COMPRESSIBLE FIBREBOARD
BETWEEN HEAD PLATE &
MASONITE

MASTIC SEALS
ADDED ONLY AFTER
STRUCTURE
FULLY LOADED

9.5 MB
+ SKIM

12.5 DUPLEX
+ 1/B + SKIM

OUT

WINDOW SET OUT
FLUSH TO
OUTER EDGE OF
PANEL VENT

1920

70 CILL
EXTENSION
STEP

FF TO WH 65 (GF BATHROOM)
SECTION

IN

F

GF BLOCK WALL TO FF
SECTION

NNC 15.9.99 REVISE BALE SKIRTING FOR GAS MAIN VENTILATION
NNB 23.8.99 COMPLETELY REDRAWN, ADD GF STUD SECTIONS

25 ∅ VENT HOLES
@ 350 C/S ON ALL
MASONITES ON BALE
SIDE OF ABS MAIN

IN OPENINGS BATS IN PLACE
SEPARATELY

VENT

ENSURE
INSULATION IS
COMPACTED
& AT NO RISK
OF BLOCKING
VENT HOLES

10 FERMACELL

32 × 50 BATTENS
@ MIN 350 C/S

CONTINUOUS
POLYTHENE
FIXED TO HEAD
PLATE & UNDER
BATTENS W/
SLACK TO
ACCOMODATE
MOVEMENT UP
TO 15MM &
AIRTIGHTNESS
TO FF

OUT

3

TYPICAL FF JUNCTION
TO BALE WALL

30 LIME RENDER

SECTION GAP RENDER STOP
BEAD

12 MDF SKIRTING GLUED ONTO 20 SW
GROUND FIXED BACK
TO TRUSSES

5MM VENT GAP TO FLOOR EDGE

EDGE PACKER TO
COMPLETELY SEAL
OFF STRAW FROM
FLOOR VOID

SW BATTEN SUPPORTING EDGE OF FLOORING,
NOTCHED TO ALLOW VENTILATION FROM
FLOOR VOID UNDER SKIRTING (FOR GAS MAIN)

25 JABLITE SB INSULATION

WARMCELL OR
ROCKWOOL INSULATION
COMPACTED AROUND
SHS

5 ∅ WEEPHOLES
(2 NO. PER BALE @
EQ. DISTANCE - PAINTED
W/ GALVANISED PAINT
BEFORE PAINTFINISH)

PERF SS +
INSECT
MESH

NOTES ON TOLERANCES DURING CONSTRUCTION:

1. ALL DIMS SHOWN ARE FOR FULLY LOADED STRUCTURE
(I.E. ON COMPLETION NOT DURING CONSTRUCTION)

2. WITH LARDER CONSTRUCTED TO 4M HEIGHT & FF/ROOF IN
PROCESS, ALLOWANCE MUST BE MADE FOR ADDITIONAL 10MM
DEFLECTION OF SPRINGS ON GRID F, 3MM DEADLOAD DEFLECTION,
5MM POTENTIAL LIVE LOAD DEFLECTION. = TOTAL 18MM MIN

3. 15MM COMPRESSIBLE FIBREBOARD TO BE CAPABLE OF
WITHSTANDING 5MM DEFLECTION W/OUT BEARING LOADS
ONTO GF STUDWORK.

4. MIN 13MM TO BE LEFT ABOVE COMPRESSIBLE BOARD @
FF/ROOF STRUCTURE CONSTRUCTION STAGE (28MM ABOVE
HEAD PLATE) TO ALLOW FOR FUTURE DEADLOAD/SPRING
DEFLECTIONS

5. ABOVE DEFLECTION ALLOWANCES ARE APPROXIMATE.
DEFLECTIONS TO BE MONITORED DURING CONSTRUCTION TO
ENSURE ISOLATION OF GF STRUCTURE FROM FF.

H/216 detail of shiplap wall to GF study at junction of bale wall

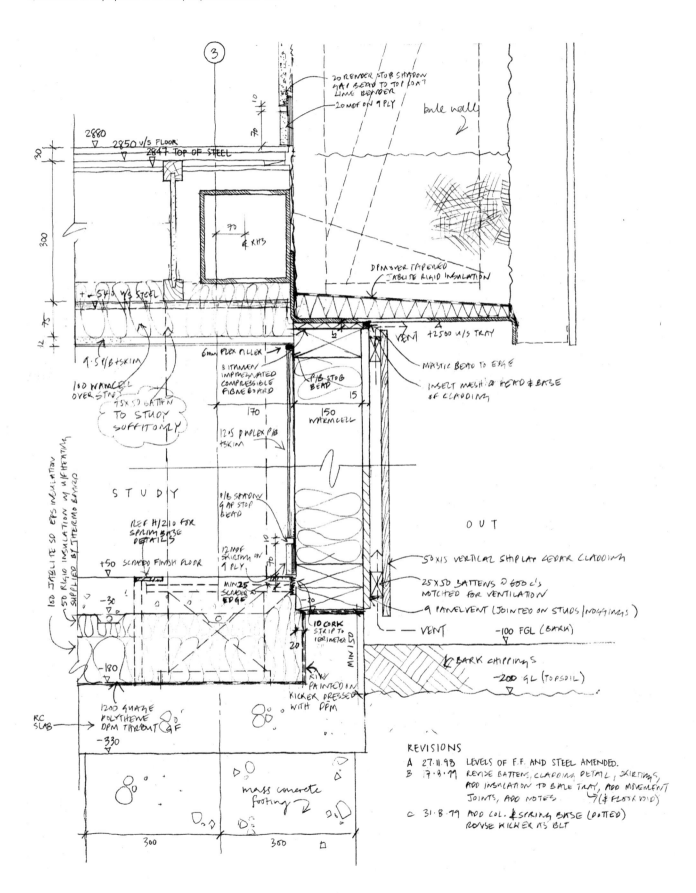

STUDY

OUT

REVISIONS
A 27.11.98 LEVELS OF F.F. AND STEEL AMENDED.
B 17.8.99 REVISE BATTENS, CLADDING DETAIL, SKIRTINGS,
           ADD INSULATION TO BALE TRAY, ADD MOVEMENT
           JOINTS, ADD NOTES   (& FLOOR VOID)
C 31.8.99 ADD COL. & SPRING BASE (DOTTED)
           REVISE KICKER AS BLT

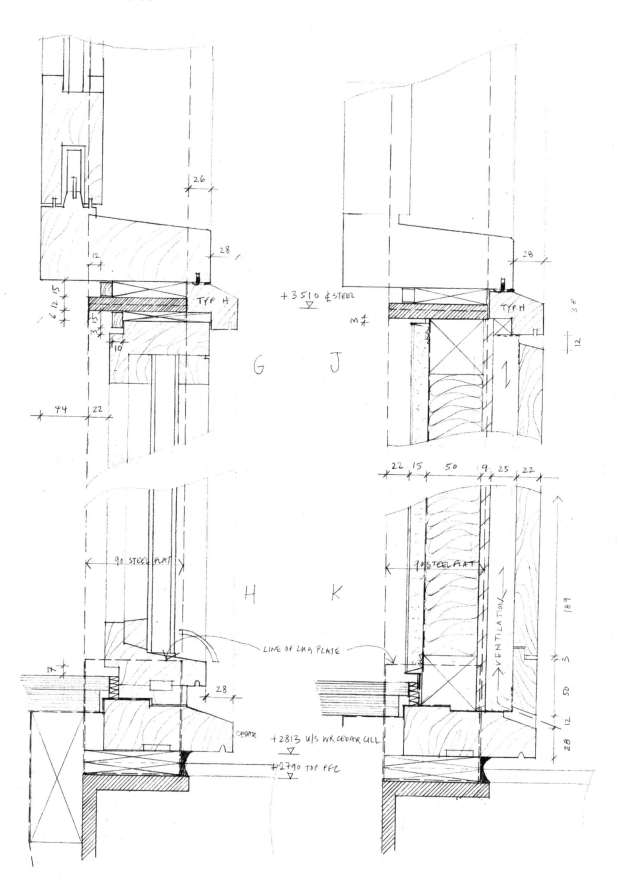

H/294 S-W elevation plan details A, B, C, C mod, D, D mod

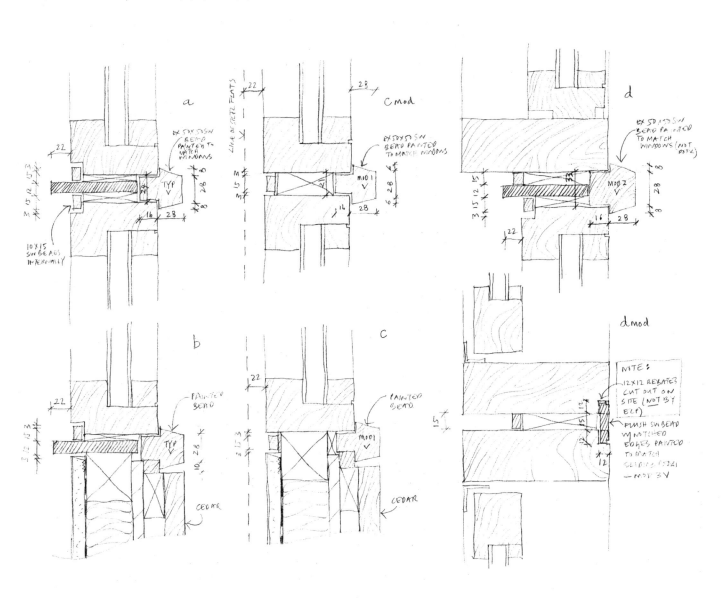

H/202 detail of house eaves with clerestorey

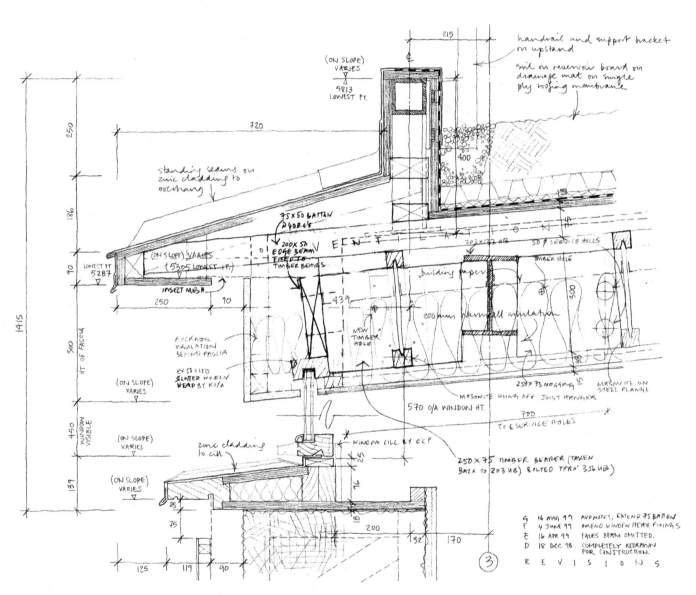

handrail and support bracket on upstand

soil on reservoir board on drainage mat on single ply roofing membrane

(ON SLOPE) VARIES
5813 LOWEST PT.

215

720

400

250

186

standing seams on zinc cladding to overhang

75X50 BATTEN 240RE's

200X50 EDGE BEAM FIXED TO TIMBER BEAMS

(ON SLOPE) VARIES
(5305 LOWEST PT.)

203X133 UB

50∅ SERVICE HOLES

building paper

TIMBER HOLE

300

90

LOWEST PT.
5287

(ON SLOPE) VARIES

INSERT MESH

250   90

439

NEW TIMBER HOLE

200mm Warmcell insulation

1415

300   HT OF FASCIA

ROCKWOOL INSULATION BEHIND FASCIA

EX 50X150 SLOTTED WINDOW HEAD BY KO/A

(ON SLOPE) VARIES

250X75 NOGGING

MASONITE ON STEEL FLANGE

450   WINDOW VISIBLE

(ON SLOPE) VARIES

MASONITE HUNG OFF JOIST HANGER

570 O/A WINDOW HT.

700 TO ∅ SERVICE HOLES

139

(ON SLOPE) VARIES

zinc cladding to cill

WINDOW CILL BY EZP

25
16
18

250X75 TIMBER BEARER (TAKEN BACK TO 203 UB) BOLTED THRO' 356 UB)

25

75

200

132   170

125   119   90

③

G   16 AUG 99   ADD NOTES, EXTEND 75 BATTEN
F   4 JUNE 99   AMEND WINDOW HEAD FIXINGS
E   16 APR 99   EAVES BEAM OMITTED.
D   18 DEC 98   COMPLETELY REDRAWN FOR CONSTRUCTION.
    R E V I S I O N S

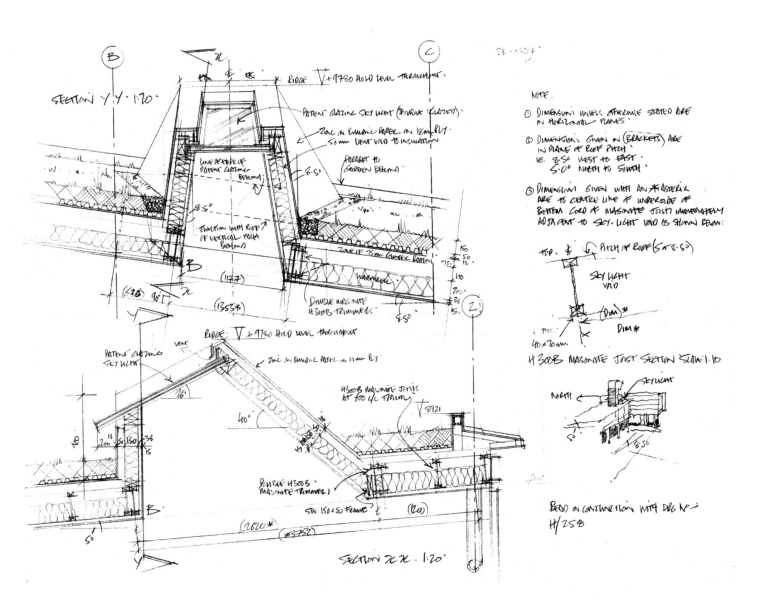

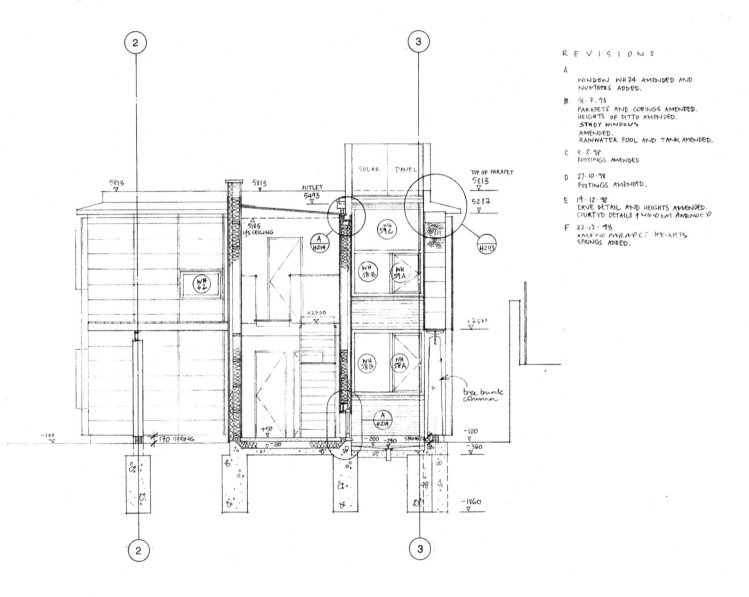

H/283 details of copings and junctions of link block to house

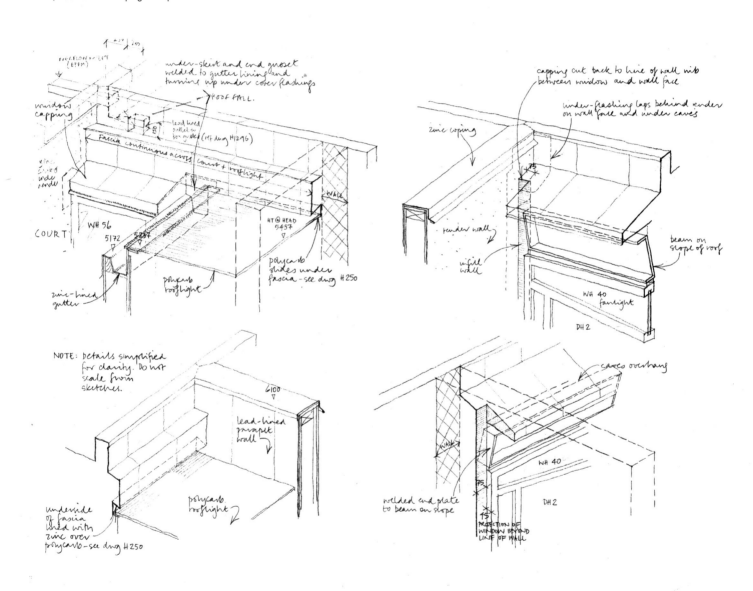

NOTE: details simplified for clarity. Do not scale from sketches.

143

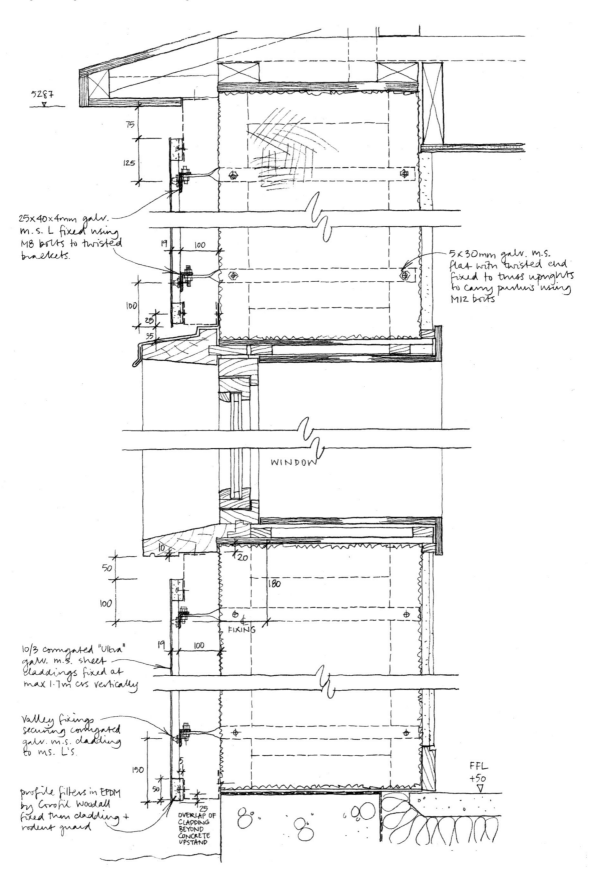

5287

75

125

25x40x4mm galv. m.s. L fixed using M8 bolts to twisted brackets.

5x30mm galv. m.s. flat with twisted end fixed to truss uprights to carry purlins using M12 bolts

19   100

100

25

35

WINDOW

10

20

50

180

100

FIXING

19   100

10/3 corrugated "Ultra" galv. m.s. sheet claddings fixed at max 1.7m crs vertically

Valley fixings securing corrugated galv. m.s. cladding to m.s. L's.

150

5

FFL +50

profile fillers in EPDM by Crosfil Woodall fixed thru cladding + rodent guard

50

25

OVERLAP OF CLADDING BEYOND CONCRETE UPSTAND

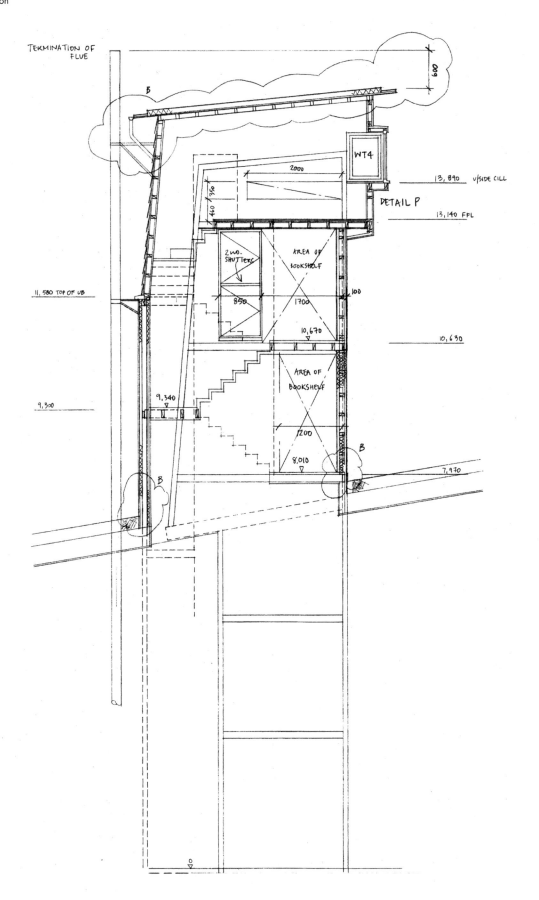

TERMINATION OF
FLUE

B

600

WT4

2000

460 / 350

13,890   U/SIDE CILL

DETAIL P

13,140 FFL

2 NO.
SHUTTERS

AREA OF
BOOKSHELF

11,580 TOP OF UB

850   1700   100

10,670

10,630

9,340

AREA OF
BOOKSHELF

9,300

1200

B

8,010

B

7,970

0

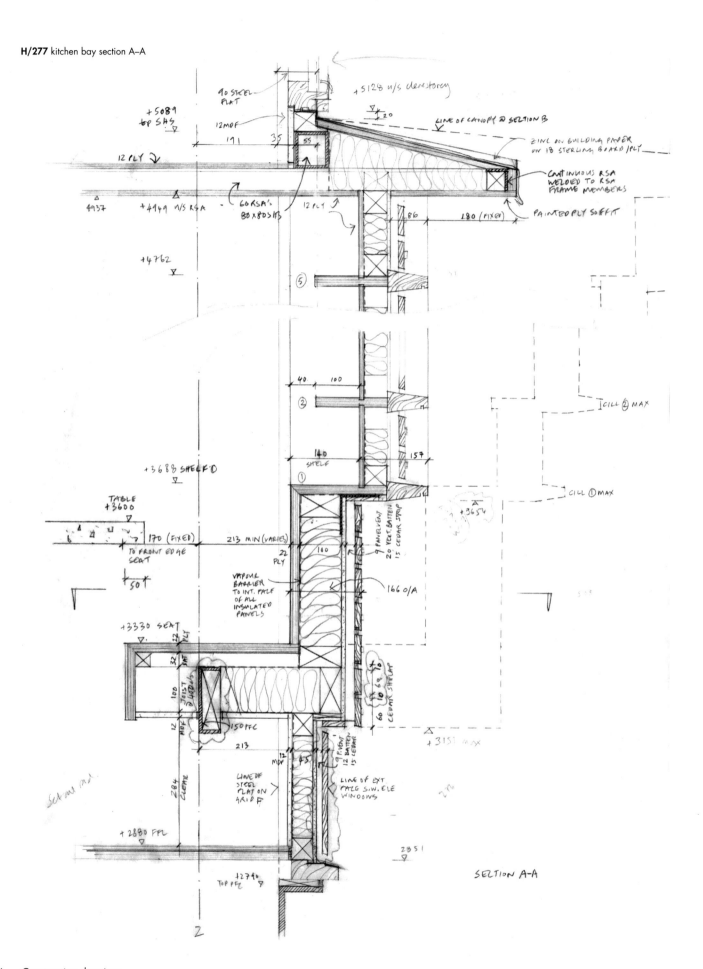

SECTION A-A

H/286 kitchen bay plan detail at WH7, WH6

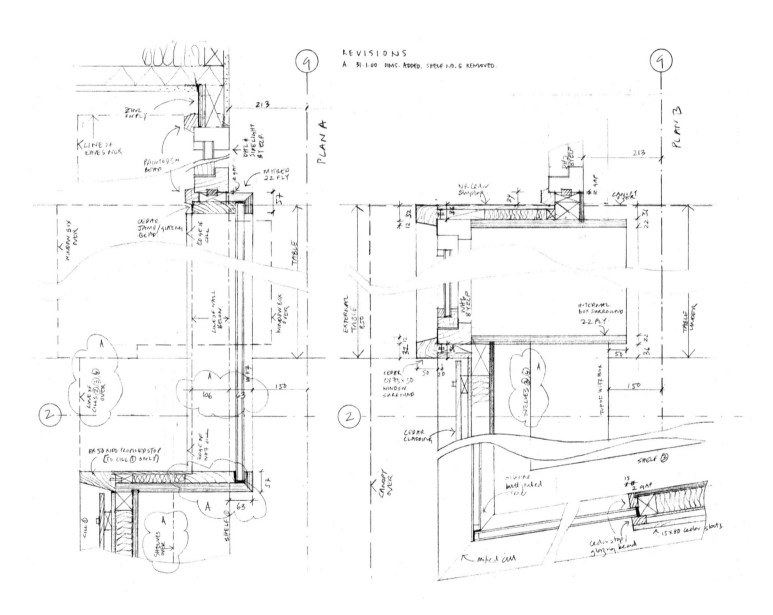

REVISIONS
A. 31.1.00 DIMS. ADDED. SHELF NO. 5 REMOVED.

147

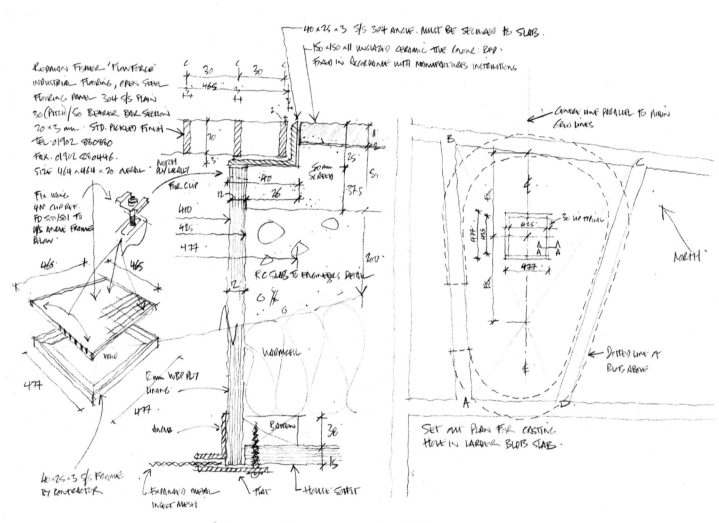

REDMAN FISHER 'FLOWFORGE'
INDUSTRIAL FLOORING, OPEN STEEL
FLOORING PANEL 304 S/S PLAIN
30 (PITCH)/50 BEARER BAR SECTION
20×3 mm. STD. PICKLED FINISH
TEL 01902 880880
FAX. 01902 880446.
SIZE 464×464×20 OVERALL

FIX USING
4No CLIP REF.
FD 500/501 TO
U/S ANGLE FRAME
BELOW.

465   465

477

40×25×3 S/S FRAME
BY CONTRACTOR

40×25×3 S/S 304 ANGLE. MUST BE SECURED TO SLAB.
150×150×11 UNGLAZED CERAMIC TILE COLOUR: RED.
FIXED IN ACCORDANCE WITH MANUFACTURES INSTRUCTIONS

NOTCH
PLY LOCALLY
FOR CLIP

50mm
SCREED

400
425
477

RC SLAB TO ENGINEERS DETAIL

WARMCELL

2mm WBP PLY
LINING

ANGLE

BATTEN

EXPANDED METAL
INSECT MESH

PLY

HOUSE SOFFIT

DETAIL SECTION THRU EDGE AA

CENTRE LINE PARALLEL TO MAIN
GRID LINES

NORTH

DOTTED LINE OF
BLOB ABOVE

SET OUT PLAN FOR CASTING
HOLE IN LARDER BLOB SLAB.

NOTE: DETAIL SUBJECT TO ENGINEER'S CONFIRMATION

H/503 details of render finish and vents to external larder blob

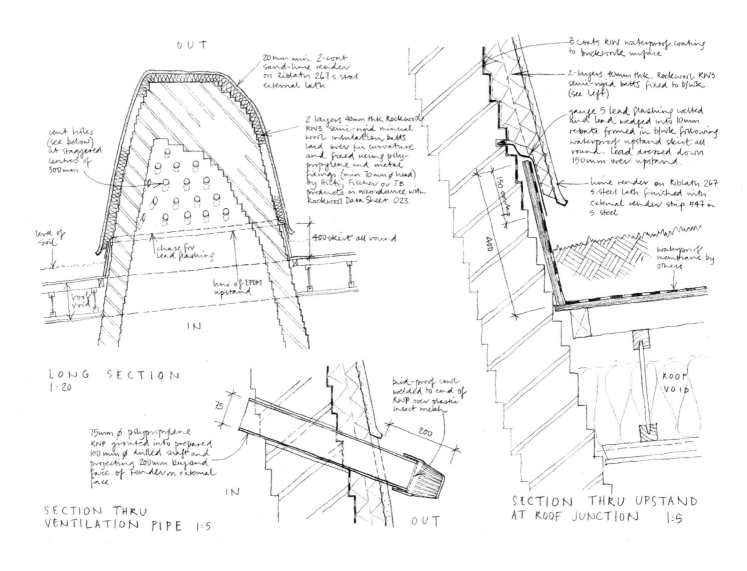

OUT

20mm min. 2-coat sand-lime render on Riblath 267 s.steel external lath

2 layers 40mm thk Rockwool RW3 semi-rigid mineral wool insulation batts laid over for curvature and fixed using polypropylene and metal fixings (min 70mm ø head) by Hilti, Fischer or JB products in accordance with Rockwool Data Sheet 023.

vent holes (see below) at staggered centres of 300mm

level of soil

chase for lead flashing

400 skirt all round

line of EPDM upstand

roof void

IN

3 coats RIW waterproof coating to brickwork surface

2-layers 40mm thk. Rockwool RW3 semi-rigid batts fixed to b/wk (see left)

gauge 5 lead flashing welted and lead wedged into 10mm rebate formed in b/wk following waterproof upstand skirt all round. lead dressed down 150mm over upstand.

150 overlap

400

lime render on Riblath 267 s.steel lath finished with external render strip 547 in s.steel

waterproof membrane by others

ROOF VOID

LONG SECTION
1:20

bird-proof cowl welded to end of RWP over plastic insect mesh

75

75mm ø polypropylene RWP grouted into prepared 100mm ø drilled shaft and projecting 200mm beyond face of render on external face.

200

IN

OUT

SECTION THRU VENTILATION PIPE 1:5

SECTION THRU UPSTAND AT ROOF JUNCTION 1:5

Office

O/107 S-E railway elevation

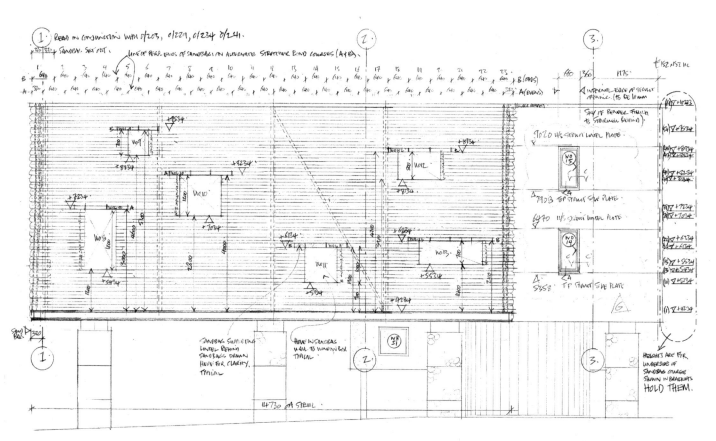

O/234 stud layout sandbag wall elevation

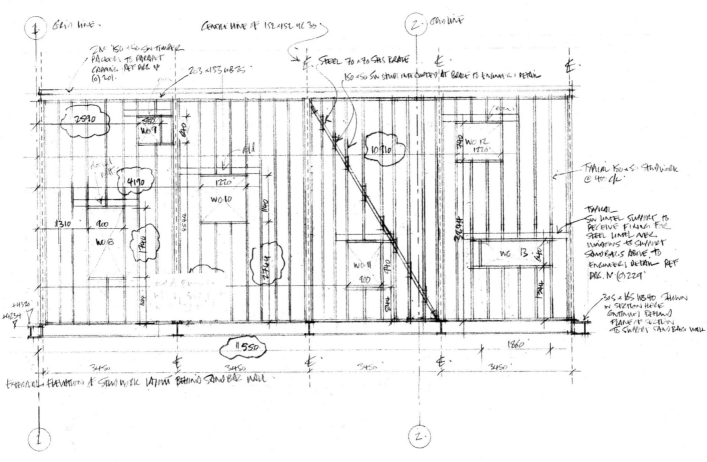

O/201 office parapets, sandbag wall

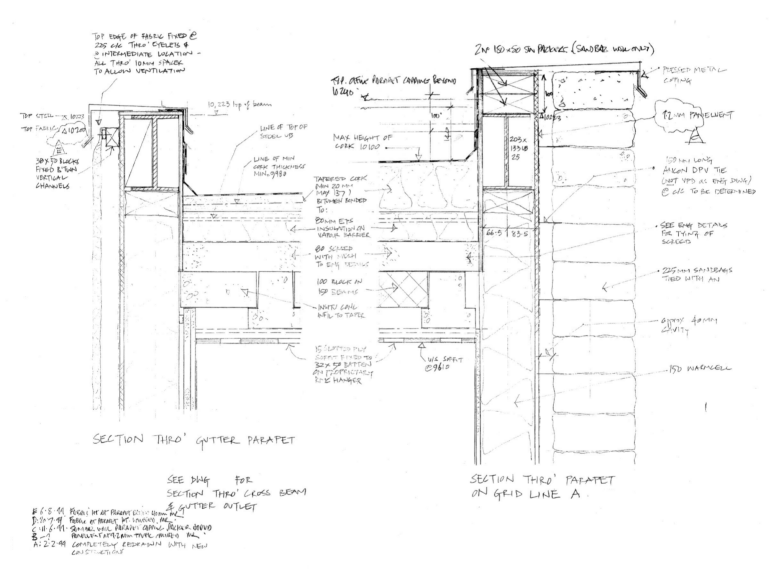

TOP EDGE OF FABRIC FIXED @
225 C/C THRO' EYELETS &
@ INTERMEDIATE LOCATION -
ALL THRO' 10MM SPACER
TO ALLOW VENTILATION

TOP STEEL ⊼ 10223

TOP FABRIC ⊿ 10200

30 X 50 BLOCKS
FIXED B'TWN
VERTICAL
CHANNELS

10,223 top of beam

LINE OF TOP OF
STEEL UB

LINE OF MIN
CORK THICKNESS
MIN=9980

TAPERED CORK
MIN 20 MM
MAX 137)
BITUMEN BONDED
TO:

80MM ETS
INSULATION ON
VAPOUR BARRIER

80 SCREED
WITH MESH
TO ENG DETAILS

100 BLOCK ON
150 BEAMS

INSITU CONC
INFILL TO TAPER

15 SLOTTED PLY
SOFFIT FIXED TO
32 X 50 BATTEN
ON PROPRIETARY
R'F HANGER

SECTION THRO' GUTTER PARAPET

SEE DWG   FOR
SECTION THRO' CROSS BEAM
& GUTTER OUTLET

2 No 150 X 50 SW PACKERS (SANDBAG WALL ONLY)

TYP. OFFICE PARAPET CAPPING BEYOND
10 240

MAX HEIGHT OF
CORK 10100

203 x
133 UB
25

66·5 83·5

U/S SOFFIT
@ 9610

PRESSED METAL
COPING

7·2 MM PANELVENT

150 MM LONG
ANKON DPV TIE
(NOT VPD AS ENG DWG)
@ C/C TO BE DETERMINED

SEE ENG DETAILS
FOR TYING OF
SCREED

225MM SANDBAGS
TIED WITH AN

APPROX 40MM
CAVITY

150 WARMCELL

SECTION THRO' PARAPET
ON GRID LINE A.

E 6·8·99 FABRIC HT AT PARAPET RAISED 40mm ML
D: 20·7·99 FABRIC AT PARAPET HT. LOWERED. ML
C: 11·6·99 SANDBAG WALL PARAPET CAPPING, PACKER ADDED
B: PANELVENT AT 7·2MM TOWER AMENDED ML
A: 2·2·99 COMPLETELY REDRAWN WITH NEW
CONSTRUCTION

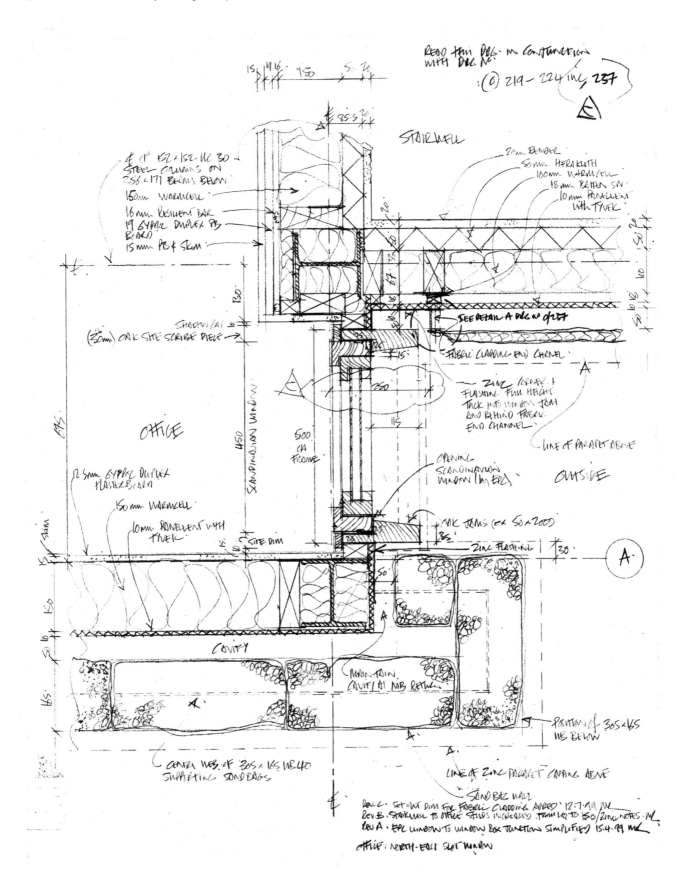

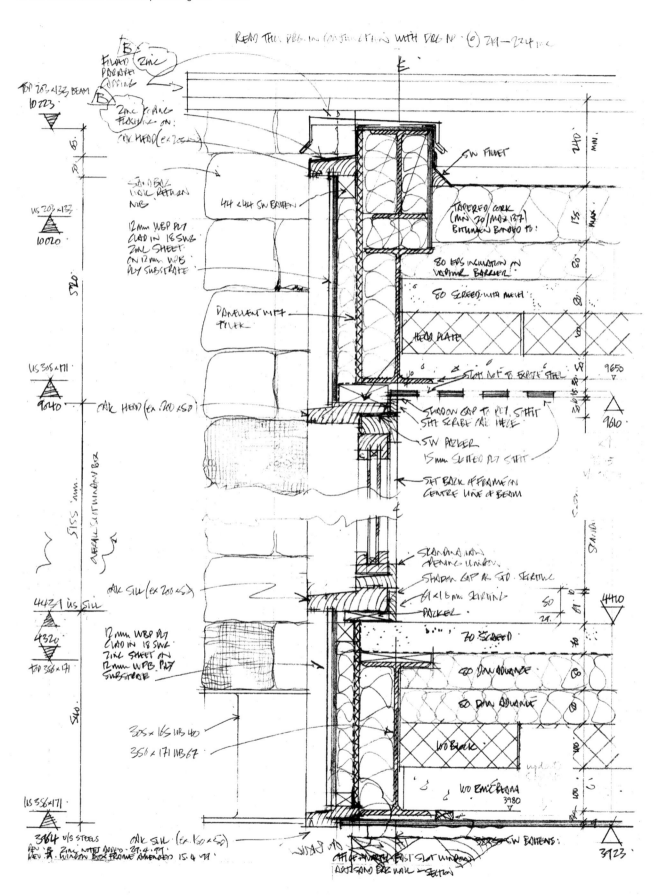

O/229 office sandbag wall window openings

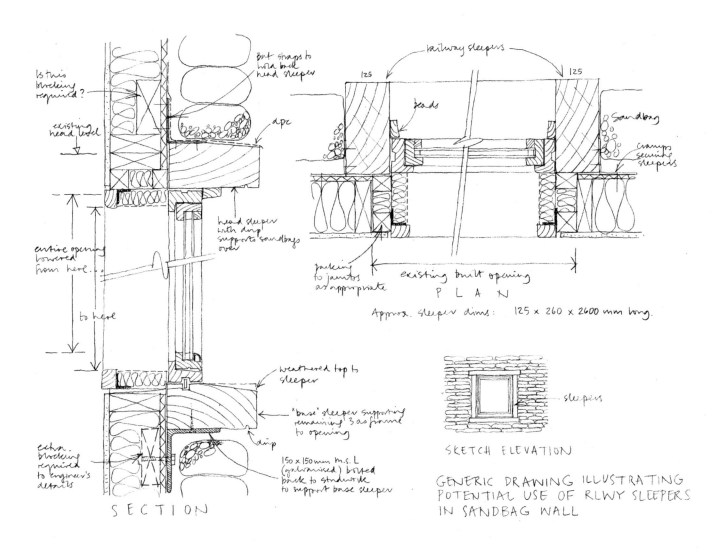

Is this blocking required?

existing head level

entire opening lowered from here...

to here

extra blocking required to engineer's details

S E C T I O N

Bolt straps to hold built head sleeper

dpc

head sleeper with dmp supports sandbags over

weathered top to sleeper

"base" sleeper supporting remaining 3 as frame to opening

dmp

150 x 150 mm m.s. L (galvanised) bolted back to studwork to support base sleeper

railway sleepers

125   125

heads

Sandbag

cramps securing sleepers

packing to jambs as appropriate

existing built opening
P L A N

Approx. sleeper dims: 125 x 260 x 2600 mm long.

sleepers

SKETCH ELEVATION

GENERIC DRAWING ILLUSTRATING
POTENTIAL USE OF RLWY SLEEPERS
IN SANDBAG WALL

O/236 setting out structural openings, garden elevation

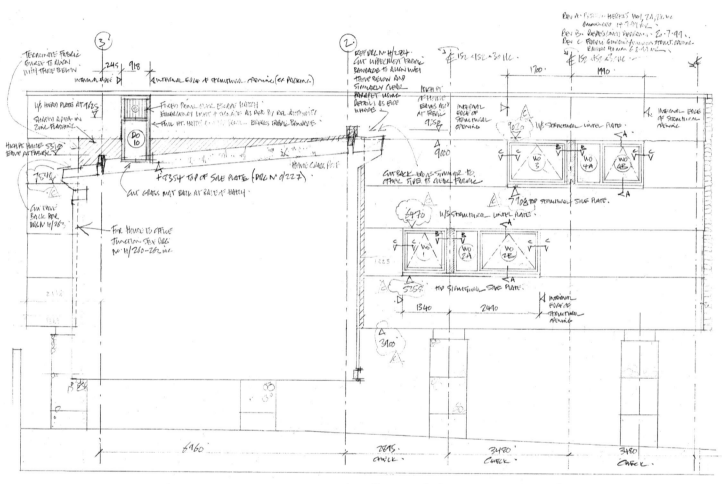

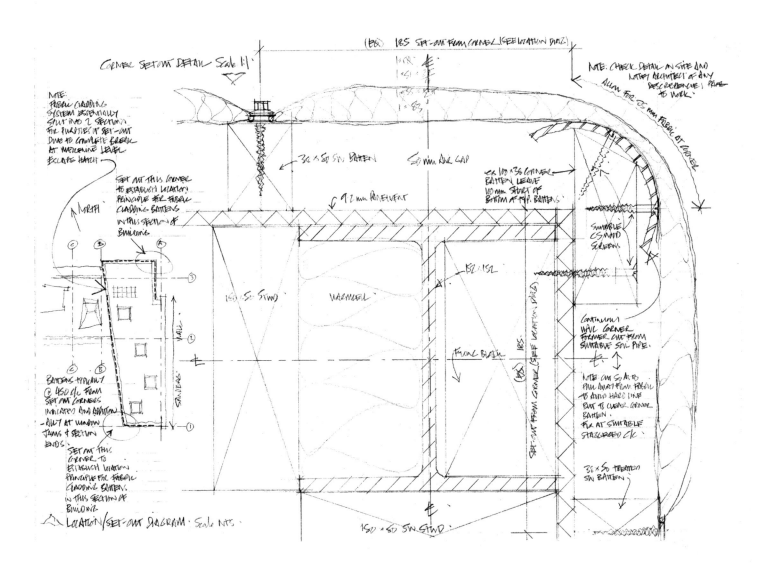

Part 3

SOS: ten years on

Gillian Horn

1999. It was the year the global population reached six billion; a neatly rounded if worryingly large end to a millennium. The year that the Euro, *Grand Designs* and Innocent were born; a time, almost now forgotten, when we could drink in a multitude of currencies but not yet get our five-a-day out of it. Google was just a wee youngster, celebrating its first birthday; it's now grown to be a verb. Starbucks too, had only just landed in our high streets, with only sixty stores, and was still a relatively safe bet for the not yet ubiquitous cappuccino experience. There were the first meetings of the Welsh Assembly and the Scottish Parliament, and the launch of Apple's first i-book. It was the year of Clinton's coup de theatre and General Musharraf's coup d'état in Pakistan, CABE, the statutory champion for good design, was launched, the Lord's Media Centre won the fourth Stirling Prize and the Reichstag re-opened in Berlin. The Dow Jones index surpassed, for the first time the 11,000 mark and Amazon, still a fledgling online retailer in a new and uncertain market, hadn't yet returned a profit. Now we have had a banking crisis that saw stock markets plummet and Amazon's profits soar.

1999. It was a time before YouTube, Facebook and Twitter entered, and in many cases restructured, our social lives and *Big Brother* was just a quirky show in the Netherlands, yet to change the profile of our TV viewing. Wikipedia, without which I couldn't have recycled these trifling facts, was not yet on hand salving our thirst for immediate, interconnected, knowledge.

1999. Stock Orchard Street was practically complete.

Ten years ago I was sitting at a drawing board in what can only be described as a store cupboard blessed with a window; the distinctively indistinct office of Sarah Wigglesworth Architects, tucked away off the Cally Road in north London, a stone's throw from the Stock Orchard Street (SOS) site, from where we designed Straw Bale House. I would have cycled up from my 'bijou' Spitalfields hidey-hole, stopping off on the way for an early bacon butty breakfast in the caff (Cally Road only had caffs, not cafés then) next to SOS. Here, with the, well let's call him somewhat over-grandiosely, Project Construction Manager I would have looked at sub-contract tender returns and the next week's programme, jointly planning our outputs and the impact on the cost and critical path of an over-buoyant zinc market affecting the completion of the roof. I would have been wearing combats and immense Fiorucci platform trainers. My hair was short, spikey and red. Sarah, sitting by my side would most likely have had an even less glamorous morning. She and Jeremy were, for that whole last year living in a caravan on the site, so for her it was from container to cupboard with no distraction, not even the Holloway Road, in between. And being the 'client' now, not the architect, she was not in the breakfast club; not party to our planning and scheduling in our adopted site office over a frothy Nescafé. So just a mud and muesli morning for Sarah. But despite the conditions she, as always, looked impeccable and sharp. On rare trainer occasions, they would be DKNY, and somehow, spotless.

So there we were, a two-girl band, (with the occasional interlude of some boy-backing-vocals) putting the world to rights in our own small way, rethinking architecture in its every possible guise, and trying to build it too. Our universe was one of bespoke one-off invention. From strategies to materials, details to the contract. In all aspects of our work we went back to first principles and looked afresh at what was available, fitting to our ecological and architectural ambitions and of course achievable. Our possibility spectrum of exploration ranged from if-only through might-just-be to not-quite. Could we hold up a building of sandbags and quilted glass fibre cloth on wire cages of site rubble alone? Alas, no – but we tried. We were rethinking ways of building. Some worked, some didn't quite make it.

> **Could we hold up a building of sandbags and quilted glass fibre cloth on wire cages of site rubble alone? Alas, no – but we tried.**

We were exploring too, the means as well as the methods and materials of building; the transition from drawing to construction, from idea to reality. We didn't want the barriers and implicit, adversarial them-and-us divisions of a traditional building contract. So Sarah and Jeremy devised a bespoke partnering contract, never actually signed, with the ideal of sharing risk and 'being friends' with the contractor. Somewhat idealistic perhaps, and certainly risky but it was not without merit or benefit, largely attributable to the integrity and trust of the individuals involved.

It was a culture of do-it-all-yourself, sometimes to the literal extreme of building parts of it ourselves. It also meant an extension to our architectural remit. A services engineer was never even considered for the job. I drew the Mechanical & Electrical schematics, did the heat loss calculations to size the radiators and boilers and became rapidly familiar with the technical complexities of manifolds and heat exchangers as well as the composters and grey water irrigation. But we did work closely with our wonderful and extremely patient structural engineers, Nick Hanika and Andy Heyne at Price & Myers, as well as, of course with the irreplaceable Martin Hughes from KOYA Construction – our project delivery man. A quantity surveyor did appear, but only fleetingly, preparing an unpalatable cost plan at an early stage that was too dream-shattering for Sarah and Jeremy to bear. So we carried on with our collective wisdom instead and put our trust in Martin and his ability to find a way of doing the right thing for the right price at the right(ish) time.

But having a non-fee-earner as the main job in the office meant that life was not all straw bales and sandbags. There were the myriad of 'grubby jobs' to deal with too; the decidedly ordinary world of other-people's-kitchens, bathrooms, and extensions, though coupled always with the unfailingly fascinating lives lived in the soon-to-be-sensational kitchens bathrooms and extensions. There were the less grubby jobs too: a quirky, turf-roofed summerhouse cabin and a feasibility study for the Siobhan Davis Dance Company studios, then targeted for King's Cross (nine years later built in Southwark), as well as our 'other' architectural lives. For we were also teaching and writing in tandem with practice. Sarah and Jeremy had not long secured their professorships at Sheffield University and I was running a unit at the Architectural Association, planning our trip touring Florida trailer parks in a convoy of motor homes. Life was intense and multi-faceted. Focused and diverse. Insular, even naive perhaps, but not introspective.

And now? Now I'm a partner in a sixty-strong architecture practice leading various large-scale education and civic projects. When I sit, I sit at a long bench desk in our large, one-room, open-plan office looking out at the city skyline of the Barbican towers. Either that or at my dining table at home, for with laptop and wireless networks, I and thousands like me can now work effectively remotely: the means for globalisation also being the means for localisation. But I am probably as much out of the office as in and as often in a meeting as not. I free-cycled the bike and now take the tube from my north London hill-top flat, having exchanged bar-life for tree-life; and I have more working lunches and eat-with-one-hand-drink-with-the-other evening dos than site breakfasts. My hair is now long, clipped up and peppered auburn and my attire altogether sharper, closer, in aspiration at least, to Sarah's; riddled with invariably ignored dry-clean-only labels and a choice of heels (no trainers, not even DKNY – never), handbags and accessories.

Now I design with systems in mind, from products to procurement, around a table of experts and specialists from engineers to artists. The culture of do-it-all-yourself has shifted to share-it-all-out and in so doing my role has moved from working alongside a singular creator to leader of a team; from the individual to the collective. This presents different challenges, different opportunities and different limitations. The challenge in my new world is to stay in control of so many disciplines that can either run away on their own tangent or stalwartly stand still and not contribute at all until everything is done. There has been a parallel shift in client profile too, from singular to group, and with that a corresponding repositioning in my role from therapist to facilitator. The need to question, listen and be diplomatic remains, and so, despite all this change, some things have held firm. I also still try to keep in touch with the breadth of architectural practice; teaching and lecturing has morphed into external examining, CABE national design panel reviewing, client consultancy, conference speaking and broadcasting.

Could my life in architecture be more different, I wonder? And is it me or is it the world out there that's changed?

Some of the external differences are certainly marked. SOS was all hand drawn save the metalwork drawings for the office staircase – my first attempt at *Minicad*. These were completed as I worked a transition period in my move to Penoyre & Prasad, where I have stayed, finishing off the last few details at SOS for half of my days and nights in the week (CAD initiation was painstaking and slow; counter-intuitive to a hand used to a pencil) and designing a new primary school in the other. Not that technology was yet much apparent at Penoyre & Prasad at that time either. Certainly general arrangement drawings were computer generated but details were generally still hand drawn and there were as many drawing boards as computers in the office then, both part of an attempt at hot-desk culture (thankfully I say as a self-proclaimed nester) not long sustained. There was also a sole P&P email i-mac in the centre of the office, with a sole email address: mail@. Now of course we're all wired, or more often than not, wirelessed, into a seemingly limitless array of virtual networks such that barely a thought is had without technology assisting, recording or distracting us from it.

The Kyoto protocol hadn't yet been adopted when we began work on SOS, and though ratified by 183 parties, this notably excluded the US. Al Gore hadn't yet run or been defeated in his presidential campaign (in which ratification of Kyoto was one of his platforms), but now climate change is impossible to ignore and little contested. SOS and the concurrent low energy, pioneering sustainable Eastbrookend Discovery Centre (designed in 1995) by Penoyre & Prasad were vanguard projects ten years ago. One-offs shouting a message that was still very little heard in the mainstream about the need for change in the way we design, build and operate our buildings. Their energy targets, whilst still better than current standards are now more the norm, though their invention and zeal is hard to replicate en-masse.

The decade saw a massive increase in public sector spending; more than fourfold in real terms, making the government, already the single biggest client in the UK construction industry, even bigger. And with this surge of public investment came a change of procurement and investment financing that brought an unparalleled injection of private sector funding into public projects. The Private Finance Initiative (PFI) was launched by John Major and implemented by New Labour just as the SOS story starts, with the first school and hospital procured through this 'initiative' completed in 1999 and 2000 respectively. It was, from one vantage point at least, a seemingly logical progression of procurement over the last twenty years as well as a response to the financing and cost uncertainty challenges the government faced in the public sector. But these successive steps in procurement transformation have brought with them a radical change for the role of the architect in the building process and with that a marked impact on the buildings that have been born out of this new system.

Could my life in architecture be more different, I wonder? And is it me or is it the world out there that's changed?

You certainly wouldn't get a SOS under PFI, nothing like it. SOS was designed by and built for a single client. The relationship between architect and client here couldn't get closer; they were one and the same. (When the project went on site Sarah and Jeremy more formally took the role of client to mine as architect to keep the necessary clarity of the respective roles in this sensitive completion stage). This meant that there was no gap in understanding between what was wanted and what could be achieved; a completely fluid, dynamic, iterative process of designing and briefing could take place. And the outcome was only possible as a result of this.

In so-called 'traditional' procurement a client engages an architect-led design team to design the scheme and a contractor to build it, with the client and architect maintaining a direct and continuous relationship from inception to handover. Under Design and Build (D&B) the architect designs the scheme typically only up to what is needed for a planning application, and then a contractor comes on board to both complete the design and to build the project for a fixed price. Henceforth the architect may either continue to work on the building, but now for the contractor, or continue to work for the client, monitoring the building works, but critically cannot do both; either the building relationship or client relationship has to be severed.

In this model the client transfers the risk, of cost and time over-runs to the contractor who takes it on for a premium. This will bring better certainty for the client but not necessarily better value.

Under Design, Build, Finance, Operate (DBFO), the procurement method within PFI that dominated the decade's pubic projects, the client–architect relationship becomes even more obscured. The project in this model is not designed at all by the client's team. Bidding is based on a schedule of outputs instead of the conventional 'inputs' of other procurement types, the client now retreating from centre-stage to the wings, saying only what is wanted not how it should be achieved. This is the leap point in the procurement progression; the bidding consortia are finance-construction led as opposed to design team led, the consequence of which is that the architect does not at any point in the process have a direct relationship with the client. In the prioritising of financing and delivery over design, the design team is relegated to 'members of the supply chain', working *for* rather than in partnership with the contractor or financier who lead the consortium team. This means the architect is at arms length from the client and users of the building they are designing for.

It's a far cry from the cosy archiclient world that was SOS. In this altered landscape even the position of 'client' as a clearly identifiable entity became disaggregated and with it a new language of 'end-users' and 'stakeholders' emerged, not to mention the host of ever-changing acronyms to describe the complex process. And the slipperiness of language masked the uncertainty of roles, such that if you asked the question 'Whose building is a school?' you would get a host of answers ranging from the pupils' (current or future), the headteacher's, the teachers', the governors', the local authority, the government's, even to the PFI consortium's. The answer, in as much as there is an answer, depends on where you place your values; with the means or the ends, the provider or the user. In the PFI procurement model the bidders' costs are converted to a single out-turn cost for the design, build, financing and operation of the project for twenty-five years that is spread over a series of unitary payments during this period. In other words, the client, in the truest sense of the word, the government as commissioning source, is buying a service, a product and the money to get it out of the ground in one.

Herein lies the complexity and fundamental flaw in the seemingly simple solution of the one-stop-shop. Design becomes a part of the overall package, which in a lowest-price short-termist culture will always be secondary. Design can be and *is* scored and weighted alongside the IT, infrastructure, legals and facilities management aspects of a bid, but with the profound misconception that a high weighting protects it. In such a system of equivalences between means and ends, the true purpose of the project is forgotten. The purpose of buildings is not that they may be cleaned or have complex contracts devised around them, but so that we can do whatever it is we do better and more joyfully. The means need to support the ends and so must be appropriate, but they do not – cannot – surpass them. For when the builders have moved on to their next job and the investors have sold on their interests (returns of fifty per cent in PFI have been known) it is the building that remains, for a lifetime, or more. The PFI model too often forces false choices: a choice between a good maintenance or IT package on the one hand and on the other, architecture that helps an organisation's efficiency and promotes well-being. We need instead a model that ensures both.

When the builders have moved on to their next job and the investors have sold on their interests... it is the building that remains, for a lifetime, or more.

Many blame the short-sightedness of government, the complacency of local authorities, the insularity of the architecture profession, the greed of the financiers or the philistinism of the contractors for getting us to this point where the point itself has been missed. Certainly we all have a part in the system and could reflect on the impact we have and/or could have within it... Over the last twenty to thirty years as a striving for certainty and control of risk in the short-term has superseded ambitions for getting-the-best for the long-term, value for money has become identified with low cost such that 'value' itself has become synonymous with 'cost'. And in this risk-averse culture of low aspiration nobody wins in the long run.

In SOS cost was just one aspect of the job that was evaluated alongside a myriad of other considerations against the real long-term value of the project: the design and the consequences of the design for people that were to live there. Had it been procured for a remote client via a disengaged representative and returns-driven contractor for a user that can only be heard through the thin walls of the inadequate building they have learnt to function in, Sarah and Jeremy might instead have found themselves living in a compact end-of-terrace brick and render house with small upvc windows, a tiled pitched roof and car-port. They would also have the close company of scores of new neighbours living in the block of flats developed on the rest of the site to maximise the return.

165

This is not to fall into the lazy trap of nostalgia and romantic dreams of halcyon days and how-it-ain't-what-it-used-to-be. Run the what-if scenario the other way and ask what would a PFI school be like if delivered SOS-style? Well, in short it would never get off the ground, or at least no more than a lick of paint and some new computers in the crumbling old school buildings as a new design would be risk-managed out of the equation due to cost uncertainty, likely programme overrun and the risks on deliverability and maintenance of untested invention. The means would prevent the ends, however noble the intentions. But what a lot would be missed as a consequence.

Is there a middle ground that could be found between these two procurement extremes of ends-and-means emphasis; of long-and short-term thinking? Because there must be accountability in the procurement of our public buildings and we cannot afford high risks of programme, cost and maintenance on them but neither can we afford to lower our standards for design, quality and invention in our public infrastructure investments. These are the buildings and environments of our future and we need to make the very best of them for their and our whole lives. So is the dream of an architecture of deliverable experimentation a deluded fantasy or a worthy aspiration? Or put another way, is there the space for experimentation and invention in public sector procurement and across the construction industry?

Is there a middle ground that could be found between these two procurement extremes of ends-and-means emphasis; of long- and short-term thinking?

In the forthcoming period of forced sobriety we might well find hope in the reflective pause, from which we may see an improvement upon the way buildings are procured and delivered. As a centralised commissioning power, the state did not step up to the mark and grasp the full potential of its massive investment with ambitious targets and demands of the industry for innovation and invention; for good value as well as low cost. Perhaps then more de-centralised commissioning of projects will bring closer relationships of clients and suppliers, users and architects and with that a place for architects to provide a more holistic service to the client. And perhaps we may find reinvention emerging from the space of this pause: of our roles in the construction industry, and of the industry itself. Perhaps.

Success in SOS was to fulfil a dream – yes it had to fit a budget for which difficult choices had to be made, but it was driven by an ambitious vision to create, through a totally co-operative process, a low energy, environmentally responsible home that would delight and inspire its occupants. In our new age of austerity, short-sighted, cost-based decision-making is set to become yet further entrenched, but to get true value from our building infrastructure investments in the future the criteria for success need to be redefined. When we look beyond just cost to the real value of a building we can see the long-term benefits of good design in the creation of places that work for us all, both users and the wider public, who thrive in well designed and considered environments.

Perhaps what is most noticeable over the last decade is what hasn't changed. It's not an enormous surprise that straw-bale building hasn't taken off a storm. But then neither has any other building technology in the construction industry. To look at the vast shift and spread in communications technology over this time is blinding by comparison. There has been no such revolution in construction; technology has certainly changed the way we do things, but not in any significant sense what we do. On a large 'Develop and Construct' new school project I worked on in recent years, for example, the design team stayed on the client side at construction stage. So executive architects took our drawings and developed them into construction details for us to first review and then for the contractor to build from. A bit circuitous perhaps, but fairly straightforward except that a further chain was added to the loop in the outsourcing of the drawing production to technicians in Vietnam who would draw through our night so that the executive architects here could correct and resend in the day for further development before being passed on to us and then back round the loop before landing on site. It somehow worked and I'm happy to say the building has won awards too.

But on site bricks are still bricks and stacked and bonded by bricklayers. That is unless they're brick slips of course, the turkey twizzler of construction – a down-grading tampering in lieu of real invention. In part this may be put down as one of the consequences of what the Bank of England laconically termed 'the nice decade'. Change requires either incentive or demand and in a boom, that's not to be found in the market and despite the billions of public investment in our buildings from the government in recent years it did not come from the client either.

And as the nice decade becomes the sober one this want for client demand of technological transformation is unlikely to change, but the struggle for survival may well provide the necessary incentive. In this tightened economic climate construction companies are not only in competition with each other, be it in the domestic or highly competitive European markets where building is significantly cheaper and quicker, but the construction industry itself will have to compete with other industries for its own endurance. The story ten years on from now may well see buildings no longer being the self-evident solution to people solving their problems that we have become accustomed to.

And there is also a glimmer of hope for an incentive-driven building revolution within these constrained parameters: that of climate change and preparing for a post-fossil fuel economy. I'm sure that straw bale houses and other low-tech solutions will have a significant place in this altogether different landscape and that the evolution of these technologies will continue. But I predict that the scale of response that is really required to climate change, when the challenge is fully met, will be the catalyst for a fundamental shake-up of how we build and what we build with; the trigger for a technological revolution. But one thing is certain; the future is going to be about the things that SOS concerned itself with. And whilst this particular solution may not be the answer, importantly the thinking that lies behind it and the concerns that it attempted to address will be those of the future and in that sense it is ahead of its time.

9 ½ Stock Orchard Street

Anya Moryoussef

I work in a sort of wonderland, an idyll in the city. There are strawberries on the roof and chickens in the garden. There is a moat of pebbles between the street and the front door. There are blankets and pillows on its faces. A tree holds up the balcony.

I work in a sort of office. There are computers and photocopiers and printers. There is a fax machine. There are phones, which ring frequently. There is an accountant, Dilip, who visits bimonthly. There are two postmen who deliver mail each morning and another who picks it up in the afternoon. Incoming post goes into a slot marked '9/10'. What's marked '10' is opened; what's marked '9' is transferred to a double tray by a large window overlooking the garden.

When I am at work on a model and require a piece of string, Sarah will slip out of the office, into the meeting room, and through a panel that blends into the wall. Twelve or so minutes later she will turn up with two large bags of ribbon and yarn, three boxes of buttons, thimbles, remnants of a board game and some tiny pieces from an old motor.

I work in a sort of house. Sometimes, while eating lunch in the meeting room, when the large sliding door is open a crack, I see into the living room. The dirty sock hiding in the shaggy rug, the rocking chair, a half-empty wine glass. Couches, scattered. The new wood-burning stove, which turns 360 degrees. And further on. The bed, which faces east, according to press photographs. The bathtub, shaped like a figure eight, according to Sarah.

Sometimes the sound of feet without shoes will blow through the office. Jeremy, in his socks, faxing or photocopying or picking up post from the tray by the large window overlooking the garden. Often he leaves a souvenir. A stack of papers, a novel, a jar of fertiliser, food, keys, his mobile. Other times things disappear – a scale rule, an old laptop, Sarah's favourite scissors. There are times, when the office is quiet, that the sound of feet without shoes can be heard in the stairwell.

I work in a sort of everyday world. In a room that hovers between house, garden, street and train tracks. Between fast and slow. Between front and back, sky and ground. Windows in the ceiling and on every wall. The street of Victorian terraces with gardens of roses and weeds and tomato vines, and laundry hanging, and murals of sheep. The blur of trains that rattle the fences. And down the street, the crowd who frequent the William Hill.

There was an evening, recently, when Sarah was caught in the stairwell. She was locked out of the office; she was locked out of the house. I thought she'd be angry. She said she sat in the meeting room and watched the sun set.

Office interior, 2009

The intimate inner

Jeremy Till

Once a year, on Open House Day, London's buildings are opened to the public. It must have been soon after we moved in that we offered Stock Orchard Street to Open House for an afternoon. We were completely unprepared for the influx of over 1,000 people in the space of four hours. They were all well-behaved in a National Trust kind of way, obediently following the hastily improvised route through the house. Except for one trait. As we were cleaning up it became apparent that drawers (of mementoes, of clothes, of cutlery) had been opened; nothing had been taken but it was a very unsettling intrusion into our most personal spaces. One might have thought that just entering the building would have been enough to satisfy curiosity, but apparently not. There was a need to go beyond the public pronouncements and displays, and delve deeper, quite literally, into our private world, as if that would offer up personal secrets and habits that the architecture did not.

On reflection, however, these unwelcome intrusions were perhaps not so surprising. An architect's own house is a poignant symbol of the tension between public and private lives. Public, because of the way in which architects' houses compact their concerns and aspirations into a single calling card, the most visible expression there is of internal thoughts. Private, because the architect has to live out her life in this public display, which at the same time becomes a manifestation of personal patterns of living, of taste, even (it appears) of choice of private belongings. Where the public and private realms are traditionally kept apart, the Open House visitors had no hesitation in putting them in a mixer, so better to soak up the spirit of the architecture. And who can blame them? We had opened ourselves up, in many ways, to this scrutiny. We had even answered the siren calls of vanity and offered ourselves up to television, hoping against the odds that our image would survive the rapacious gaze of the *Grand Designs* lens.

Sarah giving Open House Day tour, October 2008

171

Where most Londoners play out their lives behind the protective walls of anonymous, repetitive terraces, we had chosen to turn things inside-out and project an all-too-visible expression of our identities. For some, this inversion was tantamount to showing off; thus the letter to the *Architectural Review* from Shona Mordak (it took a team of us ages to crack that anagram) that somehow manages to mix sexual innuendo with architectural intemperance. But this wearing of our hearts on our sleeves was never intended as a new trick in the history of architectural gymnastics. Rather it was a consequence of an inherent aspect of the public/private tension which the architect's own house sets up, namely that it inevitably melds architect as professional with architect as person. Of course we were keen to get pent-up architectural energy out of our system (an energy fuelled by the fact that multiple ideas were pent up in our teaching and writing, and that this was our first sole-authored building, with all the expectations that brings), but at the same time this was to be the place where we would live out the rest of our lives. It was not so much a question of tempering architectural exuberance with personal and pragmatic concerns, but seeing them as one and the same.

I suspect that it is this elision of the personal with the professional, the private with the public, in architects' own houses that account for their particular character. Looking through a collection of architects' houses, *100 Houses for 100 Architects*,[i] one is struck by an unexpected gentleness, particularly in the interiors. Apart from an over-preponderance of Miesian chairs, Corbusian chaises and unlikely light fittings, these houses generally belie the aesthetic associations of order and refinement, and the behavioural clichés of architectural intolerance and arrogance. It would appear that architects are prepared to inflict their will to experiment more on others than on to themselves. The oft-repeated tales of architectural negligence – of leaking roofs, of discomfort, of deaf ears – are attached to clients who had the bravery to commission the modern masters. It is these tales that are used as sticks with which to beat up contemporary architects, as if we must all share the perceived megalomaniacal traits of the masters. But in the case of the architect's own house these simplified tales of us (the architect) and them (the client and public) do not work, because the two roles are merged. Any calamities that are inflicted are self-inflicted, and equally any delight that emerges is something to be shared by architect and dweller alike.

In the case of Stock Orchard Street, that tension between public/private, professional/personal, architect/client was always with us. Because of our relative inexperience as architects, the non-architect side probably dominated, which may explain the difficulty some have found in placing the building firmly in an architectural canon. We brought to the table all the interests, influences and ideas that had been accumulated over the years, and used the building as a means of exercising them. If other authors in this book sense the guiding hands of precedent in the building, then that is an inevitable consequence of the way in which architectural genes accrete in us all over time (it is hard to spend one's life with eyes shut and without forming allegiances) and then release themselves visually in instances, there to be read by others like tea-leaves. But that release is not fully controlled in Stock Orchard Street, which never started with the ambition on our part to place ourselves intentionally in a particular architectural genealogy.

What is less clear is how those interests, influences and ideas see the light of day in architectural projects, and why some of them emerge but not others. The standard histories of architecture tell stories of batons being passed, of X seeing Y and so doing XY, of styles evolving one out of another. The better architectural histories attempt to place these architectural tics in a wider social and cultural context. The more reductive ones attempt to wrest them from uncontrollable external forces and place them in an autonomous line of cause and effect. There is very little exposition of the mundane aspects of architectural practice,[ii] in

i Gennaro Postiglione, *100 Houses for 100 Architects* (Taschen GmbH, 2008).

ii Albena Yaneva's ethnographies of OMA are exemplary exceptions, showing how even the most famous of architects go through the most mundane of processes. Albena Yaneva, *The Making of a Building: A Pragmatist Approach to Architecture*, 1st edn (Peter Lang Pub Inc, 2009). Albena Yaneva, *Made by the Office for Metropolitan Architecture: An Ethnography of Design*, 1st edn (010 Uitgeverij, 2009).

which the unexpected minor event is almost certainly as influential as the major architectural narrative.

As I have written elsewhere,[iii] it is the tendency of architectural culture to suppress the contingent event in order to assert the authority of a discipline untroubled by external dependencies. However, the design of one's own house brings these contingencies firmly and continuously into focus, not least because one is so bound up in the economic, pragmatic and emotional aspects during the course of design and construction, and also because one must live with the consequences of that construction in the future. As Gennaro Postiglione notes: 'It is only with his own house that the architect realises that construction sites are not complete after they have been handed over.' It is not just that the actual process of construction is never complete, but that time moves on and makes continual social and spatial adjustments.

In our case economic circumstances and pressures on time (we had to get out of the caravan) meant that the building was never, and never will be, 'complete'. This incompletion was too much for the first jury from the RIBA Awards Group, who barely entered the building such was their discomfort. Measured against the standard architectural values which are perpetuated by awards systems, incompletion is seen as a mark of weakness, since only in the completion of the parts can order and perfection be found. Stock Orchard Street is not a conscious critique of these values (because that would be to replace one fixity with its equally stubborn obverse) but it does accept that accidents might and do happen, and that this is not necessarily a bad thing. It also understands, even welcomes, the fact that things do and will change during the course of construction and occupation. This does not mean that Stock Orchard Street is a random collage or a relativist architecture. Although this might sound like an interesting architectural experiment in abstract terms, the personal takes over the professional to ensure that intent about the way we might live guided the progress of

iii Jeremy Till, *Architecture Depends* (Cambridge, Mass.: MIT Press, 2009).

the design through the various competing forces. However, an openness as to exactly how that intent might be spatially realised allowed adjustments to circumstances along the way, sometimes surprising us in their outcome.

This inexactitude was helped by the relatively cumbersome state of computer-aided design at the time, which meant that the design developed through hand drawings and models rather than being exposed early on to the stage lights of a full rendering. The hand drawing works through hunch, anticipating but never fully determining the spatial experience, whereas the computer render works by foregrounding the physical structuring of space, forcing one to concentrate on its technical and aesthetic construction as opposed to its social occupation. I suspect that if we had taught ourselves to use computers earlier and better the building would have been ironed a bit flatter, losing those gawky moments and, with them, some of the surprise. Such lack of total control may appear counter-intuitive to professional behaviour, which almost by definition is about retaining mastery in order to maintain professional authority, but it is inevitable given the multiple contingencies of architectural practice. Design needs to be read as a set of continuous adjustments to changing circumstances rather than as an untroubled linear route towards a predetermined vision of perfection.

Memories are now fuzzy as to the way in which Stock Orchard Street really unfolded as a design, and how far this model of adjustment and contingent influences played out in practice. Some things are certain: the straw bales came directly out of a dinner party conversation with the environmental journalist Kate de Selincourt (but then what would the house have been made of if that conversation had not happened?). The sandbags came from a slide we often used in lectures at Kingston Polytechnic, a picture of people attempting to maintain a semblance of normality as they took tea in a Kardomah Coffee House during the Blitz, the plate glass window protected by a wall of sandbags. The raising up on stilts was a direct response to the height of the surrounding ground. The orientation and glazing of the main elevation was there to catch the sun. And so on. But other things are less certain. The tower may come from a compaction of dreamy stories of Rapunzel, of climbing through stacks of books, of retreat, of Iranian wind towers, of Tuscan hill towns, of heads with mullet haircuts, of the draw of long vistas.

This lack of certainty in the design genealogy in turn suggests an openness as to how the building might be read and experienced, so that interpretations have been thrown up that at the same time surprise and delight us: Swiss friends who stood looking up the railway line and said the expansiveness reminded them of building next to a lake at home. Giles Worsley in the dining room saying it was pure medieval manor house, a public hall with a minstrels' gallery. And Samantha Hardingham who best captures the ambiguities inherent in the project: 'Part farmhouse, part allotment, part modernist villa, part castle, part bunker… '[iv]

Such ambiguity is something that much architecture attempts to rid itself of; clarity, consistency and categorisation are upheld as strengths. It is not so much that we consciously overturned these accepted architectural virtues, but that the process of designing one's own house inevitably introduces contradictory forces. Our inclination was to accept and enjoy the ambiguities rising out of these forces, rather than suppress them in the name of order and reason. Our chapter, 'Telling Tales', presents an edited snapshot of the buffeted ride to site that any architectural project encounters. We first presented it as a lecture at the Institute of Contemporary Arts in London, an antidote to the versions of architectural history that airbrush out all the lumps and difficulties. It is the presentational equivalent of those rifled-through drawers – the intimate inner that dwells at the heart of any architectural project.

[iv] Samantha Hardingham, London: A Guide to Recent Architecture (London: Batsford, 2003), p. 184.

Raspberry canes, March 2008

Correspondence from the *Architectural Review*

The letters reproduced below appeared in *AR* in response to the publication of 9/10 Stock Orchard Street in *AR* 211 (1259) 2002, pp. 64–68

Just showing off?

Sir: At school there was a particularly unpopular boy who when trying to curry favour or make new friends would expose his genitals in the playground. It wasn't big and it wasn't clever.

While Sarah Wigglesworth may be anatomically unable to repeat the boy's act, she and Jeremy Till have however managed an architectural equivalent (*AR* January, pp. 64-68).

By clearly striving for sensationalism, they have produced their own peculiar brand of masturbatory architecture. This self-satisfying offering does not deserve to share the same binding as the finely crafted and truly creative architecture all too infrequently featured in *AR* January. That it should appear in an issue devoted to ecological matters is frankly bizarre.

Any building which encourages the critic to make references to the dark days of post-modernism is to be despised. There are no architectural jokes. The only occasions at which I have laughed aloud in response to any architectural offering is when the results are so pathetically poor it seems to be the only reasonable response. I'm sure Terry Farrell's egg cups keep him awake until late in the night as I hope the failed gabions, knackered shuttering ply and burst sacks at No. 9 Stock Orchard Street will haunt Wigglesworth and the eccentric professor for some time to come. Thank God they have to live with it.

My heart sinks when I learn that the building has already been listed as a contender for this year's building of the year. It wouldn't surprise me if the slags and the slappers of the RIBA got themselves in on 'the joke' (as the *AR* has) and dished out the gong at this year's freak show.

Yours etc.

Shona Mordak
Lincolnshire, England

Straw poll

Sir: I want to take exception to Shona Mordak's attack on the Wigglesworth and Till house in your January issue. The house is indeed a show, and is intended to be so – and be an inspiration to other architects and the general public. For instance, both the straw bales and the sacks of cement have been used to provide insulation, thermal and acoustic, cheaply and simply.

I quite agree about jokes in architecture (don't build 'em), but the house is clearly enjoyable to build and live in. And it shows that British architecture is more than tight-arsed High Tech, Will Alsop's splurges and prissy Cambridge Moderne.

Yours etc.

Henry Brandlys
Sydney, Australia

Decadent wastage

Sir: Although I'm unconvinced of its place in January's 'Ecological Propriety' issue (p. 64), I find Wigglesworth's Stock Orchard Street house quite at home in your magazine. Like many of the residences you feature, it uses decadent wastage to articulate the possession of money and property – albeit more covertly than we are used to. Consider the walls. Metre-thick walls of anything will only ever be an option for the land-rich. And the gabions. With their structural raison d'etre negated by concrete columns, they become mere cosmetic veneers – a waste of wire and perfectly good building rubble. In any case, putting a building on pilotis (of anything) is an expensive way of sheltering a garden path. This house uses lowly materials on a less-than-perfect site to articulate the traditional subtext of upmarket residential architecture. If your correspondent insists that only buildings flaunting expensive materials and value-adding processes can qualify as architecture, then she risks living in her very own house of straw.

Yours etc.

Graham McKay
London, England

What do we mean by green?

Trevor Butler

Defining what makes a green building is a complex process. The left brain would say that it is all about performance and consumption, energy reduction against best practice benchmarks; the right brain would say that we should expect a deeply moving experience which brings the joy and well-being of inhabiting a building that is 'good' for humans and for the planet. In terms of architectural and engineering practice, it is useful to reflect on how green buildings have been emerging over the past forty years or so.

As is often the case, advances in legislation came well behind the innovators and designers of ecological buildings. The modern approach to eco-design began in the late 1970s with work carried out in Europe and North America.[1] These signalled the start of an experimental approach to building efficiency, by testing the theories behind building technology. The main goals of these early experiments were autonomy of energy, water and waste treatment, inspired by a number of drivers: the remoteness of the sites, the fear of national security and testing building systems against alternative forms of living (generally self-sufficiency). The emphasis was on individual buildings with autonomous systems. 9/10 Stock Orchard Street differs from these models by its fairly unique position as a leader of eco-designed *urban* living and because it was as interested in the quality of life aspects and user control as it was in energy performance.

When looking to make these comparisons (of indeed any building), we are still seeking common parameters to demonstrate relative performance. The UK's first Building Regulations that prescribed insulation standards (U-values) were introduced in 1965.[2] The revisions in 1985 and 1990 saw progressive steps in the improvement of building insulation with the aim of conserving energy. The year 2006 saw the introduction of maximum CO_2 emissions as a measurement rather than simple energy consumption, to take into account the differences between electrical and gas heating systems.

[1] In particular, the passive annual heat storage (PAHS) house by John N. Hait (1979) and the private residence by Amory Lovins at the Rocky Mountains Institute (1982), the Dornbirn region of Austria and Jean Nouvell's Interunfall combined office/housing building in Bregenz.

[2] Since then there have been revisions in 1976, 1985, 1990, 1995, 2002, 2006 and expected revision for 2010.

The current emphasis is now on measuring energy performance and calculating carbon. Zero-carbon buildings refer to the carbon that is produced during operation, which has to be neutralised. However, it does not address the embodied energy of materials used in construction. 9/10 Stock Orchard Street set a leadership example, where embodied energy of all materials and construction processes was considered from the outset. This will become an issue of growing stature as operational carbon is reduced – leading to embodied carbon taking on a much higher life-cycle carbon quotient. Template approaches (such as BREEAM or LEED) seek to widen the remit of the calculation-based approach, yet this, too, emphasises specific outcomes and only time will tell whether this has an impact on changing human behaviour to 'greener' ways of living.

The simplest method to assess whether the design and construction principles have resulted in a 'green' building is to measure the performance of the completed, operational building. There are many methods used for assessing this, including the pioneering work by Bordass and Leaman through the PROBE Studies, and the European Union, Energy Performance of Buildings Directive. The majority of assessment methods all refer to the resource consumption of buildings in use – including electricity, gas and water utility bills. Therefore in order to assess the relative performance of the house and office, compared to best practice, the average annual energy and water consumption will be assessed.

As 9/10 Stock Orchard Street comprises a house and an office space, the first step is to identify the relative breakdown of accommodation into gross floor areas (GFA), so that estimates can be made for each type of space use. This is shown in Table 1.

	Office	House	Total
Stock Orchard Street	202m² *	236m²	438m²

Table 1 Relative GFA of 9/10 Stock Orchard Street
* includes conference/dining room

There is one main utility connection for each service that serves both buildings; therefore an estimate has been made of the relative energy consumption by building type. Without separate check-meters it is impossible to clarify precisely what the split in consumption is. The rationale for splitting the relative consumption for house and office is to some extent subjective and based on the author's experience as well as reference to best practice guides.

However, with respect to electricity, it has been assumed that the office will use significantly more than the house due to the higher IT loads of computers, printers and other electrical equipment. These will be used for the majority of the working week, and occasionally at weekends such as when there are deadlines to be met.

Similarly, while it is a smaller space than the house, the office is occupied for between eight and ten hours per day, when the house is unoccupied, so its heating load will be relatively higher. The house is also maintained at a lower temperature of 18 to 19°C during occupation and the heating is turned off when the house is unoccupied.

The water consumption for the house and office is probably more equal, but the house is likely to use more water for showers, cooking, laundry and so on, whereas the main water consumption of the office is limited to WC flushing, coffee/tea making and cleaning.

Based on these assumptions, the split in Table 2 has been adopted for the analysis, and the results that follow would enable further interpolation and hypothesising to be carried out. The base data are shown in Table 2.

	Electricity	Natural gas	Water
Utility split – house	30%	60%	60%
Utility split – office	70%	40%	40%

Table 2 Estimate of relative resource consumption per building type of 9/10 Stock Orchard Street

One more piece of baseline information is needed to complete the comparison dialogue and that is the relative global warming potential (GWP), expressed through kilograms of carbon dioxide per kilowatt-hour of energy (kg CO_2/kWh). The figure for electricity is based on how the UK generates its electricity – through the combustion of fossil fuels such as gas, oil, coal, nuclear and a small amount of renewable energy. Based on these diverse generation sources, the electricity that enters the National Grid is considered to have a common value of CO_2 per kWh as shown in Table 3. The figure associated with natural gas is based on combustion of gas in buildings – in heating systems such as boilers, hot water tanks and the respective CO_2 emissions associated with each kilowatt-hour of heat generated. These recognised 'constant' figures are taken from the UK Government Building Regulations, *Approved Document L 2006*, and are shown in Table 3.

	Electricity	Natural gas	Water
Kilograms CO_2 / kWh	0.422 kg CO_2/kWh	0.194 kg CO_2/kWh	N/A

Table 3 CO_2 factors per kWh of energy consumption
Note: the reference values for relative kg CO_2 per kWh are under review as part of the 2010 Building Regulations Part L, and subject to change.

The above data set a framework to carry out an assessment of the utility bills for 9/10 Stock Orchard Street. The bills have been collected since October 2005 to the present date, and these have been collated and averaged to give the figures set out in Table 4.

	Electricity	Gas	Water
Total annual consumption	17,968 kWh	42,40 kWh	142 m³
Total annual consumption – office	12,578 kWh	16,963kWh	57m³
Total annual consumption – house	5,390 kWh	25,444kWh	85m³

Table 4 Averaged total utility consumption for 9/10 Stock Orchard Street

Office analysis

The figures shown in Table 4 have assumed the breakdown in relative floor areas and occupation patterns as described above. In order to assess the relative performance of the office building, we have referred to the *UK Energy Consumption Guide 19 (ECG19)* for office buildings. Generally recognised as the industry standard, *ECG19* was first published in 1998 to educate building owners and operators in their understanding of energy consumption in office buildings. The guide broke new ground with respect to identifying where energy is used in office buildings. It covers:

– heating and hot water – gas or oil
– cooling
– fans, pumps, controls
– humidification
– lighting
– office equipment
– catering
– other electricity
– computer room.

The guide was revised in 2000, followed by some minor revisions again in 2003. Four different standards of office building are considered ranging from small, naturally ventilated offices to high-tech headquarter buildings; the relative energy consumption for each office type is benchmarked with the guide. For each of the four office types there are two categories of 'Typical' and 'Good practice' to reflect the difference between statutory minimum and enhanced performance. The office (10 Stock Orchard Street) does not entirely match these types, so it has been compared to Types 1 and 2 offices, whose definition is shown in Table 5.

Type 1: A simple building; relatively small and sometimes in converted residential accommodation.

Type 2: Largely open plan but with some cellular offices and special areas.

Typical size ranges from 100m² to 3,000m²

Typical size ranges from 500m² to 4,000m²

The domestic approach, with individual windows, lower illuminance levels, local light switches and heating controls helps to match the operation with the needs of occupants and tends to reduce electricity consumption in particular. There also tend to be few common facilities. Catering often consists of the odd sink, refrigerator and kettle.

This type is often purpose built, sometimes in converted industrial space. Illuminance levels, lighting power densities and hours of use are often higher than in cellular offices. There is more office equipment, vending machines and so on, and more routine use of this equipment. Lights and shared equipment tend to be switched on in larger groups, and to stay on for longer because it is more difficult to match supply to demand.

Table 5 Definitions of Types 1 and 2 offices

Based on the *ECG 19* benchmarks in kilowatt-hours per square metre per year (kWh/m²/yr), the relative utility consumption figures of 10 Stock Orchard Street (the office) have been compared with office Types 1 and 2 as described within the guide. The result of this analysis is shown in Figure 1.

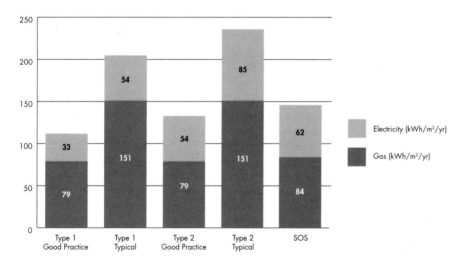

Figure 1 Energy consumption of Stock Orchard Street Office (10 Stock Orchard Street) benchmarked against *ECG 19*

The energy figures in Figure 1 for Types 1 and 2 are based on parameters that have been normalised within the *ECG 19 Guide*, based on occupancy patterns, daily hours of operation, internal comfort temperatures, lighting levels and geographic location. All of these factors should be borne in mind when comparing the relative energy performance of 10 Stock Orchard Street.

The energy consumption figures have also been converted to kilograms of carbon dioxide per square metre per year to enable further comparison of ECG 19 to be benchmarked. These are shown in Figure 2.

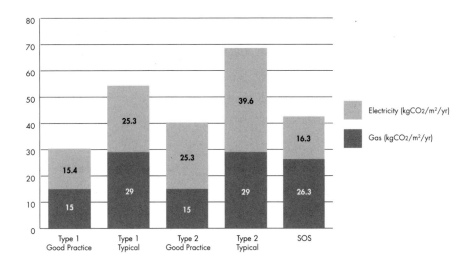

Figure 2 CO2 emissions/m²/yr of Stock Orchard Street Office (10 Stock Orchard Street) benchmarked against *ECG 19*

The water consumption for the office building is benchmarked in terms of cubic metres of water per full-time employee (FTE) per year. The water consumption of the office is an average of 5.8m³ per FTE per year. When 9/10 Stock Orchard Street was designed, the best practice guidance from the UK government was 6.6m³ per FTE per year, which has since been revised to 3m³ per FTE per year (OGC, August 2008). Therefore, based on the design criteria at the time, the office performs well. It is also understood that the government best practice figures do not make an allowance for visitors to offices, which can vary from business to business. It is considered that architects' offices would experience greater numbers of visitors, hence potential water consumers, attracting design teams of engineers, surveyors and clients, making the relative consumption higher than average. In this context, the water consumption figures are favourable.

House analysis

The performance of the house (9 Stock Orchard Street) has been compared to best practice by following a similar benchmarking method that was applied to the office. There are a number of energy guides to which reference has been made for the housing comparisons. *General Information Report 53* (*GIR53*), published in June 1996, investigates the potential for sustainable houses to be ranked in terms of 'zero heating', 'zero carbon' and fully autonomous, i.e. not connected to utility services or 'off-grid'. The report refers to the utility consumption of Robert and Brenda Vale's Autonomous House referred to in my chapter 'From Innovation to Commonplace'. *Good Practice Guide 301* (*GPG301*), published in 2002, deals with comparisons for energy-efficient heating and domestic hot water systems. This has been used to compare the best practice performance in these areas with 9 Stock Orchard Street. Comparisons have also been made to the *Code for Sustainable Homes (CfSH)*, published in December 2006, to compare the most up-to-date practice of sustainable house design standards. The code 'level 4' standard has been used as a benchmark for the study.

There are several more assessment tools that could be used with which to compare the performance of 9 Stock Orchard Street, such as the Passivhaus model (1996) that is currently gaining popularity in some circles. To be classed as a Passivhaus, the total energy demand for space heating and cooling needs to be less than 15kWh/m²/yr treated floor area; and the total primary energy[3] use for all appliances, domestic hot water and space heating and cooling needs to be less than 120kWh/m²/yr. These are tough targets that rely on super-insulation and high levels of airtightness, and go beyond the performance of 9 Stock Orchard Street, which has a space-heating load of around 77kWh/m²/yr and a total primary energy use of 184kWh/m²/yr. However, a comparison to Passivhaus performance has been made.

The comparison of these house standards is shown in Figure 3.

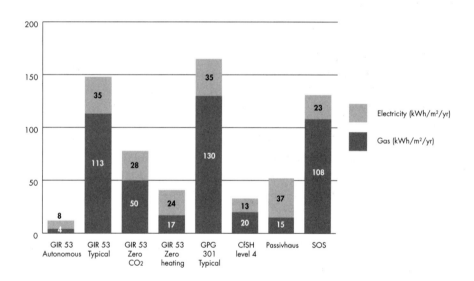

Figure 3 Energy consumption of Stock Orchard Street House (9 Stock Orchard Street) benchmarked against *GIR53*, *GPG301*, *CfSH* and Passivhaus

[3] The primary energy factors (PEF) are used to describe the relative proportion of primary energy to deliver usable energy in buildings. For example, in the UK, electricity has a PEF of 2.8 (according to the SAP 2005 calculations tool), which means that 2.8kWh of primary are required to produce 1kWh of usable electricity. Natural gas has a factor of 1.15.

The energy consumption figures have also been converted to kilograms of carbon dioxide per square metre per year to enable further comparison of the guides to be benchmarked. These are shown in Figure 4.

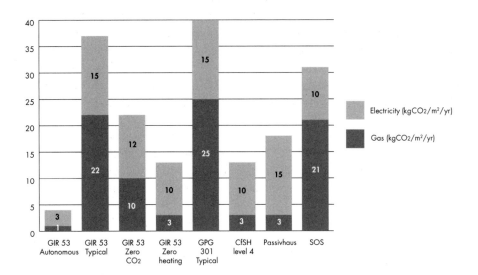

Figure 4 kg CO2 emissions of Stock Orchard Street House (9 Stock Orchard Street) benchmarked against *GIR53*, *GPG301*, *CfSH* and Passivhaus

As required under Part L of the Building Regulations (1995) submission, 9 Stock Orchard Street was assessed following the Standard Assessment Procedure (SAP) as a method of demonstrating compliance. The SAP is a UK government-approved method for calculating energy efficiency in dwellings expressed as a percentage. The higher the score, the more energy efficient the building. The calculated design score for 9 Stock Orchard Street of 92 per cent demonstrates that the proposed design should achieve a highly energy-efficient operation when constructed.[4] The SAP score is based on data such as U-values, heating and hot water systems, ventilation rates and renewable energy systems. The air infiltration rate is dealt with rather crudely by assigning a score – whether the structure is timber or masonry; there is no specific allowance for breathing walls. Given the current UK Building Regulations, it is likely that breathing walls would no longer comply due to the uncontrollable air infiltration.

Discussion

The construction methods and standards are significant factors in considering the energy consumption for 9/10 Stock Orchard Street. The buildings both have well-insulated envelopes and good-quality windows. However, the method of construction uses 'breathing wall' technology that allows moisture – and air – to pass through the building skin. While this can be beneficial during 'non-heating' seasons (spring, summer and autumn), there can be adverse effects of energy consumption during the heating season, caused by larger volumes of air leakage and infiltration. Other commentators have written

4 The maximum theoretical score is 100 per cent, although this can be exceeded through export of on-site generated electricity to the National Grid.

much on the detailed thermal analysis of breathing wall technology, and it is beyond the scope of this chapter to expand much further on the relative pros and cons of this construction technique. The author recommends further reading into their technology and examination of case study data.

In drawing conclusions from such a short-term analysis it is important to bear in mind that some factors are out of the hands of the owners/operators of the buildings and may be dependent upon external factors such as climate change. There are also possible inaccuracies in the assumptions made in the meter split estimates assumed between the house and the office. To achieve greater accuracy in the relative energy performance of the building, individual check meters should be installed on the three utility connections.

The initial comparison of data in Figures 1 and 2 suggests that the office (10 Stock Orchard Street) does not perform quite as well as a 'Good practice' office building as described by ECG 19. However, it is also shown that the office outperforms the 'Typical' standard for both office Types 1 and 2.

The ECG 19, first published in 1998 with revisions in 2000 and 2003, has now been superseded by stricter energy consumption figures through – among others – Building Regulations Part L2 2006 and the EU Energy Performance of Buildings Directive. While these new standards set higher targets for energy efficiency, in the majority of cases electrical loads associated with IT/computers – plug-loads – are omitted from the analysis. This new development in measuring energy efficiency has been brought about by placing greater emphasis on the building designers and constructors to deliver a complete product, including an efficient envelope and building services systems – heating, ventilation and air-conditioning (HVAC) and lighting. The occupants/tenants – those who actually use the building – are able to use their own preferred IT/computer systems, and the operational impact of their systems will affect the amount of energy used by the building services systems. Therefore, as the benchmarking and comparison methods stand at this stage, the relative performance of 10 Stock Orchard Street against a new building would require further analysis into the specific loads of IT/computers used in the practice, and perhaps this will be arranged through installation of sub-metering in the near future.

However, it should also be noted that the ECG 19 is produced based on sample data taken from a very limited number of buildings and should not be taken as an accurate indicator for every building type. We must be objective when carrying out a comparison of energy consumption relative to published benchmarks of performance, and to use the exercise to seek to identify how the performance can be improved.

Nonetheless, in order to reduce energy consumption in the office, building improvements could be carried out. The lower floor of the office has accommodated space for vents through the floor that could be installed to provide a means of natural ventilation – drawing air from the cooler shaded space – and exhausting the warm air by stack effect through high-level windows. This could provide natural cooling for much of the summer, and when allowed to operate passively through the night would lead to a more comfortable environment with less reliance upon the extract fans and their associated energy consumption and acoustic impacts.

Furthermore, the owners are encouraging a culture of energy saving in the office by making employees aware of the importance of switching off their computers and lights when not in use or not needed. These efforts will also continue to produce some small benefits.

The house incorporates an effective natural ventilation strategy with a secure vent provided at low level on the south-west elevation to allow air from the shaded undercroft to naturally enter the dwelling. The exhaust is provided through identical grilles close to the top of the tower, on the north-east elevation, controlled by (uninsulated) shutters. This system works well in the summer by making use of the natural stack effect, because the tower acts as a solar chimney to pull the hot air away from the occupied areas. In winter, the tower could be a sink for the warmth provided by the condensing gas boiler, thereby losing heat and, through the differential pressures that the tower creates, increasing the potential for infiltration. This is addressed by closing the door to the tower during the heating season.

In the 1990s at the time when 9/10 Stock Orchard Street was being designed, there was considerable debate about the different approaches of sustainable construction – such as thermal mass/lightweight and airtight/breathing walls. 9 Stock Orchard Street (the house) has applied the lightweight and breathing wall approach to envelope design and construction. The past ten years have seen industry recognise that breathing walls do not offer the most efficient solution for building envelopes – despite the relative U-values being to good standards. As U-values have improved through the UK Building Regulations (Part L), there is more focus on reducing the infiltration rate, and, to verify this, air-pressure testing of buildings became mandatory in the 2006 edition. The Passivhaus model insists on high standards of airtightness (i.e. low air infiltration) with background fresh air supplied by mechanical ventilation with heat recovery (MVHR). This has been shown to work well in Scandinavia and Germany – where the majority of the estimated 15,000 Passivhaus buildings have been constructed – but in the UK's milder climate and a less carbon-efficient electrical grid, this is harder to deliver.

The direction that is generally recognised as 'Best practice' is to make the building envelope as airtight as possible to minimise accidental – or background – air leakage, and to allow deliberate ventilation strategies to be applied to provide adequate air change. For all times of the year, except during heating season, the ventilation strategy for houses is to use openable windows and ventilation grilles to give a good fresh air supply. During the heating season, the preferred method is to use compact mechanical ventilation systems with heat recovery (MVHR) that use efficient fans to supply fresh air that is heated by the outgoing exhaust air. The compact MVHR units provide a means of providing fresh air, when the outside air temperature would be too cold to open windows, so that the health and well-being of building occupants is maintained. It does this through controlling CO_2 buildup, moisture and mould, which would become problematic from an overly sealed building envelope. One of the industry's mantras for envelope and ventilation design has been 'build tight; ventilate right', and this seems to sum up the approach fairly well.

The house (9 Stock Orchard Street) is provided with fresh air via a compact MVHR system for use during the heating season. This approach was adopted in the late 1990s when the debate over MVHR and breathing walls was being carried out, and it represents a belt-and-braces aspiration that doesn't realise the potential that the owners would, perhaps, have hoped for. This is most probably because the breathing walls, by encouraging air leakage, increase the heating load when there is a greater temperature difference between indoors and outdoors which the MVHR unit cannot mitigate. Now that more is known about the impact of heating energy associated with breathing walls, this may have led the designers of 9/10 Stock Orchard Street to adopt a different system. In addition, the undercrofts of both buildings are also likely to be major contributory factors to the relative higher heating energy consumption. By having exposed building on walls, roof and floors, it means that there is a larger surface area, as well as increased infiltration through which heat can be lost.

The large volume of 9 Stock Orchard Street (the house) combined with the huge area of glazing, the exposed ground floor and the lack of thermal mass undoubtedly contribute to the heating load in winter, despite the obvious benefits of good light and pleasure in contact with the external world. A more balanced approach to these factors would result in improved energy consumption.

In summary, the performance of 9/10 Stock Orchard Street as a green building has been assessed using utility bills and an estimated split between house and office. This has shown that, overall, the energy efficiency is somewhere between 'good' and 'typical' practice for the era in which it was designed. The use of benchmarks as exact relative determinants of performance should be used with caution, as every building is different in intensity and use. Furthermore, it is notable that the buildings proposed for benchmarking studies are usually not 'average' buildings; they are often more refined, with the owners seeking to display their better-than-average performance.

As a final note, the 9/10 Stock Orchard Street office still performs in the same ballpark estimate of good practice and, with ongoing improvements to operation through user habits and adjustments to the construction, the performance will likely improve further. When a building's performance is analysed and made public this puts the owners in a vulnerable position, and as a result this exercise happens far too rarely for any lessons to be learned. Therefore the owners of 9/10 Stock Orchard Street should be applauded for taking this step and making a significant contribution to the knowledge of helping to define 'what is green'.

As green building slowly becomes mainstream, legislation and societal drivers will push developers and owners to achieve greater efficiency and conservation of resources. The mainstreaming process, while exciting to observe and an essential requirement for the twenty-first century, is at the same time being exploited through 'greenwash' because standards are not agreed across the industry. One of the clearest examples of this is in energy modelling of building performance for Building Regulations compliance. As the modelling procedures become more onerous (as required for carbon minimisation and resource protection), the calculations become more complex. This makes the checking of design applications significantly more time consuming and expert, and in practice can lead to building designs being approved on paper although they would not meet the standards in practice.

Ultimately, utility meters present a true picture of consumption, and over-ambitious design claims will be revealed during the early period of occupation. Discrepancies between predictions and actual measurements will need analysing and may be caused by many factors including (but not limited to) misunderstandings, poor construction workmanship, over-optimistic predictions based on limited data, user behaviour and lack of knowledge. This is a call for truthfulness and honesty across the whole industry – and those who rise above the greenwash and the exaggerated claims will become leaders of design and construction. This subject is not simple, since differing views exist and multiple parameters are used to determine what is truly green. We are in a season of education and learning that will probably last until 2020. By then, if we do not know what we must do to produce green buildings as part of our sustainable lifestyles, it may well be too late.

The drive must come from clients who, as energy costs increase and the carbon footprints of new buildings are publicised, will demand that their design teams produce buildings that (in all senses) perform better. We may never be rid of those who falsely exploit the green-building movement, but as clients, municipalities and design teams work closer together there may be some hope in achieving the spirit of the law, even if the letter of the law proves unattainable. It is my own view that the design of the built environment must be pursued and implemented in an inclusive, interdisciplinary process in order to deliver a fully integrated solution that addresses primary ecological issues as the priority driver.

A house among houses: the idea of 9/10 Stock Orchard Street

Matthew Barac

What image does 'the idea of a house' conjure up in your mind's eye? Alarm bells are already ringing for the suspicious reader, who can see right through this trick question. It is a question designed to provoke rather than frame an argument, playing as it does on the weakness of so many architects for ideas – especially ideas that some would consider to be the domain of philosophers or sociologists. It is also designed to draw attention to the weakness of almost all other disciplines, especially those explicitly concerned with ideas, for architecture. Architecture does, after all, make its own particular claim to ideas, even if it is a claim that we as a discipline tend to overlook.

For architects, routinely caricatured as black-clad aesthetes standing resolute against the clutter of messy, disorderly life, ideas hold designs together. This shared belief has been expressed in diverse strands of architectural theory (Hillier 1996, Rykwert 1972) but, for the unsuspecting public, architects who concern themselves with ideas are too often guilty of being out of touch with everyday life. In this line of reasoning, 'ideas' and 'the real world' are opposing poles of an argument that separates the abstractions of form from the grit, cost and compromise of actuality.

This is not just the fault of the public out there. We within the profession do it too. The institutionalised motif of the 'ideas competition' is just one example; many take the view that competitions today should be seen as a warning against the way in which ideas, especially seductive ideas, can stand in the way of reality. Ideas competitions frequently result in a sense of waste, with the intellectual capital embodied in concepts generated by the design process compromised by their failure to take root in real situations. The relationship between the words 'concept' and 'conceit', summarised in the Renaissance formulation of the *concetto*, captures both the tendency of ideas towards autonomy and their nature, within matter, as representational potential (Minor 2006). This etymological synthesis historically grounded the *concetto* in ethical implications that have been largely lost in the trafficking of ideas convened by today's competitions. We are, instead, faced by a fusion of mystification and marketing, resulting in objects of desire that used to fall under the rubric of 'paper architecture' but that now appear, more often than not, on screens, in streams of bits and bytes, in dazzling 'visualisations'.

Yet, for all the risk of being seduced by ideas – of being caught playing with concepts rather than constructing real things that matter – the best architects' houses do engage actively with ideas. Well-worn in criticism, the motif of the architect's house is often considered interchangeable with that of the ideas building and naturally refers, sometimes deprecatingly, to the more widely appropriated notion of the 'ideal home' (De Botton 2006). Given that many of the readers of this book will be architects, the question we started with may be put differently. Rather than calling up personal associations and memories we could be more objective. What are the thoughts and references that make up the conceptual framework of 'house'? And what is the status of this assembled idea in our thinking – in our discipline, our research and our practice? How, then, do we assess and define the position, within this discourse, of a new work of architecture? Will we know, when we see it, whether or not to describe it as something really new and worthy of praise; as a contribution that takes debate about houses forward – a house among houses?

The argumentative house

Houses don't just appear out of nowhere; they all start with an idea. Discussion of ideas usually turns first to origins – to the conceptual rather than the literal origin of a house in its primordial or absolute form. This notion of a house that is at the beginning and perhaps also at the end of all houses is embedded in architectural as well as other traditions. When Joseph Rykwert (1972) wrote about the primitive hut in architectural history, he called his book *On Adam's House in Paradise*, drawing attention to his example's originary status as a cornerstone of the first grand design. The word 'origin' gives us 'original', pointing to the parallel dominant interpretation of 'idea' – that it refers to inspiration, which is related to the attributes of originality: to uniqueness and a capacity for representation. Inspiration and creativity are necessarily connected, and architecture's processes naturally mediate the creative dimension of inspiration's manifestations through representation. In the creative act, originality combines with genius to bring the power of the source, imagined as a geographical, historical or metaphysical origin, into dialogue with future possibilities. Channelled through design, which stands in for what Marcel Duchamp (1957) described as the 'mediumistic being' of the artist, this dialogue provides a basis for measuring innovation. It is within the exchange between a shared understanding of what home means and experimental forms, technologies or methods that the architect's house operates as a test bed for new ideas.

Assuming that a house is, first and foremost, a home, can it be authentic if its purpose has more to do with trying out new ideas? Should design not

Well-worn in criticism, the motif of the architect's house is often considered interchangeable with that of the ideas building.

focus on making a house do what it is supposed to do – keep out the cold and divide space in a way that suits our needs? It will be argued that architecture must perform both symbolic and practical functions if it is to be original, and the architect's house is useful for exploring how this comes to pass because both its reading and its design are always biographically determined. Seen as the architect's calling card, it must also support personal and professional life. If it fails to do so, it risks being lampooned as a non-house, as many architects' houses are, perhaps because the 'conceit' of the *concetto* has outrun the concept of what it is to be at home. Striking a balance between the technical and representational functioning of domestic architecture is a challenge, even though many feel it should perhaps be second nature to those who would imbue their architecture with the spirit of innovation.

The 'trick question' with which we started preys on the historical tendency of so many to get that balance wrong – to try to build 'an idea' rather than a house. Yet from the moment a house is just a twinkling in the eye, an architect must consider more than just hearth and home. A house is also geometry, history, regulation, technique and business. It demands allegiance to shared beliefs; it involves references and cleverness, back-to-basics dumbness and quiet professionalism. Architects cannot reduce the idea of the house to a single thing. Ask them what 'house' means and they will worry themselves into a pile of monographs, setting their own ideas off in a game of tag with Frank Lloyd Wright's Falling Water (1936), Eileen Gray's E1027 (1926–1929), Philip Johnson's Glass House (1949), Frank Gehry's Santa Monica house (1978–1979), Tony Fretton's Red House (2002)… The house is everything to an architect that the layperson thinks it isn't: sculptural, abstract, intricate, profound, always extending beyond itself, and in its perfect form – as a paradigm or an idea – the house is rarely the basis for agreement.

Instead, as demonstrated by the formula of UK reality-TV house-hunting programme *Location, Location, Location*, the idea of the perfect house is an excuse for an argument. The house that we want – especially if we are a couple – is an assortment of contradictions and demands. It must be at once both spacious and cosy, it must be urban but rural. We would have our homes impress our neighbours and yet portray modest restraint. What this tells us is that a house, for an architect, is never alone. In its newness it is in the company of everything that has gone before it, yet always aspiring to be something apart. In its singularity it offers conditions for a world of possibilities. This line of thinking, that a house is not so much an idea as it is an argument, begins to suggest how it can contribute to debate.

As any reader with even a passing knowledge of 9/10 Stock Orchard Street will know, these observations – about the house as an 'idea'; about a tendency in grown-up architectural concepts towards plurality; about the centrality of argumentation to meaningful design – all capture something of the Straw House. Much that has been said and written about the building, and there is plenty, has observed that it rejects conventional analysis.[1] Instead of being a house that can be pinned down by a single idea, this house has many – indeed, 'too many', as Jeremy Till has defiantly agreed (2000). This

Striking a balance between the technical and representational functioning of domestic architecture is a challenge.

[1] Almost everyone who is anyone in architectural criticism today has written a review of the Straw House, from Rowan Moore, to Dominic Lutyens, to Peter Davey.

makes the house unwieldy as a tool for argument, because it can mean so many things. By the same token, in the hands of a practised rhetorician it has multiple uses; Till (2000) uses it as a platform for arguing about the politics of research by design. My argument in this chapter is somewhat different. While acknowledging, as I have done elsewhere (2002), that the Straw House brings us to the sweet counter of twenty-first-century architecture, I want to rein back to recognise order in its multiplicity. More than just a sack of ideas jangling around, this design is an assemblage of intellectual and practical explorations, seasoned by the personality of authorship, and – in this way – not so very different from other architects' houses. It contributes to debate through its capacity to transform and test ideas, opening up possibilities for different interpretations and working with new technologies. And, so my argument goes, it does all this architecturally. The claim that I am moving towards is that the Straw House merits a position among the pantheon of ideas buildings, many of them architects' houses, because it attempts to reconcile concepts with place, in itself and in discourse. Knobbly and gawky, it does this in a way that is not tidied up for the camera. Yet it has elegant angles and a winning charm.

Therefore it affects a greater claim to being 'real' architecture. It pushes and pulls the idea of the house in directions that say: 'Don't be smug with the idea of house that you have. A house could, after all, be *me*, and through the kind of house that I am we can glimpse a whole new world.' It reaches beyond the conceptualisation of one kind of house or another as representing a choice; of the architect in history having 'tried a range of things' in order to come up with a catalogue of options. The house that claims its place in discourse is more than the sum of its parts, not as an exemplar or as a stylistic exercise *par excellence*, but as a manifold of meaning.

The Straw House challenges interpretation because it eschews the categories with which historians expect to be able to measure value.

This chapter makes the case for the Straw House to be seen in this light. A preamble invited the reader to consider the tension, in architecture, between 'ideas' and the 'reality', establishing the need to revisit our expectations if we are to acknowledge innovation. In a discussion about the motif of the architect's house, this section – the first section – has suggested that the Straw House challenges interpretation because it eschews the categories with which historians expect to be able to measure value. Instead of providing a manifesto suited either to the old school credo of purity and closure, or to a new generation of critics brought up on sound-bites and software, this house is argumentative: that is its style. The second section will explore the implications of this style by returning to the theme of the architectural idea. Tracing the efforts of thinkers such as Colin St John Wilson to understand the ethics of contributing to debate through design, we will consider how claims to originality come with their own obligations. The Straw House is unconventional; Rowan Moore has called it 'stilted, multiform, (and) rambling' (2001). Yet this does not imply that the house has no order. Indeed, its sense of wholeness is vital to its capacity to offer itself up in worldly terms. So many architects' houses (and city plans) turn their claims to wholeness into a strait-jacket, masquerading as a vision of a better life. The Straw House deftly avoids this trap. In the third section we reflect on how its architecture is, in fact, orderly and responsible, in step with the incidental

Not only is the dining table the literal origin of the design... but it is also the metaphoric anchor for the house.

rhythms of everyday life rather than the 'unstoppable drive' of modern times (Till 2009: 85).

From maverick to role model

The idea for the Straw House is, quite clearly, difficult to pin down. Many have tried – not only critics but also students, researchers, passengers on the train in and out of King's Cross, and the architects themselves. The most recent edition of *Sarah Wigglesworth Architects' Office Catalogue* (2009) provides a typically unsatisfying depiction of what gave rise to the design: that it aimed 'to provide a model of sustainable living in an urban setting'. Anyone who knows the house would agree that there is more to it, and – in all fairness – the catalogue text does go on to mention a variety of innovations. This parlour game could go on: Peter Davey wrote about 'overlapping storytelling' (2002), Hugh Pearman echoed the idea of a 'working prototype' (2001), William Tozer advocated 'the construction of ideas' (2002). But such efforts to capture the design concept in a reader-friendly quip seem wide of the mark. Acknowledging this difficulty, Wigglesworth has built a narrative that is more faithful to the architectural process – one that captures the idea both as origin and in metaphor.

This is the idea of the dining table. Not only is the dining table the literal origin of the design – the site of many meals during which the house was the topic of discussion, and also the site of design: drawing, model-making and meetings – but it is also the metaphoric anchor for the house. The traditional, phenomenologically powerful notion of 'hearth' as domestic centre is here eclipsed by the dining table, which 'quite literally assumes a pivotal position between work and home' in plan (Tozer 2002). The dining table was where it all started, but it also provides an analogy for the authenticity of architecture. Wigglesworth claims that the dining table is more faithful than most theory to the spatiality and temporality of everyday interpretations of architecture – of how we inhabit and imagine places. This is because the table's rhythm of order and disorder, of being neatly laid and routinely messed up, reflects the decorum of human situations.

Linking the idea behind the design to humdrum, ordinary situations is not to suggest that it is prosaic. Indeed, the case being made draws on a tradition of interpreting places in poetic terms associated with philosophy. One of the fathers of this approach is Gaston Bachelard, whose primer *The Poetics of Space* (1969) remains a key text for understanding how ordinary things can inspire. Much of Bachelard's writing depicts spaces, furniture and situations that evoke a kind of solitary melancholy. The intellectual provenance of Wigglesworth's dining table is, in many ways, the opposite, perhaps owing more to the industrious communality captured in Herman Hertzberger's phenomenological figure 'the sociology of the table' (2000: 154). The capacity of the table to represent both a world of possibilities, oriented to society at large, and an anchor for a moment shared between two people, points to an attribute that Bachelard (1969: 183) sums up as 'intimate immensity'.[2] This is the principle of the microcosm, underpinning not only the extensive referential faculty of the dining table but also its intensive, symbolic function: its depth. The idea of the dining table is able to represent the whole by virtue

[2] Bachelard emphasises daydreaming rather than the motif of the microcosm, but the principle remains relevant.

of its status as a conceptual anchor for the design, a witty manoeuvre that recalls the principle of the *concetto* discussed earlier.

To some readers, the prospect of so many long words coming to rest on a table-top composition of dirty dishes, breadcrumbs, coffee rings and wine spills will, no doubt, appear ridiculous. But it is in the play between profound metaphoric power and mundane everydayness — after all, it is just a table — that the value of the idea is made evident.

Clever and witty this idea may well be, verified as authentic, providing both an origin and inspiration, and — through references and symbols — drawing secondary ideas, ideas that promiscuously attach themselves to the conceptual superstructure of the design, together into a whole, but does the house contribute to debate? What, if anything, is really new about its design? Is newness even relevant to the definition of a 'contribution'? Research students are prone to panic when they hear this word, faced as they are with the task of backing up the claim that their work contributes something new. But the 'how-to' pages of any dissertation manual typically offer up to fifteen ways to make an 'original contribution' to knowledge. For architecture, in a debate constituted less in words and more in built form, this question can be controversial. Consensus about what making a contribution means would certainly help to bring greater order to the academic house of our discipline, with a positive impact on wider debate so that our currently anaemic concept of originality could adapt to the diversity, scope and politics of the knowledge out there. Too much of the 'design as research' being rolled out today does little to further this objective. Instead, it promotes formal exercises that lead to compositions characterised by their emptiness. A lack of depth and weight, of connection to the ground (which we will later address as an attribute of 'responsible architecture'), creates difficulties for wider debate by implying that a contribution can be made out of something that is hardly there: that is, to paraphrase the oft-quoted Marshall Berman, about to 'melt into air' (1988).

It has been argued that for a work falling within the privileged category of the architect's house to be admitted to the pantheon of designs that have genuinely moved debate forward, it must engage with ideas. Alongside demonstrable innovation, it must perform both symbolic and practical functions and, in so doing, support and enhance life. While this list of demands clearly reaches beyond the expectations of many conventional academic programmes, setting goals for architecture that would claim a place in history rather than occupying a dusty shelf in the university library, the concern for content does not disappear. Of course, the enormous scope of disciplinary knowledge and the funding dynamics of research mean that a technical bias will inevitably endure. But this should not steer the criteria for contributions that aim to provide orientation to debate. To take up a position alongside other major figures, is it enough to contribute by continuing a line of inquiry started by another architect, adding a variant or an alternative approach to the pool of knowledge? Will a major contribution not need to do more than simply focus on a single original technique or use of materials, or bring familiar material together in an original way? The argument

No matter how articulated and sophisticated they may be, houses that qualify as 'homes' are anchored by their embodying attributes: their weight.

developed here certainly calls for more. To meet the terms already outlined, a contribution should matter. Drawing on the idea that meaningful architecture will carry weight, it should be substantial. It should certainly offer something new, but greatness is unlikely to be defined by novelty. Our conceptualisation of newness may therefore need some clarification.

Few have written as eloquently about the meaning of innovation in design as Colin St John Wilson (2000). In 'The Historical Sense' he transcribed T.S. Eliot's celebrated 1919 analysis of the relationship between tradition and the individual talent from literature to architecture.[3] Wilson insisted that there is always a dialogue between the works of the past, which constitute and reside within a tradition, and the capacity of something new to contribute. What Wilson calls a 'paradoxical interpretation of tradition as the springboard for innovation' (2000: 67) reveals within newness an obligation to history. Adding to the existing pantheon of significant works of architecture is not, therefore, simply about getting attention:

> It involves in the first place, the historical sense, which... involves a perception, not only of the pastness of the past, but of its presence... a simultaneous existence (that) composes a simultaneous order. This historical sense... is what makes an (architect) traditional. And it is at the same time what makes an (architect) most acutely conscious of his place in time, of his own contemporaneity.

Arguing for a reconciliation between modernity and history, against both the dominant strand of modernism and historicist tendencies, Wilson rails against design that raids the surfaces of historical forms without due regard for their depth. He wants architects to innovate, but in a manner more attentive to context. This is not simply a complaint against 'kitsch', but a condition of true innovation – of the 'really new' (1992: 68). Wilson adds that the innovative architect will therefore be aware of the 'great difficulties and responsibilities' that attend to adding something new to debate. Ideas are not just for fun; they come with obligations.

Ideas that measure up to their obligations are a precondition for architecture that matters. 'Really new' design will reach ahead into a temporal zone not yet known but, at the same time, keep one foot in the past. This past is common ground: a shared historical territory. Hence it is both permanent and essentially human, a ground with which we identify and to which we all belong. Phil Tabor (1994) navigates between phenomenological and psychological interpretations of this observation to note that the 'house identified as the self is called *home*'. No matter how articulated and sophisticated they may be, houses that qualify as 'homes' are anchored by their embodying attributes: their weight. While such architecture should not be frivolous, it may well be light-hearted – the Straw House certainly is, celebrated by Davey (2002) as 'the most sexy and witty building I have seen for years'. But to usefully add to the pantheon of works – to be a 'house among houses' – it must carry the burden of tradition. It will be noted that such a claim takes issue, after Wilson, with the likes of many of Modernism's fathers, including Gropius (Menin and Kite 2005: 263), and also with the

[3] 'The Historical Sense: T.S. Eliot's Conception of Tradition, and its Relevance to Architecture' was first published in 1984 in the *Architectural Review*, 176(1052): 68–70. The reference given here is to its republication as a chapter in *Architectural Reflections*.

drift towards play for its own sake in architecture aligned with strands of postmodern theory. Peter Eisenman's celebrated house designs of the 1970s, which are 'against the traditional notion of how you occupy a house', indulge in self-referential games; they demonstrate formal cleverness rather than architecture.[4] Eschewing their obligations, these design ideas attack tradition, mocking the notion of common ground.

Quite clearly the Straw House is also far from traditional. Yet, despite its quirky heterogeneity, its 'playful mix (of) conflicting architectural styles' (Lutyens 2002) and the drama of its interiors, much about it is familiar and reassuring. It has walls, roofs, windows; the rooms are room-like, and the curious, gawky tower, front door, gabion piers and kitchen table all remind us of other towers, doors, columns and tables. While these are things we can use as markers in relation to other homes, here they have their own claim and place. Turning traditional ideas upside-down, the Straw House offers new configurations of work and home. It raises the living room above a chicken coop; it uses straw for its walls and plants a meadow on its sloping roof. But these playful ideas are not jokes. They are serious games, respectful of the environment, responsive to context and attentive to tradition.

Playful and quirky, this house is also respectful, responsive and attentive. As several critics have observed, much of its charm grows out of its capacity to be many things at once: to be an architectural maverick, evading categorisation, and at the same time a role model – a prototype for sustainable urban living. Discussion has begun to characterise the house as a work that matters, arguing for its contribution to debate according to criteria of innovation, meaningfulness and paradoxical wholeness, a point to which we will return. Its manipulation of spaces and materials, of reference and function, situates everyday problems within the issues of our times. We have noted that it does these things in a manner that allows the home to exert a place-making claim, celebrating the specific capabilities of architecture. As opposed to other, possibly cleverer, more perfect but less animated houses, the Straw House herds its unruly flock of ideas together in a manner that reflects more accurately the realities of life in the city – certainly this part of the city – than the regimented precision of what Till refers to as the 'juggernaut' of 'Enlightenment fundamentalism' that continues to exert power over architectural discourse (Till 2009: 48). At the Straw House, ideas are claimed by, through and in the architecture, so that architecture's way of being is allowed to flourish. Ideas are used to connect things, reminding us of the characteristic integrity of space and its bond with culture (Barac and McFadyen 2007: 111). This spatial integrity opens the design up, allowing it to mean many things to many people and, in the same moment, to bring its material and intellectual components together to form an architecture that is substantial.

Ideas with obligations

So how, exactly, does this house – a house made of straw – bring something substantial to debate? What about it is profound, what makes its materials matter, and what gives its intellectual ideas body? Following Wilson, we have drawn upon ideas in literary criticism to understand better the idea of the

At the Straw House, ideas are claimed by, through and in the architecture, so that architecture's way of being is allowed to flourish. Ideas are used to connect things.

[4] Eisenman quoted in *Deconstruction: Omnibus Volume*, A. Papadakis et al. (eds) (1989).

new. Weaponising Eliot's insights, in his battle with architecture that shirks its ethical obligations, Wilson navigates between the politics of representation and the judgements embedded in notions of taste. His aim is to rehearse the case for an 'other (Modernist) tradition' (Wilson 1995), but ours is to explore how an architecture that is maverick in relation to the established canon and, at the same time, a role model for future works, can be responsible. It will be suggested that the Straw House achieves this through its capacity to belong to its place and in its time, a belonging played out in architecture of substance that mediates between the personal, particular narratives of everyday occupation and collective, larger cycles of shared experience.

In our global times of connectedness and separation, our world of networks, inequality, and consumption, the topic of responsibility in architecture is inevitably controversial. Even as it levels everything out in capital flows and rapid adaptations, globalisation spurs a desire for that which it threatens to erase. The twentieth century's love affair with everything artificial has given way not to a backlash, but certainly to a call to order – a desire to make architecture that is *not* unbound from place and time, and that is *not* so removed from human concerns that it cannot tell which way is up: in short, a call for architecture to get grounded. This aspiration concerns techniques to improve the built environment's relationship with material resources and also to address the concrete conditions of everyday life. The demand for concreteness would recover architecture's social and cultural role, one in which it is able to tether us down in a world spinning ever faster. Responsible architecture therefore makes places. It matters in the sense of being grounded, providing an anchor for negotiating the challenges of communication and productivity that characterise today's practices of work and play.

Despite the sometimes awkward disposition of the house, a house clearly unlike anything around it, it exhibits a keen desire to be a part of local life alongside its efforts to belong to the cycles and rhythms of the planet.

The Heideggerian drift of this argument is hardly surprising, given that Till and Wigglesworth were both part of (and set themselves apart from) a school of thought at the University of Cambridge that drew extensively, during its flowering, upon the tradition of phenomenological hermeneutics. For more than twenty-five years, architectural history and design were taught and debated as part of a broad interest in contemporary culture (Menin and Kite 2005: 241). Although approaches to design were diverse, with stark contrasts between 'positivist' and 'phenomenological' studios, much of the school discourse argued for politically responsive renderings of spatial experience. In particular, the teachings of Dalibor Vesely and Peter Carl promoted an engagement with the ontology of places: with their material and formal associations, and with their meanings.

Ontological concerns are embedded in the use, choice and manipulation of materials at the Straw House. At once tentative and assertive, this building neither bullies nor sucks up to its surroundings. Rather it belongs by offering something new and, at the same time, by responding to its visible, tangible context. This responsive belonging wants to 'do the right thing'. Despite the sometimes awkward disposition of the house, a house clearly unlike anything around it, it exhibits a keen desire to be a part of local life alongside its efforts to belong to the cycles and rhythms of the planet. It wants to have friends just as much as it wants to stand apart. Material claims are made explicit from the moment the visitor steps, with a crunch, across the gravel threshold, and even before. Viewed from the street approach, the material iconography of the woven willow fence panels of the entrance façade celebrates garden sheds and the culture of allotments. Viewed from a passing train, the material character of the office wing, complete with 'sleeper' window surrounds and cement-sandbag cladding, could not be more demonstrative. The gabion piers, despite their questionable authenticity, reclaim and reinvigorate the concrete found on the site, by smashing it into pieces and piling it into wire cages which are then used to prop up the new accommodation.[5] This materialist account binds the building's physical constitution to a broader concern with climate change – a key challenge for our epoch, yet one that was, when the Straw House was designed and constructed, struggling to find its feet in debate.

What the house did very well, at the time it first appeared on the horizon, and continues to do, sometimes dividing opinion, is to stimulate discussion about the architectural iconography of sustainability. Notwithstanding a number of brave innovations and the rise, during the 1990s, of a cohort of 'green' practices, environmentally responsible architecture remains widely associated with dullness and worthiness. Setting out to revolutionise the way we think about sustainability, to make it cool and stylish, the Straw House addressed the challenge of opinion-forming, positioning itself as an architectural agent of change (Soane 2003: 200). Style, even the stylistic category of 'timelessness', is always a form of engagement with temporality. The temporal dimension of the belonging of the Straw House is also expressed in its character as narrative. The house itself takes the role of storyteller: a self-styled pioneer, offering its autobiography as a vehicle for learning that starts with its own beginning. This 'personal' beginning migrates into the public domain as the story of the house becomes appropriated and diversified through wider narratives of sustainable architecture, and in discussions about the meaning of the home in twenty-first-century debate.

Certainly it may be seen that the house raises public issues and also responds to personal problems. It makes claims to greatness but it is also modest, and even, at times, humble. Positioned at the turn of the millennium, looking back to architectural traditions that include is own witty reference to l'Augier's primitive hut in a tree column next to the front door, and forward to a future in which sustainability is embedded in architectural culture rather than a technological add-on, the design has the good sense to leave questions unanswered; to present itself as an unfinished project rather than as the answer to everything. Yet it is brave, carrying a torch for architecture. Rather than using 'ideas' to escape from the contingency of everyday life, it develops concepts and conceits that celebrate the fact that the world is unpredictable, divided and untidy.

We have considered the substance of the Straw House design not only in its material sense but in terms of time, investigating how its architecture of ideas fulfils obligations and acts responsibly. But writing about the house in its material and temporal components runs the risk – a risk in all criticism – of

The house itself takes the role of storyteller: a self-styled pioneer, offering its autobiography as a vehicle for learning that starts with its own beginning.

5 Sterner critics have found fault with the gabion piers as they do not actually support the office wing; the structural work is performed by concrete columns hidden within them.

There is an order to this storytelling architecture, and it is an architectural order in which space is the primary vehicle of orientation.

breaking the house up into pieces and thereby erasing the object of study. Many critics, myself included, have written about 9/10 Stock Orchard Street as an assembly of vignettes. What and where is the whole of this house? It is certainly a substantial building in terms of its material manifestation and the life it reflects and supports, but is it more than the sum of its parts?

The paradoxical wholeness of the Straw House is defined by the narrative style of its architecture: its myriad ideas and its episodic manner. While the stories it tells may be diverse, sending us off in a number of different directions, they belong together, nested within bigger shared stories. There is an order to this storytelling architecture, and it is an architectural order in which space is the primary vehicle of orientation.

The richness and referentiality of the Straw House makes it softly amenable to appropriation; indeed, the way in which the building invites people in (particularly students) underpins its heuristic character. And not content with inviting you in, the architecture carries you in the wake of its storytelling dynamic. Marshalling different narratives of everyday life, it brings them together in a three-dimensionally expressed manifold of meanings: in routes, activities and conversations that inhabit, attach themselves to or spin out from the building. The architecture structures this simultaneity of experience, creating a backdrop that anticipates events and at the same times brings richness to their interpretation. Any visitor will recognise this palpable sense of anticipation. As ideas track back and forth through the building, ordinary life goes on. Chickens wander around the garden, avoiding the slippery uplights embedded in the gravel pathway; the afternoon sun tracks across the gable wall, offering a shadow-play tableau to Sunday stew; while the Caledonian Sleeper whistles past on its nightly rush north, wild strawberries grow on the roof at their own pace; the new year-out student gets to work, in the office, on a CAD plan for a new sustainable school on site in Wakefield; up in the study at the top of the tower, it's a choice between working on a research paper or typing out a design and access statement for a masterplan…

This simultaneity is the whole. Not the fact of 'lots of things happening at the same time', but the fact that the architecture provides a continuum in which such events have their place. The means by which place is allowed to be claimed, fostering tangible and memorable ways (with material and temporal implications) in which to belong, brings order to the house rather than turning its multiform variety into so much architectural noise. Making all of this work depends upon a keen awareness of the capacity of typical human situations to bring orientation to the diverse stimuli of urban life today (Vesely 2004).

Architectural awareness links into practical knowledge in the mobilisation of ideas at the Straw House: into a kind of knowledge embedded in design practice. Mediated by the methods of making buildings, the challenge of maintaining authorial control over the whole is played out in the layering of spatial vignettes. These diverse moments – constructional decisions, scenes from domestic life, daydreams, concepts – can be imagined like doodles that always end up the same. The image of their convergence, for the designer, offers a glimpse of the order that positions them in meaningful relationships with one another. Revealed more clearly in the sectional configuration of the building than in the plans, and in Wigglesworth's 'time-lapse' drawings of her dining table, the vertical order of the house pivots, as I have written elsewhere, around its 'principal room': the dining room (Barac 2002). While this may not be the biggest or even the best room in the house, it provides orientation for everything above and below, to the left and to the right, what is yet to come and what has passed. The room offers a moment at rest in an otherwise complex weave of narratives. In so doing it centres the composition. Compared to what many authors have said about the house, this analysis may appear old-fashioned. But the dining room is, I would argue, the place where the many moving parts of this infernal machine may be understood in alignment. Moreover, I suggest that it is in the table conceptualised as a *wunderblok* of ordinary occupation, which is the origin of this room and the hinge of the house, that the responsibilities and obligations of the architectural order are revealed – more so, perhaps, than in the higher profile sustainability credentials of the architecture. Borrowing from Wilson again, affording ethical concerns their rightful place in architecture entails the pursuit of 'that which is most fruitful in the weaving together of innumerable patterns of operation in day-to-day life' (2000: 45).

Interpreting the order of the Straw House thus makes available to us a sense of its architectural wholeness, which – in turn – gives each of the many ideas within the design its own place. At its most articulate, representing a more elevated register of its order than the concrete attributes that confer weight upon the architecture, the house is able to stake a claim to significance in discourse. Healthily contested at times since the building was first published, this claim has already served to define the house as a touchstone for thinking about sustainability in architecture as a cultural endeavour. Yet, I have argued, its contribution adds up to more than this. I have drawn attention to how the house – its expressive language and the experiences it bestows – is faithful to architecture's way of being. Its ideas make connections between things, reinforcing the integrative potential of space.

The house – its expressive language and the experiences it bestows – is faithful to architecture's way of being. Its ideas make connections between things, reinforcing the integrative potential of space.

Moreover, the way in which architecture's spatial mode of organising ideas is celebrated supports the case for seeing this house as a work of substance; its playfully narrative style is grounded in material and temporal terms. The resulting sense of place in time reflects the way in which architecture, through the mobilisation of spatial ideas that connect, is able to mediate, to paraphrase sociologist C. Wright Mills, between the personal problems of everyday life and the wider issues of the day (1959) in a manner that underwrites the architectural order of the work.

The innovative architecture of the Straw House has brought new ideas to debate, contributing something new in a manner that respects tradition. Despite maverick tendencies, this is a grown-up architecture that matters; unafraid to address the domain of the symbolic, it is at pains to fulfil its obligations. It brings itself into being in a substantial way by virtue of its material presence, and also by embedding itself in rhythms of everyday life, rising to the contextual challenge of narrating correspondences between ordinary problems and the issues of our times.

Understanding the argumentative temperament of the Straw House has helped to explain how its architectural order depends less on completeness – on a vision of architecture that can be divided by the steps of a mathematical proof – than on its character as an imperfect whole. This theorisation of ideas marks architecture out as different from disciplinary knowledge that depends on the internal logic of concepts. There can be little doubt that this house is significant: that it has things to say, points to make, and takes a position. But the fact that it does these things in an authentically architectural manner most convincingly makes the case that we should consider it no ordinary house, despite its love affair with ordinariness, but a house among houses.

References

Bachelard, G. (1969, c.1958) *The Poetics of Space*, trans. Maria Jolas (Boston, MA: Beacon Press).

Barac, M. (2002) 'The Ideas Factory' in *World Architecture* 102: 39–42.

Barac, M. and L. McFadyen (2007) 'Connected Space' in *Home Cultures* 4(2): 109–116.

Berman, M. (1988) *All That is Solid Melts into Air: The Experience of Modernity* (New York: Penguin Books).

Davey, P. (2002) 'The Slick and the Hairy' in *Architectural Review* 211(1259): 64–68.

De Botton, A. (2006) *The Architecture of Happiness* (London: Hamish Hamilton).

Duchamp, M. (1957) 'The Creative Act', paper presented at the Convention of the American Federation of Arts, Houston, Texas.

Hertzberger, H. (2000) *Space and the Architect: Lessons in Architecture 2*, (Rotterdam: 010 Publishers).

Hillier, B. (1996) *Space is the Machine: A Configurational Theory of Architecture* (Cambridge: Cambridge University Press).

Lutyens, D. (2002) 'Clutching at Straws' in *Observer*, 13 January.

Menin, S. and S. Kite (2005) *An Architecture of Invitation: Colin St John Wilson* (Aldershot: Ashgate).

Minor, V.H. (2006) *The Death of the Baroque and the Rhetoric of Good Taste* (Cambridge: Cambridge University Press).

Moore, R. (2001) 'Grass Roof, Straw Walls, close to King's Cross, Would Suit Green Couple' in *Evening Standard*, 26 June: 24–25.

Papadakis, A, C. Cooke and A. Benjamin (eds) (1989) *Deconstruction: Omnibus Volume* (London: Academy Editions).

Pearman, H. (2001) 'House of Straw' in *Sunday Times*, 1 July.

Rykwert, J. (1972) *On Adam's House in Paradise: The Idea of the Primitive Hut in Architectural History* (New York: Museum of Modern Art).

Sarah Wigglesworth Architects (2009) *Sarah Wigglesworth Architects' Office Catalogue* (London: Sarah Wigglesworth Architects).

Soane, J. (2003) *New Home: Architecture and Design* (London: Conran Octopus).

Tabor, P. (1994) 'Striking Home: The Telematic Assault on Identity', paper presented at the conference *Doors of Perception 2 – @Home*. Netherlands Design Institute and Mediamatic, Amsterdam.

Till, J. (2000) 'Too Many Ideas', paper presented at the EAAE conference in Delft.

(2009) *Architecture Depends* (Cambridge, MA, and London: MIT Press).

Tozer, W. (2002) 'Wigglesworth Till: House of Straw', *Monument* 46: 56–61.

Vesely, D. (2004) *Architecture in the Age of Divided Representation* (Cambridge, MA, and London: MIT Press).

Wilson, C. St John (1995) *The Other Tradition of Architecture: The Uncompleted Project* (London: Academy Editions).

(2000, c.1992) *Architectural Reflections: Studies in the Practice and Philosophy of Architecture* (Manchester: Manchester University Press).

Wright Mills, C. (1959) *The Sociological Imagination* (London, Oxford and New York: Oxford University Press).

External kitchen table,
October 2008

Left **Pond, April 2009**
Above **Rustic court, January 2009**

Fading light,
October 2008

Left **Window, 2008**
Right **Kitchen, October 2008**

Left **Office stair, March 2009**
Right **Minstrel's gallery, October 2008**

Above **Living room, October 2008**
Right **Mezzanine study, October 2008**

Above **Door to roof, April 2009**
Right **Hillside roof garden, March 2008**

Left **Overlooking, April 2009**
Above **Daybed in tower room, April 2009**

Out of time, out of frame, into the box

Kester Rattenbury

Out of time

The 'problem' with Wigglesworth and Till's straw bale house is exactly what gives it its peculiar powers. It's too big. The site would hold at least two of its comfortable late Victorian neighbours in Stock Orchard Street, and four or five of the smaller, and less comfortably gardened, 1980s-ish successors, in the cul-de-sac which backs the other side of the site. Instead, it holds one medium-sized office, a two-bedroomed house, off-street parking (of a kind, in a buddleia bush) for one small car and a largish garden. It's a next-door-to normal building with a density way below its place and time.

At the time it was built, the gossip was always that the size of this big house (which clearly wants to be a shack) was a mistake: that the site must have been much bigger than they imagined. But perhaps not: because this 'mistake' plays magical tricks. Maybe because it was conceived on holidays, talked about rather than drawn, developed as a self-build, it doesn't behave like the commercially pressured buildings around it. It makes you feel like you're somewhere else: in a slightly different time or place.

Mind you, time and place are changeable things. Old and new maps show scales shifting vastly around this site – from those apocryphal fruit trees to prison, asylum, grand house, shanty town, mammoth Victorian food market. Stock Orchard Street is in a curious part of north London, a service hinterland between Islington and Camden; both opened to and severed from the city to the south by the mainline railway, and with its historic landmarks largely absent. The corner pubs alone mark the vast nearby site of the vanished Caledonian Road market; they were built over the infamous Belle-Isle horse-butchery and Pleasant Grove, with its dust heaps; the model for Dickens' Harmony Jail and Bowery dust heaps in *Our Mutual Friend* – and one of his great examples of places where names can mean their opposite.

Plan of the parish of
St Mary Islington, 1841

221

But any fans of Peter Ackroyd's ideas of continuity of site will love to know that between Belle-Isle and the Stock Orchard Street site were 'Experimental Gardens'; a short-lived community self-build programme, in the manner of Robert Owen, set up in the 1840s, just down Caledonian Road and opposite Pentonville Prison.

Most recently, the site of 9/10 used to be a forge, and the current building deliberately retains that B1-ishness: it's a workplace for maybe eight to fifteen people, maybe more, with two people living next to the shop. So it's sometimes busy, sometimes empty, with a shifting intensity of usage over any given period: the undercroft, the stacks of things in spare spaces next to the railway or down the back of the house; a rambling density which is unfamiliar in this place and age. Whatever the architectural language may be, 9/10 uses its site like a cross between farmhouse and small family works – things that might once have been there – in a place and time where the development norm would be a small block of flats. Or a big grand villa with a garden, designed to show off your space for all you were worth.

There seems to be something about this space-slack that visitors notice. In the many, many reviews of 9/10 (in an unusually wide range of places, from interiors magazines to guidebooks, from ecological magazines to esoteric journals), rather than the usual architect-y comparisons, you get non-architect-y, personal and holiday ones. I always have a strong sense of semi-converted farmhouses in Spain, France, Italy here, but also a nagging memory of a holiday inter-railing around Denmark. One visitor compared Stock Orchard Street to a beach on a lake in Switzerland. The obvious architect-y suspects – Le Corbusier, Walter Segal, Rem Koolhaas – somehow don't get talked about so often. I don't think it matters *where* it reminds you of, but that it's simply somewhere else.

Or in a different time frame. I've been to three parties there: the first, featuring straw bales, the old foundry sheds and peach Bellinis; the last,

a smart and very friendly work do in Sarah's office. The most memorable was their 'centenary' birthday; an exceptionally generous event at which Martyn Ware of Heaven 17 was DJ-ing (keep your eye on that music) while we lazed around the whole site; spent hours sitting on the grass roof in the night; sat talking in the small, central kitchen. Those few hours felt like we had at least had a weekend in the country. It felt strange to get home so fast on the night bus.

This residual peculiarity, this sense of time-slip, seems to operate because Wigglesworth and Till have ignored at least one of the conventions ingrained in the normal architectural psyche – that sense of the reasonable use of space in London. It's an odd thing to focus on: it could be a mistake; it's not something you can easily capture in photos, and our ways of expressing it are poor. It is not something that is normally represented in architectural books or articles. But our sense of it is strong, and it's that mismatch between what you notice and what you normally represent which for some reason dogs my ideas in trying to figure out this building.

I have to admit that I find 9/10 an incredibly difficult thing to write about. In many ways it is not that unusual, or it is only unusual in the way that other architect-designed houses are: atypical configurations and use of materials; new variants, evolutions or combinations of existing types. Definitely of its time, though it is far easier to see that now that it is ten years older, and its time has settled around it – and indeed has followed what has turned out to be its lead. Just a medium-sized live/work building: the type of thing that you'd expect a normal magazine feature on; not the sort of thing about which you could persuade a batch of writers to cook up a whole book.

I had always imagined it as a villa which wants to be a shack; a Petit Trianon of ethic and social concerns. Very much an architect's own house as experiment; and a very English one at that; more Clough Williams Ellis than Corbusier. But to me, the ways in which it is unusual – the

Edward Weller's Map of London (section), 1859

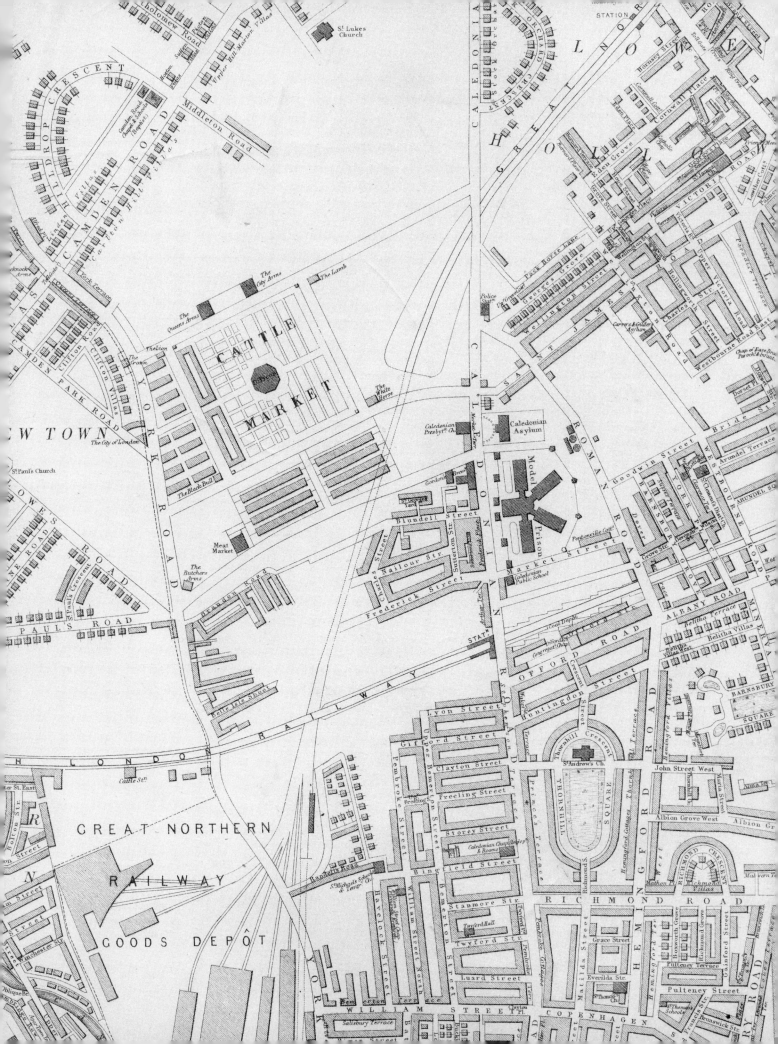

ways in which it is different from its architectural peers – seem to be to do with representation, or rather to do with side-stepping the tropes we use for representing architecture. That makes it difficult to discuss – without sounding pretentious, anyway – or even to understand.

This house is too eclectic to be in a single style, and it's too curated and composed to be truly eclectic. It doesn't fit the usual conventions in which we not only publish, but actually often design and imagine projects: as a coherent set of pictorial visualisations. It wasn't designed through drawings but through conversations; and so unsurprisingly, its ideas cannot quite be captured: the set of photographs or drawings which usually act as a distillation, or shorthand code, for the 'architecture' of the project (whatever that is). 9/10's architecture is only partly (if at all) about what it looks like. Whenever I see drawings or photos of it, they never look like the house I am thinking of.

Perhaps this is one of the ways in which 9/10 remains a theoretical project – one that does help expose the conventions of architectural behaviour. Perhaps it does this by picking a few conventions and selectively ignoring them (as well as in re-combining some others, many of them about how things get made) and seeing what type of architecture you get.

One factor excluded here is that an architectural idea should be visually discernible within a single frame – that somewhere there is a perspective view or a photo which really expresses the project. That is our underlying norm, and it is only a few types of really influential projects (CLASP schools, Cedric Price) which evade it and they're notoriously difficult to describe. 9/10 too. It is not a set style and there is not a visual or formal family which stitches the dissimilar ideas together. It is not even really a polemic collage, like Koolhaas' Villa dal'Ava, though it clearly shares its free reconfiguring of modernist and vernacular forms. It's full of styles, and forms, and ideas (I did manage to identify the Mosque of Cordova as an organising principle for how you move through the interrupted grid). But

to me it's more notable for what it isn't, overall, than what it is.

The most overt attempt at excluding a normal trope in this house, though, is the attempt to avoid the myth of being 'finished' – that image of perfection purveyed by drawings and magazines and aspired to, but so rarely found, in real-life projects. Its deliberate attitude to time is also of its time. This house came directly out of academic and theoretical work – Desiring Practices;[1] *Architectural Design: The Everyday and Architecture*[2] – which are now so pervasive it is hard to remember that once, people had to (sort of) invent them. But if ever a project should have earned itself a Ph.D. or two through working out some theories and then building, it is this one.

To give an inexpert outsider's view of this branch of theory: it was the new (or anyway, latest) mix of theory and practice – and the active questioning of which was which. This was an argument for theory as a form *of* practice; the interest in the drawing as 'site'; the deliberate withdrawal or reversal of the boundaries of a set 'high' architecture; the questioning of the notions of purity, perfection and completeness implicit in the architectural drawing, and particularly the presentation drawing. The theories of this time – the late 1980s and early 1990s – sought to draw and design in a way which evaded that (apparently) implicit underlying assumption of perfection and completeness.

So the straw bale house was not just an experiment in new (or old) techniques, it was also designed *not* to be 'finished', and it was meant to change over time, in polemically avoiding that notion of perfection, of completeness, of the perfect moment in time. The sandbag wall, for instance:

Where most walls are designed to shrug off the effects of time, this one encourages time to pass through, and thereby modify it. Over the years, the bags will decay, and the mixture will harden, so that eventually a rippling wall of concrete will emerge, left with the rough imprint of cloth.[3]

[1] Wigglesworth, S., McCorquodale, D. and Rüedi, K. (eds) *Desiring Practices: Architecture, Gender and the Interdisciplinary*, London: Black Dog, 1996.

[2] Till, J. and Wigglesworth, S. *Architectural Design: The Everyday and Architecture*, London: Wiley Academy, 1998.

[3] Till, J. and Wigglesworth, S *9/10 Stock Orchard Street: A Guidebook*, London: The Bank of Ideas, 2001, p. 5

I have to say that if this were one purpose of the 9/10 experiment, its findings may not have exactly matched its hypotheses. Although many people have called it unfinished (I'm coming to that later), to me the house as a thing is just as 'finished' as any other project ever is. Of course it changes over time, and of course those perfect drawings exclude use, wear and tear, mistake, and the huge, unknowable differences of personal perception. But built buildings almost always, to my mind, look substantial, and inevitable, and there is always a visceral shock when one is demolished – to which one quickly adapts as a new inevitability.

9/10 is certainly not, to my mind, at all untidy or incomplete as a piece of architecture; and if overturning that myth was part of its theoretical intent, I don't think it succeeded. For me, anyway, it is much, much harder to suggest that buildings are provisional, temporary, and capable of disappearing altogether than that. It takes something as extreme as Inter-Action or the Aviary to do this, and then only if you shift your focus to look at it in that way. Oddly, though I was lucky to know Price well enough to be asked to write about his work, I only really 'saw' the aviary in this provisional way after his death – indeed, I think we do think about buildings like life. We know they can vanish but we simply don't believe it.

The incredible difficulty of getting people to see buildings as mutable to me is the Cedric Price (and Dickens) argument – that buildings, being slow, expensive things that allow you to privatise space and organise how people use it – tend to ossify anyway. That it requires at least as much work – more in fact – to prevent them from ossifying, to make them change, as it does to 'finish' them.

In fact those bags rotted immediately in the first year, leaving ragged, hairy fragments still floating from the façade. The building is only as unfinished as other buildings are. It feels extremely reliable. But it is in that odd sense of time-lapse; that it remains hard to represent; that there is some way in which it never quite fits where you put it.

4 A detailed analysis of press bias in architectural journalism during the 1980s may be found in Rattenbury, K. 'Naturally Biased' in Rattenbury, K. (ed.) This Is Not Architecture, London: Routledge, 2002.

Out of frame

I have an unreliable memory of asking, at Building Design, the UK weekly architectural newspaper, why we weren't publishing the straw bale house or when we would publish it, and being told that we weren't going to. It was a curio: it had already been published in AJ, peculiarly as a construction site. And it still 'wasn't finished'.

That, effectively, broke two of the absolute rules of newsworthiness and ethics for architectural journalism. The media are a highly systematised process – not necessarily developed or controlled by anyone in particular, but arising from a vast array of commercial and cultural interests and conventions (what Gramsci would call hegemony), which mean that both the mass media and the more specialised architectural media are fiercely selective, partial, extremely conventional interlinked bodies operating on a series of unwritten codes, always slowly evolving but fiercely maintained at any one time.

Under normal circumstances – the circumstances Wigglesworth and Till didn't evolve for themselves – their project would fit in well. To be publishable, a project must be new, innovative (mildly so, in the greater scheme of things: really fundamental innovations are much harder to identify and take longer to show up). It should be of a type and style which are currently deemed fashionable to readers (the neo-classicists are quite right to point out that the system is stacked against them), it is normally by someone people already know of, or rate – or have been in some way sanctioned by those that do – through awards, competitions and so on. And it's probably in London, because most of the country's architects and money are there – and because most of its magazines and hence journalists are there, and can get to see things easily, quickly and cheaply. Architectural journalism, like a more intense form of all other types of journalism, also operates principally on a network of friends and contacts, largely centred in London, and ideally with a fair dose of, and interest in, youngish people. All of these fit 9/10 like a glove.[4]

However, to get those big building reviews in the architectural journals, a building must also be new, finished and (unless it is of really 'world-class' importance) it must not have been published by any direct rival papers. That is a classic media rivalry, but a rivalry of which in architecture, at that time, there was really only one example in the world: *AJ* and *BD*.

Wigglesworth and Till had deliberately kicked over the traces on this one. 9/10 was a polemical objection to notions of finished purity, and the architectural press clearly took it at its word: one magazine publishing it unfinished, the other refusing to publish (1) because it was already published, and (2) because it wasn't finished.

In fact, it would have been perfectly possible to construct a 'finished' publication of 9/10. Jonathan Hill's study of the constructed visions of purity suggested by photos of the original Barcelona Pavilion – which was in fact partly mocked up in paint and timber, with only the good bits photographed – is only a high-flown example of the weekly routines of the architectural press.

The finished, complete and virginally unseen project – the ideal of the architectural press – is, in my experience, almost always a constructed fiction; sometimes dramatically so. Projects are normally photographed painfully incomplete, with workmen, tools, unfinished areas kept out of shot. The readers, in their heads, put together this empty, perfect space. Far more so than those 'perfect' finished architectural drawings which the theories of the late 1980s challenged, the architectural publication constructs a fib: trying (broadly speaking) to make the project look like the drawings: 'perfect', 'ideal'. Or like the drawings might have done if there had been any.

In fact, 9/10 as a subject for the media to represent *isn't* all that different from other houses – it took a little longer to build and used rather more peculiar materials. My own theory is that it is far more important in our inability to pigeonhole it that there are no 'definitive'

pictorial views of it; or that they don't work together to form a set with visible, agreed meanings in the normal way. But the unpictorial focus through which Wigglesworth and Till themselves developed the project switched it out of that one key part of the media's framing techniques – the finished, perfect, unseen house – the white wedding of architectural publication, where SOS had gone for cohabitation. If Wigglesworth and Till had wanted that core, glossy, one-off project feature (did they?) they had, with extreme acuity, shot themselves in the foot.

Into the box

But that's no big deal. They just missed their chance to get one main building feature in the architectural magazines of the time. But 9/10 had anyway stolen a march on those architectural magazines. They were already trying to persuade someone to make a TV programme about their house. And here they were right on the cusp of a different age.

This was the end of the old media era; the one that had stretched (broadly) from the 'death' of modern architecture (13 July 1972 at 3.32 p.m., according to Charles Jencks)[5], through the Prince of Wales' 'carbuncle' speech (30 May 1984), and was only starting to break up in the 1990s: the age when UK modern architecture was officially deemed unpopular, and certainly not a subject the public would be prepared to watch on TV. Wigglesworth and Till's proposal to make a television programme about 9/10 met with the stock response of the time – inevitably, some variant of the late Sir Huw Weldon's dictum 'you can't do architecture on TV'.

Then, six months later, a researcher from Talkback, the production company which brought *Big Brother* to the UK, phoned, pushing a 'new concept for a programme' and expecting Wigglesworth and Till to be excited by the names Daisy Goodwin and Kevin McCloud. They had never heard of them. They didn't have a television. They were practically strong-armed into signing the release document. So there 9/10 was,

[5] With the demolition of Pruitt Igoe in St Louis, Missouri. Jencks, C. *The Language of Post-Modern Architecture*, London: Academy Editions, 1977.

as the grand finale to, and what looked like the first serious bit of architecture in, the first series of a new architectural representational form: *Grand Designs*.[6]

This piece of prescient subject placement was something of a 'mixed bag', Wigglesworth says. Like all media, TV has its own shifting template for its representations, and those of reality TV – then a new idea in this country – had yet to emerge in all their tongue-in-cheek, stereotypical, belittling and aggrandising splendour.

This was light years away from the relationship between the specialised architectural journalists and their subjects, which, like parliamentary lobby journalists, operate as a sort of mutually dependent society; appearing to challenge, while essentially supporting, the subjects on whom they depend. But it soon became clear that the subjects of reality TV officially give up – through that release document which Sarah and Jeremy were so unwilling to sign – all power of control or influence over how they are represented.

In their case, for instance, when Martin Hughes, the Contract Project Manager, chose not to appear on camera, *Grand Designs* edited the script so that another workman (who trained with Walter Segal and had been on television before) seemed to be running the site. Thus when he, perfectly reasonably, said, 'I don't know what I'm going to be doing from day to day' it could have looked like professional incompetence.

Wigglesworth and Till felt 'bruised', says Sarah.[7] It was 'terribly boring' doing endless generic retakes to avoid the noise of a train. Sarah and Jeremy were – as we used to be back in those less informed, less cynical days – somewhat shocked to realise how thoroughly things (e.g. a neighbour visiting to see the model) were staged. The part where the job architect, Gillian Horn, told Kevin McCloud not to pick up a spring – 'much too heavy' – and he didn't listen was their best moment.

Of course, Talkback also turned them into stereotypes: 'Jeremy the egghead, me the long-suffering person.' The whole process, she says, felt 'belittling' and – it looked this too, in the first series, at the time – misogynistic. She was the only female professional in the first series, and was running the job while Jeremy was teaching in Sheffield, but the editors preferred taking Jeremy's comments. Either the later edits in the updates have corrected this, or perhaps we've all just got used to it.

This major engagement with the media was jammed with paradox. Sarah and Jeremy really wanted to do the programme for good old Reithean reasons – education, explanation, as well as democracy and debate – but they got picked up by reality TV, which aimed to remake real life as a spectator sport. They were in the forefront of the wave of television programmes that did indeed popularise architecture, that did indeed open a dialogue with the everyday – but, like all media, on its own financial, practical, cultural and economic terms. It had no particular interest, for instance, in describing how things were made, which was something Sarah and Jeremy had particularly wanted it to do. *Grand Designs* was a major player for the interests of the property and the DIY industry – incredibly powerful economic forces. Most bizarrely of all, Jeremy and Sarah's strong theoretical, democratic reasons for making a television programme were – in its own peculiar way – just what this commercialised, popularised, stereotyped format wanted.

To the would-be democratic, entertainment-led culture of late twentieth-century Britain the gentle eccentricities of this house were jam. It *loved* the fact that it could pigeonhole Sarah and Jeremy as nice but mad professors trying to build their own theories and running hopelessly over time and budget. That was *exactly* what the programme wanted. Their building was late. Very late. It didn't make the grand completion finale at the end as the others had; they had only got the frame up by the final edit, and Kevin McCloud gratuitously built his own straw bale office to fill what

[6] *Grand Designs*: Series 1, Talkback for Channel 4, 2001.
[7] Wigglesworth, S., interview with the author, 2009.

was at first perceived to be a hole in the programme.

But it was clearly the best in the series, and the series itself began to adapt; to recognise that this was more of an opportunity than a problem. Quickly, the series maker was beginning to get the point – these projects extend over a long time; they're slow, and though there is a point when you can say it is finished, it isn't when you thought it would be. *Grand Designs* became a forerunner of a new form of budget TV, allowing the revisits to work in their favour. Three programmes for the price of one. *Grand Designs* helped to remake the architectural world as we know it, popularising and to some extent de-professionalising architecture in favour of a sort of fusion of DIY and high design culture. In retrospect, Wigglesworth and Till and 9/10 were the factors that may have started pushing the original, not-that-architect-friendly series into what it was to become. *Grand Designs* may have developed at least partly in 9/10's image.

The process and ideas of the house (albeit in a somewhat limited theoretical format) fitted *Grand Designs* far better than it fitted the equally self-serving conventions of the design magazines. In some ways – highly stereotyped of course – the media's notions of popular appeal played out well with some of the theoretical concerns of the time. If *Grand Designs* isn't the everyday (of a sort), I don't know what is – debunking professionalism, promoting the messy everyday experience, voicing a range of highly personal takes on, and approaches to, ecological concerns. The inevitable TV screwball comedy take on reality – though vastly partial, limited, selective and inevitably fuelled by the drive of the big economic interests and organisational conventions behind it – was not a million miles from Sarah and Jeremy's real concerns. Yet *Grand Designs* has become a powerful branding tool of the DIY and property industry, with its own highly selective, highly partial view of reality. Be very careful what you wish for.

The 1980s/out of time

At their centenary party, Martyn Ware played his brilliant record '(We Don't Need This) Fascist Groove Thang' about three times. I have never got it out of my head as part of the theme of this article. Then, at Jeremy Till's inaugural lecture as Dean of the School of Architecture and the Built Environment at the University of Westminster, launching his book *Architecture Depends*[8] – which argues in favour of mess and against the myth of control, but in the most ordered, managed and stylish presentation I have ever seen – he played 'Shipbuilding', the heart-wrenching Elvis Costello ballad about the warmongering of the 1980s putting the great decimated shipyards of the north-east, temporarily, back in work.

Music helps. Since I had mainly known them professionally, this was an obvious fact I had missed. Sarah and Jeremy are children of the 1980s – the era of concerted, intelligent resistance to Thatcherism; which contained both the grains of the Third Way and the grains of the radical resistance to it. You can still see it (just) in their haircuts. You can hear it in their music. You can see it in the house. For all their professional, academic successes, that house is a pocket of idealism in resistance to a potentially hostile world.

Architecturally, the 1980s – the counter-culture era (the things we did while Damian Hirst was planning his first show in London's then-derelict Royal Docks) – had a lot going on. There was Decon and its grungy British variants; the growth of Minimalism in the luxury and art worlds; the conversion of High Tech from radical experiment to mainstream commerce, the commercial demonisation of PoMo; the growth of community architecture and then its 'stylistic' banishment from the magazines – later to be replaced by a more abstracted but widespread interest in the 'everyday', gradually re-linking some of these scattered ideals. There were the germs of the mainstream evolution of a commercialised form of 'green': all the things we have well-established versions of taking up the mainstream now, in fact. That is how long it takes architectural ideas

[8] Till, J. *Architecture Depends*, Cambridge, MA and London: MIT Press, 2009.

to grow from pockets of polemical resistance into real things.

There is always a time-lag in architecture – especially in teaching; which exists in a sort of pre-echo, where young teachers develop their thoughts and ideas through teaching, exhibition and sometimes theory in the schools – a sort of *de facto* laboratory – before they can persuade anyone to build. So a second generation, taught by these people, comes through the schools before the original work has been built, or even designed. This means that to teachers and critics, things can seem retro or derivative before the first versions have even appeared on site.

9/10 works in this more normal time-slip too. It's ten years old, but now it looks bang-on-the-money contemporary – so contemporary it seems normal, just as once it seemed strange without it being quite clear why (like wearing the wrong shape of jeans). That is almost inevitable. It was done as part of a theoretical advance, and as part of a teaching programme. Lots of the ideas it came up with went into production before it did (like Philip Johnson with Mies, to use a somewhat grandiose example). Those gabion walls in Herzog and de Meuron's Dominus Winery (1996–1998) were worked on by someone who had been taught by Jeremy (beating 9/10 into physical reality). The Bartlett and Sheffield have taught hundreds, probably thousands of architects by now; so 9/10 looks natural in its heterogeneity, where once it appeared peculiar. Time has settled around it. It will read well in history books, as all those projects do which you think have been wrongly dated – and where a single image is quite clearly meant to help you find the building rather than an attempt to visually translate it.

At the same time, it does look exactly of its time: descriptive of its time, in fact. Accurate prediction almost always goes unnoticed – something which once seemed a strange fit is now unnoticeably normal – like starting to wear a fashion before anyone else does. It is usually brash or exquisite people one has confidence in for these stylistic predictions, but this house is remarkably modest, and it's not as well known as an incunabulum – as an original source document – as it might deserve, and this must surely be because it accurately criticises, and refuses to adopt, the fictional constructs by which things become famous. The project accurately predicted a more eclectic architectural ideology; a more active perfect-imperfect which did all it could not to be dogmatic. In some ways, and bizarrely for something so hugely and intensely designed, it doesn't feel like it's designed at all, but like a piece of entirely natural academic vernacular: entirely normal of its time and place. Except that I cannot think of anyone else who does it.

'To make wonders plain': the ethics of Stock Orchard Street

Adrian Forty

Is Stock Orchard Street ethical architecture? Possibly. Its experiments in sustainability, its respect for its context, its protection of the dignity of its users all fit the ethical bill. Since the building was completed, Jeremy Till has written an abrasive attack on architectural ethics, taking architects to task for having muddled ethics with aesthetics. Ethics, he insists, is not to do with things but with actions – 'a brick has no morals', as he puts it. The architect's ethical duty, he says, 'lies not in the refinement of the object as a static visual product, but as contributor to the creation of empowering spatial, and hence social relationships in the name of others'. An ethical stance, claims Till, citing Zygmunt Bauman, means 'to assume responsibility for the Other'.[i] Quite where this leaves Stock Orchard Street, not a public building, and with only a limited engagement to the Other, we will regard as an open question.

A different interpretation of what ethics means in architecture comes from the philosopher Karsten Harries, who says that a work of architecture is ethical insofar as it provides an answer to what it means to be at home in the world.[ii] While this is quite unlike Till's definition of architectural ethics, both Till and Harries see ethics as the business of setting up principles, against which we can then measure the results. The risk of this is that we end up arguing about the principles, rather than concentrating on the consequences. Another way to think about ethics in architecture would be to shift attention away from principles, and look instead at procedures and results.

This alternative interpretation of ethics is suggested by reading Sir Francis Bacon's *Essays*, or to give them their full title, *Essayes or Counsels, Civill and Morall*.[iii] Bacon (1561–1626), best known as the founder of the inductive scientific method and father of the English seventeenth-century scientific revolution, has been out of favour for the last half century or so on account of his alleged culpability, in the eyes of Adorno and others, for the rise of scientific materialism. But Bacon can surprise us – he was a more diverse thinker than the Frankfurt School gave him credit for. Bacon wrote several versions of the *Essays* during his lifetime, augmenting and changing them. The final version appeared in 1625, the year before his death, and included fifty-eight essays on all sorts of moral subjects – Truth, Revenge, Envy, Love, Cunning, of Seeming Wise, Friendship, Ambition, Anger and so on. Within the 1625 edition are two essays that do not obviously fit with the subjects of the others, one 'Of Building', and another 'Of Gardens', which together are unique in that they deal with material practices, rather than with vices or virtues. These two essays are sandwiched between 'Of Deformity' and 'Of Negotiating'. To the best of my knowledge, Bacon's 'Of Building' was the first time that anyone had placed a discussion of architecture specifically within the context of morality and ethics, and this alone makes it worth a second look.

The essay 'Of Building' has been largely ignored by historians of architecture, nor have commentators upon Bacon's other essays shown much interest in it. It does not appear in either of two recent anthologies of architectural texts from the early modern period.[iv] The German critic Hermann Muthesius, however, in his classic *The English House* of 1904, quoted the first part of the opening sentence of the essay, not just once, but twice – 'Houses are built to live in, and not to look on; therefore let use be preferred before uniformity, except where both may be had'.[v] Muthesius clearly regarded Bacon as a spokesman for the properties that he saw and admired in late nineteenth-century English domestic architecture: practicality and unostentatiousness. And on the very few other occasions that architectural writers have paid any attention to Bacon's essay, it has almost always been to claim Bacon as some kind of proto-functionalist. These references to 'Of Building' seem to me to miss the point of the essay, since they entirely ignore its context – and indeed most of its content.

It is not hard to see why Bacon's 'Of Building' has been overlooked. It is very short, and after a brief and largely derivative discussion about the siting of buildings, is mainly devoted to the description of an ideal country house, something like an Elizabethan prodigy house, a type that had already been superseded by the date when he was writing. In other words, on the face of it, Bacon's essay has nothing new to say about architecture. Compared to Sir Henry Wotton's *The Elements of Architecture*, which was published a year earlier, in 1624, it lacks originality, and contains no useful architectural prescriptions.

If 'Of Building' is something of a puzzle, so are Bacon's *Essays* as a whole. People have argued about their relationship to Bacon's other philosophical works, and there has been uncertainty as to how to read the *Essays*. 'Of Building' is not alone in being a seemingly 'weak' essay, disjointed, lacking in coherence, and without a conclusion: compared to Bacon's other writings, which are sharp as anything, the *Essays* seem wanting in rigour and clarity. And curiously, the essays that he rewrote from the previous editions ('Of Building' was not one of these) became not more but even less coherent in their rewriting, suggesting that this was precisely the effect that Bacon was after.

Bacon's disinclination to provide unambiguous advice on any of the ethical issues he wrote about appears to be connected to his generally low opinion of moral philosophy as a branch of philosophy. For Bacon, the purpose of learning was to study nature, and to gain knowledge; the tendency of moral philosophy had been, as he saw it, to divert men away from investigation, and into disputation. Philosophy had been, as Bacon put it, 'fruitful of controversies, but barren of works'.[vi] Bacon's writing was intentionally fragmentary, since, as he saw it, his project would be hindered by presenting a body of work that appeared overly complete. Too systematic a philosophy would be a disincentive to the kind of investigation that Bacon advocated: it was not his purpose to replace one system by another. Bacon's aim was to invite interrogation of all received knowledge – especially that coming from ancient philosophy – and to put in place an ongoing and necessarily inconclusive investigation, whose destination was uncertain. For this reason he recommended an aphoristic way of writing, because, he explained, 'aphorisms, representing only portions and as it were fragments of knowledge, invite others to contribute and add something in their turn; whereas methodical delivery, carrying the show of a total, makes men careless, as if they were already at the end'.[vii] Bacon's way of writing about moral philosophy was wholly consistent with these general precepts; both in their style and in their contents, the *Essays* were not meant to endorse any particular rules for behaviour, but rather to raise questions about the value and status of ethics, and to create uncertainty rather than offer guidance as to how men should act.

Most readers of the *Essays* seem to have approached them expecting to discover clear advice on human behaviour, and, finding this lacking, they have been at a loss to know what to say about them. An exception is the American literary critic, Stanley Fish, who in his book *Self-Consuming Artifacts* – by far the best and most inspired interpretation of the *Essays* – argues that the *Essays* provided Bacon with a means of demonstrating, in the field of ethics, his general philosophical approach.[viii] According to Fish, the confusion induced by reading one of Bacon's essays is intentional, and is meant to force readers to change their minds, often several times, during the course of a single essay. The subject of each of Bacon's essays is not its nominal topic – love, friendship, revenge – but rather what men think about these things, and how inconclusive and contradictory those thoughts have been. Each one replays Bacon's basic theme, the need 'to rid ourselves of excessive respect and admiration for things discovered already'.[ix]

The pattern of many of the essays is to start with a statement that seems a generally accepted truth, but then to sow the seeds of doubt, by introducing other, contradictory, assertions, leaving the reader at the end entirely unsure what to think about the matter under discussion. Fish situates this formula within the context of Bacon's general approach to knowledge. Bacon's main concern was with the inadequacy of the human mind, and he saw his task as to protect the mind against itself: his advice in the *Novum Organum* was 'let every student of nature take this as a rule – that whatever his mind seizes and dwells upon with peculiar satisfaction is to be held in suspicion'.[x] In particular, Bacon was concerned by the tendency of the human mind to move too quickly to general explanations: 'the mind longs to spring up to positions of higher generality, that it may find rest there; and so after a little while wearies of experiment'.[xi] Bacon's aim was to prevent the mind's tendency 'to jump and fly from particulars to remote axioms and of almost the highest generality'.[xii] Another counterproductive tendency identified by

Bacon is for the mind to find order where there is none, 'to suppose the existence of more order and regularity in the world than it finds'.xiii And in enquiry, the mind, having once found a credible explanation, will tend to ignore contrary evidence:

> The human understanding when it has once adopted an opinion (either as being the received opinion or as being agreeable to itself) draws all things else to support and agree with it. And though there be a greater number and weight of instances to be found on the other side, yet these it either neglects and despises; or else by some distinction sets aside and rejects; in order that by this great and pernicious predetermination the authority of its former conclusions may remain inviolate.xiv

If these were the ideas that guided Bacon's approach to all investigation, the *Essays* were, Fish argues, a demonstration of these principles in practice, within the realm of morality, notoriously prone to the kind of monstrously dogmatic judgements of which Bacon was most contemptuous. While pretending to be a good moralist, Bacon ends up destabilising thought. Where, then, does this leave the essay 'Of Building'?

In some respects, 'Of Building' follows the same formula as many of the other essays. It starts with a generalisation – in this case possibly taken from Wotton, who had similarly pleaded the primacy of use in determining the arrangement of the parts of a building. Bacon then goes on to a discussion of the siting of houses, a topic addressed by Vitruvius at the beginning of *De Architectura*, and, likewise tediously by most subsequent Renaissance writers on architecture – including Wotton. But Bacon, rather than setting out yet again the criteria for choosing a site, shows that the received ideas of what makes an ideal site are irreconcilable, and that in practice no such site will ever be found. His conclusion is that if you want a perfect situation, you must have several houses. This is true to form for Bacon – the principles of the established authorities turn out, when examined closely, to be nonsense. We are intended, I suspect, to take this little demonstration of the illogicality of the customary precepts for the siting of houses as a lesson in the worthlessness of all the other so-called principles of architecture laid down by the authorities. If we are to doubt what they say about sites, why take any more seriously the rest of what they have to say?

Having disposed of all 'principles' of architecture, Bacon turns his attention to the ideal house. At first reading, this appears to be a straightforward description of a large Elizabethan country house, laid out around courtyards. (It has been suggested that the description resembled his own house at Gorhambury.)xv Bacon begins his description by emphasising the importance of a division between the two sides of a house, 'a side for the banquet... and a side for the household; the one for feasts and triumphs, and the other for dwelling'. In other words, a distinction between the public side of the house and the private, a division marked on the front of the house by a tower. But having emphasised the division of the house into two, Bacon proceeds to describe the parts behind the front, and in these, organised around a succession of courtyards, the distinction between the banquet and household sides dissolves, and the ranges around the several courtyards are not clearly dedicated to one or other of these two functions. The essentially bi-axial division of the front is replaced by a distinction based upon depth, with less and less formality as one draws away further from the front. Finally, the description of the house ends, confusingly, with the entrance courts, through which you would have had to pass to reach the front of the house, with which the description began.

This scrambled account of the house may again be deliberate. Bacon had started the essay by railing against the poetic descriptions of houses: 'Leave the goodly fabrics of houses, for beauty only, to the enchanted palaces of the poets; who build them with small cost.' Bacon is suspicious of both literary descriptions, and of architectural magnificence, and seems to be at some pains not to allow his readers to be seduced by words. But there is also the fact that the mind has to be protected against its tendency to oversimplify things, to look for more order in the world than actually occurs. Contrary to the mind's (and the architect's) compulsive tendency to render the world into a satisfying neatness, Bacon seems determined to preserve something of the disorder and confusion with which we actually experience the world. The world is not as tidy as we like to think.

The presence of this essay among the other essays is still perplexing. Is 'Of Building' about building, or architecture, at all? There is always the possibility that Bacon, in common with other philosophers before and since, was using building as a metaphor for his own philosophical system. However, we should be cautious about this, since Bacon was in general resistant to metaphors, both on account of what he saw as their misuse by the scholastics, and their tendency to encourage the mind to fly to generalities, and more particularly because of his view that what he was proposing was not a 'system' such as could be represented in terms of an analogy. Bacon was much more concerned that whatever method should be capable of exposing its own errors – 'I… make the things plain for all to see, so that my mistakes can be spotted and separated out before the body of science is further infected by them';[xvi] any metaphor, but especially one of building, would tend to conceal the errors. In fact, Bacon did use metaphors to describe his procedure, but the metaphors he preferred were either of voyaging and navigation or of gardening, all of which were more accommodating of temporality and movement, and also of accidents; architecture and building were far too static for Bacon's purposes. Nevertheless, Bacon was certainly aware of the potential of the architectural metaphor to describe his project – according to his chaplain William Rawley, he complained that in his intellectual task he was condemned to be both architect and labourer. 'Having … collected the materials for the building, and in his Novum Organum set down the instruments and directions for the work', no one had come forward to carry out the necessary experimental research; and, Rawley continued, 'I have heard his lordship speak complainingly, that his lordship (who thinketh that he deserved to be an architect in this building) should be forced to be a workman and a labourer, and to dig the clay and burn the brick'.[xvii] Even so, given his general avoidance of metaphors within his writing, it does not appear that Bacon intended the essay 'Of Building' to be an analogue of his philosophical method.

What then are we left with? Bacon's 'Of Building' seems to be more than just a jumble of derivative and out-of-date notions about architecture. Rather it is the first piece of *critical* architectural theory, the first time that anyone had turned architectural thought back on itself, made it question itself, and exposed its own shortcomings. Traditionally, it is the Frenchman Claude Perrault who has been credited with this achievement; but while Perrault, an inductive thinker after Bacon's model, was far better informed about architecture, and gave a more sophisticated analysis of the arbitrary nature of architectural beauty, it was Bacon who first saw that architecture was just as suspect as any other practice that based itself upon ancient authority. But more than just a critique of architectural knowledge, Bacon's essay is, it seems, an anticipation of a form of architectural criticism not otherwise encountered until the late twentieth century, an attempt through architecture's own precepts to draw attention to the way that architecture leads the human mind astray, causing it to believe that there is more order in the world than is actually the case. Bacon's comments on building correspond to his warnings against conventional philosophy, which seduced the mind by the elegance of its structures; too easily these gained the upper hand and ended up regulating thought.

But what does Bacon's essay tell us about the *ethics* of architecture? Taken together, *The Essays* indicate that ethics is not about applying principles – whose origins are always dubious; the general message of *The Essays* is that expediency is a better guide to action than principle – ends justify means. Bacon, himself a politician (he was James I's Attorney General and then Lord Chancellor), was a Machiavellian, believing in a rigorous separation between public and private or personal morality: envy, vanity, revenge, ambition, were all defensible qualities in public life, even if inappropriate in private life. When it comes to intellectual practice, what concerned Bacon were not principles, but the transparency of the procedure for arriving at the result. As he wrote in the essay 'Of Truth', it is not truth itself that matters so much as the enquiry after truth, 'the love-making or wooing of it', that is the 'sovereign good of human nature'.[xviii] In the way we go about things, Bacon wanted to disinhibit us from all the usual nostrums and formulae about what constitutes the proper and the good.

If Stock Orchard Street is ethical it is not because it satisfies some previously declared principle of ethics, but because, like Bacon's essays, it forces us to ask what an ethics of architecture might be. Specifically, in its general shagginess, its hairiness, it is unusually transparent about its own design procedures. Another of Bacon's works, the *Sylva Sylvarum*, throws more light on Bacon's attempts to find a form to express the unresolved and the contradictory. The *Sylva Sylvarum* (which could be translated as 'The Forest of Materials', though it is known as 'The Natural History') belongs to a now forgotten genre, the *sylva*, which, on the analogy of felled timber ready to be sawn and worked, contained raw knowledge, awaiting refinement and processing.[xix] It was a genre that appealed to Bacon, and which he developed, because it allowed for an unelaborated, plain style that contrasted with the more usual rhetorically finished embellished literary forms, and it enabled him to avoid imposing a contrived order upon findings and observations that he had made. Things that he had noticed, but had been unable to explain, should not be swept away out of sight, nor tidied up so as to seem that they had been resolved. Better to expose them, raw and unresolved though they were, in the hope that someone in the future might make sense of them. There is a lesson here for architects, and one that Stock Orchard Street takes advantage of. Rather than the usual compulsion to conceal the messy compromises, the fudged solutions inevitable to all works of architecture, at Stock Orchard Street at least some of these persist into the finished work. According to William Rawley, Bacon's ambition was 'to make wonders plain, and not plain things wonders':[xx] Stock Orchard Street is a *sylva*, whose ethics lie in its acknowledgement of at least some of the unresolved business of architecture. Like the best moral philosophy, it makes us question our assumptions about what is right, while leaving us still unsure, though wiser.

Acknowledgement

With thanks to Christine Stevenson for her suggestions.

[i] J. Till, *Architecture Depends*, Cambridge, MA, and London: MIT Press, 2009, pp. 173–8.

[ii] K. Harries, *The Ethical Function of Architecture*, Cambridge, MA, and London: MIT Press, 1997.

[iii] The two most recent editions of *The Essays* are F. Bacon, *The Essays*, edited by J. Pitcher, London: Penguin Books, 1985; and F. Bacon, *Essayes or Counsels, Civill and Morall*, edited by M. Kiernan, Oxford: Clarendon Press, 1985. The latter is more authoritative, but the former is more widely available.

[iv] C. van Eck and C. Anderson, *British Architectural Theory, 1540–1750: An Anthology of Texts*, Aldershot: Ashgate. 2003; H.F. Mallgrave, *Architectural Theory*, vol.1, Malden, MA, and Oxford: Blackwell, 2006.

[v] H. Muthesius, *The English House*, edited by D. Sharp, translated by J. Seligman and S. Spencer, 3 vols, London: Frances Lincoln, 2007; vol. 2, title page, p. 239.

[vi] F. Bacon, *The Works of Francis Bacon*, edited by J. Spedding, R.L. Ellis and D.D. Heath, London: Longman & Co., vol. IV, 1858, p. 14.

[vii] Ibid, p. 451.

[viii] S.E. Fish, *Self-Consuming Artifacts: The Experience of Seventeenth-Century Literature*, Berkeley, Los Angeles and London: University of California Press, 1972, pp. 78–155.

[ix] F. Bacon, *The Instauratio Magna Part II: Novum Organon*, edited and translated by G. Rees with M. Wakely, Oxford: Clarendon Press, 2004, p. 11.

[x] Bacon, *Works*, vol. IV, 1858, p. 60.

[xi] Ibid., p.50.

[xii] Ibid., p. 97.

[xiii] Ibid., p. 55.

[xiv] Ibid., p. 56

[xv] Bacon, *The Essays*, ed. M. Kiernan, p. 276.

[xvi] Bacon, *Novum Organon*, 2004, p. 21.

[xvii] W. Rawley, 'Preface' to F. Bacon, *Sylva Sylvanum*, in *The Works of Francis Bacon*, edited by J. Spedding, R.L. Ellis and D.D. Heath, London: Longman & Co., vol. II, 1857, p. 336.

[xiii] Bacon, *The Essays*, ed. Pitcher, p. 62.

[xix] See F. De Bruyn, 'The Classical Sylva and the Generic Development of Scientific Writing in Seventeenth-Century England', *New Literary History*, 32, 2001, 347–373.

[xx] Rawley, in Bacon, *Works*, vol. II, 1857, p. 336.

Appendices

Gazetteer

The street

Stock Orchard Street is a London backwater; it is a street where cars come to die. On one side of the street is the main East Coast railway line, on the other a row of Victorian railway workers' houses. At the end, the site for 9/10 Stock Orchard Street was once an old forge, sold off at an auction in 1994 by British Rail in the last throes of privatisation. A planning application was made to Islington Council in May 1997 and permission was received eight weeks later under delegated powers with no amendments to the design requested. The building is L-shaped; one arm along the railway contains the office, the other the house, with a hybrid conference/dining room at the junction of the two arms. A five-storey tower pins the building to the ground, as well as acting as a marker to the end of the street. A room (maybe a head) at the top watches; it can be seen from Caledonian Road underground station and at night acts as a beacon to the tired home-comer.

The gate

The front gate is made of willow hurdles held in a galvanised steel frame, hints of medieval rural juxtaposed with contemporary industrial in a blatant disregard for the normal separation of these categories. The gate thus introduces the building beyond, which enjoys crossing the boundaries of the slick and the hairy. The making of the gate took some persuasion: hurdles are made to agricultural tolerances ('that should stop the sheep getting through'), steel frames manufactured to millimetres. It took over twenty drawings and countless telephone calls before agreement between the two was reached. This level of involvement was indicative of the project as a whole which took over 350 drawings and nearly two and a half years to construct, employing a core team of six craftsmen who turned their hand to all the multiple construction techniques used in the building.

The house elevation

The main elevation to the house is south facing, harnessing the natural heat of the sun. The projecting steel fins support a sunscreen which protects the glazing on hot summer days, while allowing in low-level winter sun. The elevation was designed from inside out, allowing the domestic life of the interior to come to the surface. A continuous clerestorey allows the roof to float above, while below the play of solid and open reflects the activities behind. On the left, the design changes scale, coming to a more crafted and bodily enclosure that huddles around the kitchen table. The main floor of the house is lifted up on columns, perched on springs, bringing it to the same floor level as the surrounding houses. The resulting undercroft, the home of chickens, reveals the full scale of the site (40m x 20m). The two-storey west wing contains the bedrooms and bathrooms.

The entrance

The house is entered like a farmhouse, through the back door, reached by a long path across the garden. Louvres next to the door let in air, which naturally rises up through the house to another louvre in the tower, cooling the space during the summer. A small low-level slot window opposite the door gives on to a pond at the bottom of a courtyard. Views are restricted into this private court, but a watery light is admitted on to the entrance hall floor. A continuous roof light above accentuates the slot-like, transitional character of the hallway and beckons the visitor upward. The stair is on wheels that take up the movement between the solid bedroom wing and the sprung main living area.

The living room

At the top of the stairs on the left wall is a Piranesi etching, a convivial conflation of time, provisionality, ruins, scales and objects which serves well as an introduction to the living room beyond. The room is conceived as a table top, on to which domestic items are placed. A grid of steel columns provides an order, which is then disturbed by the insertion of large elements (the library tower, the blob of the larder, the dividing wooden wall). The resulting juxtapositions are an honest expression of fruitful domestic clutter and foster a variety of living conditions. The two-way slope of the roof accentuates this diversity, so that in the back corner the space is low and enclosed, whereas towards the front the feel is more expansive, even one of display, consistent with a reading of the room as a *piano nobile*. The living room is intended to encourage and accommodate the whole gamut of activities, moods and degrees of privacy that one desires in a domestic interior. While large, the space is not overbearing. There are two coffee tables: one a cable reel found on site, the other an early piece by Thomas Sandell.

The larder and kitchen

The most prominent interruption within the living room is the lump of the larder. Where many living rooms are focused on a fire (dad's slippers laid out to warm in front), this one is organised around a place of cool – the larder, storehouse of provisions. The larder was based on the structural principle of the mud-brick vaults found in Mali, and is built out of a skin of self-supporting brickwork. It is then wrapped in insulation and finished with lime plaster. The larder projects through the roof and has vents at the top as well as in the floor. This combination of thermal mass, protective insulation and natural ventilation maintains a constant cool temperature inside, even on the hottest days. Hidden behind the larder is the kitchen. A canopy over the table brings the space down to bodily scale, a sense reinforced by the surrounding built-in seats and shelves, which appear as if a separate structure has been inserted into the corner of the house. The table is cast out of products using recycled glass as its main constituent; it floats through the wall to the deck outside.

The library tower

A tower rises through the building. Skewed in plan and with raking columns, the tower is designed to provide a set of unexpected nooks, glimpses and shadows in and around it. The oversized columns are the depth of a large book, and the tower is lined with shelves to form a vertical library. The staircase has treads of various depths and is provided with cushions for when a spontaneous dip into a book turns into something more compelling. A staircase weaves through this tower, stopping first at a mezzanine which projects into the living room, rising to a door which gives out on to the meadow roof before climbing two further storeys to the room at the top. This retreat contains a day-bed and small desk, and is used as a writing room, nourished by the vertical library below.

The dining/conference room

The dining/conference room is situated at the junction of the house and office in the tallest space in the building. When entered from the main stair, the room assumes the sense of a medieval hall, with dining table laid out below and galleries above. The room recognises the joint claims of both work and play to occupy the surface of the large table. At times the space is used as a conference room for the office. At other times, with the timber dividing wall pulled back, it is united with the house and serves as a dining room. This wall is finished in rough ply in alternating striped and dotted planks, a decision made at the end of the contract when there was no strength to do another drawing. Instead a verbal instruction was given to the builders – 'do it in alternate tiger bands and leopard bands'. The window at low level is at the same height as the train windows; sitting in the living room one can share a table top for an instant with passing passengers.

Selected materials specification

The gabions

The office is raised up on walls made of recycled concrete held in wire cages. The walls are spaced at 5.5 metre intervals, the rhythm of a typical London terrace, evoking compacted ruins of the houses that might once have stood on the site. On top of each pier are green boxes containing springs, like massive bed springs, which damp the vibration from the passing trains. Raising the office up allows the passing life of the railway to enter the site, as well as permitting views up the disappearing tracks, taking the imagination beyond the confines of the site. Before the introduction of landfill tax, construction waste accounted for 30 per cent of all waste in the United Kingdom. Now materials from demolished buildings are in abundant and cheap supply. It was cheaper to bring a lorry load of recycled concrete to the site than it was to a take a lorry load of spoil away, though finding concrete lumps that were not so small as to slip through the holes in the cages, but not so big as to not form a consolidated filling, was more of a problem. The concrete is held in wire cages called gabions, which are normally used in civil engineering. They arrived as flat packs, an Ikea engineering, and are then filled by hand with the concrete lumps. The walls, though excessive, are structurally efficient: the steel of the cages is in tension and the concrete in compression, so each material is working in its most efficient manner. Tests with the manufacturers and university engineering departments suggested that the gabions could have supported a six-storey building. However, this did not persuade the building inspector, who was worried about the risk of fire melting the wire cages, and so insisted that rough columns were cast in the centre of each pier.

Specification
Recycled concrete, filtered with 100mm min/200mm max screens. Placed in Macaferri 8/2.7 galvanised gabions, each 2m wide, 1m deep, 1m high.

Concrete capping 200mm deep to spread load. Springs by GERB mounted on top, each designed to specific point load and spring frequency to reduce railway vibration.

The quilted wall

Offices are usually seen as places set apart from the home and architecturally assume an identity of decorum and order, of efficiency, solidity and of progress. This contrasts to the nature of domestic life, which is habitually regarded as a place of comfort, leisure and nostalgia. The standard garb for offices is thus that of corporate modernism – shiny, refined, façades adopting the appearance of fashionable technology. This aesthetic is gendered: the 'rational' male associated with the virtues of the efficient office while the home is the place where the personal, the wilful and the uncanny – 'feminine traits' – are given free rein. At Stock Orchard Street such categorisations are challenged and disrupted. The office is wrapped in cloth, puckered and buttoned like a domestic quilt. It looks fragile, but is designed to last for years, and then it will be unbuttoned and replaced with something quite else – a provisional architecture resisting the demands for eternity, fixity and progress.

We invented our own DIY method of achieving this effect, but were nervous about it, and so consulted experts who have worked with the knights and lords of British architecture. An architectural genealogy has established itself in the recent architectural use of fabric. Frei Otto–Hopkins–Horden–Rogers. It is clear from the expert's reaction that our proposed solution does not fit into this family tree. It will flap and tear, he says. It will pucker irregularly, he says. It will not be absolutely tight, he says. We are convinced enough by his arguments (in our nervousness we overlook how he conflates technical and aesthetic criteria) to ask him to quote for a highly stretched skin which only they can erect. Unfortunately their price for all this

is four times our budget. It is a Mies Barcelona Chair when we can only afford an Ikea Chesterfield. So it is back to the DIY. A small sail maker makes up the lengths that are then wrapped like bandages around the office. The cloth is silicone impregnated woven fibreglass, used on North Sea oil rigs for machine covers, which was then quilted with an insulating layer and an inner lining – the quilting buttons being replaced with a grid of steel eyelets, through which roofing screws hold the quilt back to the timber frame of the office.

Specification
– Outer layer: Alpha Maritex 3200/2/SS in rolls 1500mm wide and 1270mm wide.
– Interlining (wadding): 25mm thick wadding, water resistant and fireproof to BS FR Sleepware BS 5722/Pt. 1 Upholstery BS 5852 702 Wadding.
– Lining: fire- and fungal-retardant treated polyester backing sheet to match sample supplied.
– Eyelets: 9mm internal diameter opening in stainless steel. Eyelets are to compress the wadding to form 'quilted' effect.
– Thread: Nomex MX 40 BS EN ISO 9002. (strength 2.9 Kg/m, colour: natural).

Sandbag wall

The wall was inspired by a wartime picture of the Kardomah Coffee-house during the Blitz, its plate glass widow protected by a wall of sandbags, with refined Londoners attempting to maintain some semblance of normality behind this crude architecture. It was also designed for technical reasons – we needed a lot of mass to reduce the noise from the railway, but casting a concrete wall so close to a working railway line was ruled out on safety grounds, so we invented our own DIY version. Where most walls are designed to shrug off the effects of time, this one encourages time to pass through, and thereby modify it. Over the years, the bags will decay and the mixture will harden, so that eventually a rippling wall of concrete will emerge, left with

the rough imprint of cloth. To find a bag that would allow this to happen took endless research. Standard hessian bags would have decayed too quickly, allowing the filling to dribble out. The plastic bags used in military architecture would not have allowed any water through and so the filling would never have hardened. Eventually we found a loose weave polypropylene bag, which was semi-porous and decays under the effects of ultraviolet light. Because the standard bag size would have meant the wall would have weighed 60 tonnes, we had to get the 1700 bags specially made up in a reduced width, but even so they came in at just 44p each.

The bags are filled with a mixture of sand, cement and lime, a laborious hand process which meant that only 100 bags could be made a day. They were laid in a brick-bonding pattern, and hosed down with water when each course had been completed, thereby starting the hardening process of the lime and cement. They are tied back to the timber frame with stainless steel cavity ties. The window surrounds are made from railway sleepers left on the site. The elevation is designed to be seen from a passing train, a glimpse of the random splattering of openings confusing the sense of scale and place, introducing a moment of strangeness as commuters look up from their papers.

Specification
1700 no. sacks made by Rapbond Ltd from beige uncoated woven polypropylene size no less than 260 x 700mm. Sacks to have one end and one side double-stitched and one end open with no frayed edges. Filled with 1:1:4 cement/lime/sand mix, and open heads closed using polypropylene electrical tie. Stainless steel non-standard wall ties, Ancon ref. DPV (type D dowel head, type P shank and type V 90-degree bend head), 150mm long from tail end containing dowel to right angle bend at head: 460 no. required.

Laying: Start at both ends and centre. Work from centre outwards, adjusting each course vertically (to finish 100mm high) and horizontally for evenness. Gauge vertical coursing carefully, especially approaching lintels over windows. Ensure courses do not sag to sides of windows. At ends of wall and window reveals lay tied ends of bag inward. At window openings or where fractional bags are required, tie off bags at suitable places. Wet bags as work progresses.

Straw bales

Straw bales have been used in construction for years – there are reports of 300-year-old straw houses in Germany. The technique has recently been revived in the USA, where there is a buoyant straw bale movement. 9 Stock Orchard Street was the first straw dwelling in the United Kingdom to receive building control approval and planning permission. Straw bales may be used either as a load-bearing system, or as a walling infill to a frame. For the two-storey sections at Stock Orchard Street, a non-load-bearing system is used in which vertical timber ladders take the roof and floor loads. These ladders are made using gang-nailed roof truss technology, and placed at the width of straw bale (1050mm) to form a balloon frame. The straw bales are then stacked between, forming the insulation and the substance of the wall. The straw was baled in the Cotswolds by a farmer who took pride in the precise size of his bales and who was glad to find a client who appreciated his tight tolerances. Straw is clearly a cheap way of building a wall; it is also a highly sustainable form of construction, using a surplus material with no embodied energy and providing an insulation value greater than current requirements (with an approximate U-value of 0.15). Bales are also quick and easy to build with; large sections of the walls at Stock Orchard Street were built by amateurs.

In the most commonly found forms of bale construction the straw is rendered both inside and outside with a lime plaster. However, there are technical doubts as to whether this system is suitable for the wetter and more humid UK climate; it is also disappointing not to be able to see the straw. A completely new system was developed for Stock Orchard Street. This protects the straw using a rainscreen, behind which is a ventilated cavity that allows any trapped moisture or condensation to escape. In an early prototype, all the bales were sheathed in a skin of transparent polycarbonate, revealing the straw in its golden glory. As built, the design is a mixture of galvanised steel cladding and polycarbonate, with perforated metal closures at top and bottom allowing air in but keeping out rodents and insects. The straw can be seen and inspected through the polycarbonate 'window', like an exhibit in a science museum, openly revealing the secret life of the building inside. Prior to cladding and plastering, the walls were sprayed with a Borax solution, which is recommended to reduce potential insect breeding.

The inside face of the straw is covered with a lime plaster applied directly to the surface of the bales, with small strips of expanded metal bridging across the wooden trusses to prevent cracks. Because the dry straw sucked all the water out of the first coat of the plaster, it was first necessary to soak the bales. The application of the plaster demanded some deskilling on the part of the plasterers, who normally aspire to complete smoothness and verticality. On this occasion a less perfect surface was sought, reflecting the origins of the wall beneath. Lime is a forgiving material, allowing the straw to breathe as well as accommodating movement. Fire tests have shown that a plastered straw bale wall passes a two-hour fire test, the compaction of the straw meaning that it only smoulders.

Specification
– Straw bales: 550 bales from barley straw, each 36 inches long by 18 inches deep by 15 inches high, supplied by Abbott & Co Ltd (Wessex) at a total cost of £825 delivered to London. Bales laid stack bonded between softwood gang-nailed timber trusses, 35mm thick, 490mm wide and of varying length, supplied by Cox and Long. All trusses made of softwood chords 35 x 72mm with 'Tim-Bor' timber preservative. Bales are pinned to each other with 8mm reinforcing bars, passing through two bales, and are set on a standard concrete strip foundation (resilient insulation should have been included between straw and concrete to reduce possibility of condensation forming where the straw bales meet the cold concrete, but was not specified).
– Lime plaster: one part natural hydraulic lime with two parts sand, applied in three layers and finished with a timber float. Lime supplied by Hydraulic Lias Limes Ltd.
– Exterior cladding: 'Ultra' 19/2 embossed galvanised mild steel corrugated panels by Corrugated Sheets and Cladding Ltd.
– Polycarbonate: Maxlite Suntuf corrugated polycarbonate sheets 8/3 corrugated iron profile, supplied by Century Plastics Ltd. Fixed with Dural finish steel self-drilling hex head screws with integral washers, size 5.5mm diameter. x 25mm long.
– Rodent Guard: 2mm-thick perforated pre-galvanised steel sheet (with 3mm holes to give approximately 40 per cent openness) with insect guard spot welded to internal surface. All supplied by Potter and Soar.

Water and fuel systems

Buried under the house are two large tanks, each of which stores 3000 litres of rainwater collected from the office roof. One tank provides water for the washing machine and office toilets. Water from the other tank is pumped up to irrigate the meadow on the roof of the house which is planted with wild flowers and strawberries. Water from the roof drains into a large hopper and from there into a downpipe which feeds the pool in the back courtyard. This is an outdoor room surrounded by private spaces (bathroom, utility room and studies). North facing and enclosed by the bale wall at first-storey level, this is a damp, mossy grotto. Water consumption in the house is further reduced by the composting toilet, a permanently ventilated, waterless chamber that over time produces a rich liquid manure (completely sterile) and a small amount of odourless solid compost. Finally, a solar panel over the bathroom provides hot water and reduces gas consumption. The house is heated by a condensing gas boiler. The bedroom wing has under-floor heating within the ground screed, while the main house is heated by radiators, some of which are hidden in trenches under the large south-west-facing windows. In summer, the water which irrigates the grass roof cools the building as it evaporates and helps reduce internal temperatures. Natural ventilation is encouraged to enter the house from the louvre vent beside the entrance door and is drawn by stack effect up through the living area to a high-level louvre on the leeward side of the tower.

Specification
– Composting toilet: Clivus M2 by ClivusMultrum.
– Rainwater tanks: 3500 litres concrete tanks by Albion Concrete Products, one fitted with Boss 120 submersible pump (for garden and roof water), the other pumped with a OSIP suction pump (for toilets and washing machine). Rainwater filter and diverter by Wisy.
– Whole house ventilation system: Baxi WH400.
– Solar panel and cylinder: Zen Aquasol Duo Sloar thermal system supplied by AES Ltd.

Areas: 9/10 Stock Orchard Street

House ground floor
59.78sqm

House first floor
179.142sqm

House mezzanine
14.679sqm (per floor)

(Conference/dining room
+ lobby 32.14sqm)

House total
253.59sqm

Office ground floor
17.24sqm

Office first floor
93.27sqm

Office mezzanine
62.48sqm

Office total
172.99sqm

Whole ground floor
77.01sqm

Whole first floor
272.41sqm

Whole mezzanine
77.60sqm

Building total
427sqm

Plot size
800sqm

Contributors to the building

**Project management and main
contractor**
KOYA Construction Limited
Martin Hughes

KOYA craftsmen
Steve Archbutt
(site agent and cement bag wall)
Steve Fitzjohn
(fabric wall and kitchen 'cabin')
Martin Francis
(joinery, tower stair
and library shelving)
Pat McMahon
(gabions and ground
floor timber wall)
John Watson
(fabric wall and tower
timber cladding)
Matt Bloom
(carpentry)

Architects
Sarah Wigglesworth Architects
and Jeremy Till
*Sarah Wigglesworth, Jeremy Till,
Gillian Horn and Michael
Richards*

Structural engineers
Price & Myers
*Nick Hanika, Andy Heyne and
Richard Seville*

Acoustic consultants
Paul Gillieron Acoustic Design
Paul Gillieron and Mark Hornsby

Electrical installation
AJA Electrics

Finance
The Ecology Building Society

Fire protection consultant
*Professor Roger Plank, University
of Sheffield*

Larder blob consultant
Loci
Jason Armstead

Lighting advice
Claudia Clements

Mechanical and electrical advice
Richard Pearce

Project photographer
Paul Smoothy

Planning consultant
Peter Kyte Associates
Peter Kyte

Plumbing installation
MAN Plumbing and Heating
Mick Nolan

**Springs consultant and
manufacturer**
GERB
Hans-Georg Wagner

Steelwork
Joy Steel

Straw suppliers
Abbots & Co Ltd (Wessex)
Ian Pearman

Water consultants
Elemental Solutions
Mark Moodie and Nick Grant

Notes on contributing authors

Matthew Barac is a senior lecturer at London South Bank University. His academic career follows time spent in practice, including his own office (Cape Town) and several years at PTEa (London), where he helped to establish a 'third age housing' division and co-authored the findings of HAPPI – Housing our Ageing Population: Panel for Innovation (2009). His Ph.D. won the RIBA President's Award for Research (2007) and the International Bauhaus Prize (2004). Current research explores the spatial order of informal urbanity, as part of an international theory-building initiative convened by the African Centre for Cities. He has taught at several schools of architecture; he speaks at conferences and chairs public events. As well as contributing to academic journals and books, he writes for mainstream publications including *Icon* magazine, *Building Design* and *Il Giornale dell'Architettura*. In 2007 he guest-edited a special issue of the *Architectural Review* on South Africa. He chairs the board of charity Architecture Sans Frontières.

Trevor Butler began his career in the UK, developing specialist sustainable engineering practices to make green design mainstream. With over sixteen years' experience in leading the engineering of green buildings and infrastructure projects, his experience in this field is both broad and deep. A proven team player, he has led the engineering design for several award-winning projects in the UK, Iraq and Canada. In 2007, he was voted the UK Sustainability Champion by his industry peers and clients. He strongly believes that design of the built environment needs to be holistic and interdisciplinary to create fully integrated designs that address ecological and social issues within a competitive commercial context. Critical to achieving this approach is an understanding of risks, transparent analysis and communication to deliver simple sustainable solutions. Maintaining a balance between learning and practice, he is founder of Archineers Consulting, serves as Adjunct Professor at Dalhousie University, and is currently undertaking a Professional Doctorate.

Adrian Forty is Professor of Architectural History at The Bartlett, UCL. He has written on design (*Objects of Desire*, Thames & Hudson, 1986), and on architecture. His book *Words and Buildings: A Vocabulary of Modern Architecture* (Thames & Hudson, 2000) is about the ambivalent relationship modern architecture had with verbal language, both suspicious of it, but also creating a new vocabulary to talk about architecture. As well as a variety of essays and articles about diverse architectural topics, he co-edited with Suzanne Kuechler *The Art of Forgetting* (Berg, 1999) and with Elisabetta Andreoli *Brazil's Modern Architecture* (Phaidon, 2004). He is currently engaged on a worldwide study of the relationship between concrete and culture in the twentieth century.

Frances Holliss is an architect and an academic who has taught for many years in the Department of Architecture and Spatial Design at London Metropolitan University. She is also a Research Fellow at the Cities Institute. She has practised architecture in England and worked among the rural poor in Central America, building settlements in a war zone. Her 2007 Ph.D. on the architecture of home-based work uncovered the old but little-written-about building type that combines dwelling and workplace ('workhome'), and made an analysis of its contemporary form and governance. In 2009 she received Knowledge Transfer funding from the Arts and Humanities Research Council for a two-year project to develop an open-access, online design guide for the workhome. She lectures internationally on her research, and her book, *Beyond Live/Work: The Architecture of Home-based Work* will be published by Routledge in 2012.

Gillian Horn is a partner at Penoyre & Prasad. She joined the practice in 1999 following the completion of the Straw Bale House at Stock Orchard Street for which she was project architect. She studied at the University of Cambridge where she graduated with distinction before continuing her training at Harvard. She enjoys teaching and has run design studios for the Architectural Association, Kingston University and Greenwich University as well as design and dissertation supervision at the University of Cambridge. She is a regular conference speaker and contributor to Radio 4's *Learning Curve* as well as acting as an architectural expert on a series of programmes for Teachers TV.

Martin Hughes has been working in design and construction since 1979 and founded KOYA in 1998 as a way of getting Stock Orchard Street built. He trained in architecture at Cambridge and product design at Central School of Art. He was a director of Support Architects (1982–1987) and worked for Architype (1992–1997). He has managed the construction of over 200 projects and specialises in the use of timber and steel frames and the integration of new technologies. Besides Stock Orchard Street, he has won awards for the CUE Building at the Horniman Museum (1997) and for three self-build housing schemes in Lewisham (1992–2001). He has contributed to the Part 3 course at Cambridge School of Architecture since 2003. Since 1998 KOYA has partnered with consultants, contractors and subcontractors to produce a range of innovative and environmentally sustainable buildings. Its current workload ranges from an office refurbishment for Transport For London at Oxford Circus to the construction of a house from rammed earth in Petersfield.

Jan-Carlos Kucharek grew up in a run-down Jacobean house in Wiltshire. He studied architecture at Canterbury College of Art, spent three years working in a practice in Tokyo, travelled, and gained his Diploma at The Bartlett, UCL, with Jeremy Till and Jonathan Hill, in 1996. He qualified as an architect in 2002 working on commercial projects at Foster and Partners. Realising that corporate practice really wasn't his thing and finally reconciling himself to the fact that sentences too are constructions, he left in 2005 to become Assistant Editor of the *RIBA Journal*. He still holds this position, writes for other journals and continues to work freelance in practice. He lives and works in London.

Katie Lloyd Thomas trained as an architect and currently teaches history and theory at The Bartlett. She is the editor of *Material Matters: Architecture and Material Practice* (Routledge, 2007) which was long-listed for the RIBA International Book Awards 2007, and a founder member of **taking place**, a group of artists and architects concerned with feminist spatial practice. Recent publications include 'Building While Being in It: Notes on Drawing "Otherhow"' in *Altering Practices: Feminist Politics and Poetics of Space*, ed. D. Petrescu (Routledge, 2007); 'Jigging with Concrete: Matter and Form in the Making of Wall One' in *Fabricformwork*, eds. A. Chandler and R. Pedreschi (RIBA Publications, 2007); 'Specifying Materials: Language, Matter and the Conspiracy of Muteness' in *From Models to Drawings*, eds. M. Frascari, J. Hale and B. Starkey (Routledge, 2007); and 'Going into the Mould: Process and Materials in the Architectural Specification' in *Radical Philosophy*, 144 (2007). She completed a Ph.D. on concepts of materials and the architectural specification at the CRMEP at Middlesex University.

Anya Moryoussef, recipient of the Royal Architectural Institute of Canada student medal, graduated from the University of Waterloo, with a Master of Architecture, in 2006. Her thesis, 'The Criminal, The Cartographer, The Carpenter', comprised three creative non-fiction stories, set in Toronto, which explored the processes and origins of architecture and the city as works of artifice created by non-architects. Currently practising in Toronto, she is working towards her architectural licence. Previously she worked and studied in New York, Istanbul, Rome and Bergen, Norway, where she taught design studio at the Bergen Arkitekt Skole. As a student in 2002 and then again from 2006 through 2009, she worked at Sarah Wigglesworth Architects. The time she spent at 9½ Stock Orchard Street continues to strongly affect her personal and professional development.

Kester Rattenbury is an architectural journalist, writer and teacher, and is Reader of Architecture at the University of Westminster where she runs the EXP research group and teaches a Diploma design studio. Her books include *This Is Not Architecture* (Routledge, 2002), which is partly based on her Ph.D. on the coverage of architecture in national newspapers in the 1980s; *Archaeology of the Air: O'Donnell and Tuomey* (Navado Press, 2004); *Architects Today*, with Robert Bevan and Kieran Long (Laurence King, 2004); and *Supercrit 1: POTTERIES THINKBELT* and *Supercrit 2: Learning From Las Vegas*, both with Samantha Hardingham (Routledge, 2007). She was also Principal Investigator of the Archigram Archival Project (http://archigram.westminster.ac.uk) which made the works of the seminal architectural group available online.

Jeremy Till is an architect and educator. He is widely seen as a leading figure in the contemporary debate about the built environment and lectures worldwide on architecture and education. He is Dean of Architecture and the Built Environment at the University of Westminster. His written work includes *Architecture and Participation* (edited with Peter Blundell-Jones and Doina Petrescu Spon Press, 2004) *Flexible Housing* (with Tatjana Schneider, Architectural Press, 2007), which was winner of the 2007 RIBA President's Medal for Research, and *Architecture Depends* (MIT Press, 2009). As an architect, he is a Director in Sarah Wigglesworth Architects which is best known for their pioneering building, 9/10 Stock Orchard Street (the Straw House and Quilted Office), which has received extensive international acclaim and multiple awards. In 2006 he was appointed to represent Britain at the Venice Architecture Biennale.

Sarah Wigglesworth heads her own practice based in London. The practice won awards for, among other projects, Mossbrook Special School Classroom of the Future (2005), Siobhan Davies Dance Studios (2006) and Cremorne Riverside Canoeing Centre (2008). One of the five practices selected to design one of the government's BSF Exemplar Primary Schools, the practice is now building a version of this, Sandal Magna School in Wakefield, which opened in September 2010. She is also Professor of Architecture at The University of Sheffield where she is responsible for establishing a new Ph.D. by Design. She has published extensively and, in addition to authoring numerous essays, she is joint editor (with Katerina Rüedi and Duncan McCorquodale) of *Desiring Practices: Architecture, Gender and the Interdisciplinary* (Black Dog Press, 1996) and (with Jeremy Till) *Architectural Design: The Everyday and Architecture* (Academy Wiley, 1998). She was awarded an MBE for services to architecture in 2003.

Acknowledgements

In the production of this book
I would like to thank the following
people:

Ellie & Katya Duffy
Tom Ebdon
Fran Ford
Mark Hadden
Paul Smoothy
Jeremy Till
Ben Woolhead

Image credits

All images © Paul Smoothy
unless otherwise stated below.

Introduction
p. 4 © Sarah Wigglesworth/
Jeremy Till

The client's tale
Figs 1, 3 © Sallmann
Harman Healy
Figs 2, 5, 8–17, 25–7, 33, 34,
39 © SarahWigglesworth/
Jeremy Till
Fig 18 © David Grandorge

Telling tales
All © Sarah Wigglesworth/
Jeremy Till except:
p. 45 left © Sallmann
Harman Healy
p. 46 middle and bottom
right © Christine Sullivan
p. 49 top left and middle
and p. 57 left © David
Grandorge

Ordinariness and perfection
pp. 63–6 © Sarah
Wigglesworth/Jeremy Till

Design drawings
pp. 72–5 © Sarah
Wigglesworth/Jeremy Till
pp. 76–81 © Sarah
Wigglesworth Architects

House with associated office?
All © Frances Holliss except:
Figs 1, 15, 25, 26
© English Heritage. NMR.
Fig 6 © Nick Hufton
Figs 8, 17 © Sarah
Wigglesworth/Jeremy Till
Figs 11, 13, 18, 21, 22
© Mark Hadden
Fig 12 image from *La Maison de
Verre, Pierre Chareau's Modernist
Masterwork*, 2007 Dominique
Vellay, Thames and Hudson
© Francois Halard/Trish South
Management/trunkarchive.com
Fig 16 image from Le Corbusier's
Oeuvre Complete © FLC/ADAGP
Paris and DACS, London 2010
Fig 24 © Colin Davies

Getting it built
pp. 98–9 © Martin Hughes

**From innovation
to commonplace**
pp. 104–11 © Sarah
Wigglesworth/Jeremy Till

The model: deconstructed
pp. 114–17 © Sarah
Wigglesworth/Jeremy Till

**The excessive materiality
of Stock Orchard Street**
pp. 118–31 © Sarah
Wigglesworth/Jeremy Till

Construction drawings
pp. 134–57 © Sarah
Wigglesworth Architects

**Out of time, out of frame,
into the box**
p. 220, p. 223 © Islington Local
History Centre

Index

Dominus Winery 229
doorbell 86–7, *87*
Dornbirn region, Austria 178 n1
drawings 15–16, 19–20, 22, 24, 46, 48, 49–51, 55, 57, 63–6, 70, 72–81, 101, 102, 115, 117, 134–57, 163, 167, 173, 202, 224–6
dual-use buildings *see* live/work environment
Duchamp, Marcel 192
dwelling, use of term 84

Eames House 86, 87, 89, *91*, 91, 93
eco-concrete 99, 106
ecological architecture 2, 11–12, 22, 105–12, 163; environmental principles *109*, *111*
Ecology Building Society 20
economics 2, 17, 84, 93, 94, 95, 101, 102, 105–6, 121, 130, 167, 173, 227, 228
Eisenman, Peter 121, 198
Eliot, T.S. 197, 199
elitist projects 94
energy consumption 5–6; good practice 181, 182, 186, 188; role of construction methods and standards 185; typical standard 181, 182, 184, 188
energy performance 179
Energy Performance of Buildings, European Union 179, 186
energy storage 103
energy systems, renewable 195
Enlightenment, fundamentalism of 198
entrance 25, 87, 89, 92, *109*, 200, 235, 240, 242, 243
essentialism 121
ethics 2, 5, 11, 192, 194, 199, 202, 222, 225, 231–7
ethnographies of OMA 172
everyday, the x, 66, 70, 227, 228
excess 5, 118–21; decoration 123; material, and the feminine 121–4; materialisation of 130; possibilities of 129–30; and proper materials 125–9
experiment, experimental 2, 14, 22, 76, 92, 106, 112, 116, 129, 166, 172, 173, 178, 192, 222, 224–5, 228, 231, 233, 235; self-experiments vii
Experimental Gardens 222

expertise 3, 70, 87, 120, 131
extrafunctional 118, 123, 125, 127, 129
extra-structural 127

fabric cladding *see* cladding
Façades for the Future 17
'fat' architecture 118
female space 5, 62, 67
feminine viii, 118–31, 242
feminist, feminism 5, 11, 118–31, 246
feminist material practice 11, 118–31
fetishistic minimalism 70
finance 6, 18–19, 20, 25, 57–8, 96–7, 103, 133, 165
finished 26, 224–5, 226, 228, 236
finishes 18, 25
Fire Brigade 56, 127
fire safety 20, 127
Fish, Stanley: *Self-Consuming Artefacts* 233, 234
fleshiness 121
fodder merchants 17, 54
Forty, Adrian 5, 7, 245
Fraser, Mariam 130
Fretton, Tony 193
Fulbright Fellowship, the 10
Future Systems 17, 54, 57

gabions ix, 5, 20, 22, 23, *24*, 69, 70, 97, 102, 108, *122*, 123, 200, 200 n5, 229, 242
GANTT chart 97
garden x, 28, 34–5, *36*, 38–9, 40–3, 69, *71*, 87, *175*, 200
garden cities 93
gate, the 69, 86, *86*, 87, 240
Gedge, Dusty 110
Gehry, Frank vii
General Information Report 53 (*GIR 53*) 183
gentleness vii, 172, 227
geometric line 121–3
GERB 23
Gillieron, Paul 23
glazed elevation 102
glazing 69, 84, 88, 97, 102, *107*, 174, 186, 188, 240
global warming potential (GWP) 180
Goff, Bruce vii, 96
Goodwin, Daisy 226
Gramsci, Antonio 225
Grand Designs 1–2, 58, 171, 227–8
Gray, Eileen 193
green building design *see* ecological architecture

green buildings 5, 178, 189
Gropius, Walter 197
Grosz, Elizabeth 5, 118, 121, 123, 127, 129–31
GUI 103

Hait, John N. 178 n1
Hanika, Nick 161
Hardingham, Sam 174
Harries, Karsten 231
heat pumps 103
heat-recovery system 109–10
heating systems 106, 178, 180, 181, 182, 183, 184, *184*, 185, *185*, 186, 188, 195; central heating system 111, 243; underfloor 26
Heidegger, Martin 199
Hertzberger, Herman 195
Herzog & de Meuron 229
heterogeneity 198, 229
Heyne, Andy 161; Martin Hughes message to *119*, 120
High Tech xi, *177*, 181, 228
Hill, Jonathan 53, 226
Hirst, Damian 228
Hockerton Housing Project 106
Holliss, Frances 245
home, houses as 192, 197
home-based work 93, 94–5
Horn, Gillian 4, 18, 19, 22, 25, 55, 127, 227, 246; architecture practice 162–3
Horniman Museum 19
Housing Design Guide 94
Howard, Ebenezer 93
Hughes, Martin 6, 18–19, 21, 22, 28, 57, 58, 59, 161, 227, 246; message to Andy Heyne *119*, 120
hybrid 2, 5, 14, 69, 84, 107, 127, 240

idea of a dining table 195–6
idea of a house 191–2; debate 196–7; designs 192–3; and obligations 197–203; origins 192; philosophy 195–6; and reality 194
ideal home 192
incomplete, incompleteness 2, 70, 225, 226
Ingraham, Catherine 121–3, 128, 130
insulation 26, 103, 108, 123, 178
integrative design 106, 202, 249
intelligent building 106
intentionality xi
Inter-Action studios 225

Interbuild 17–18, *18*, 54, 55–7, 127, 132
Intermediate Technology 132
Irigaray, Luce 130
Islington, London Borough of vii, 14, 27, *87*, 91, *125*, 220, 221, 240
Islington Gazette 53, 54
IT system 165, 179, 186

Jencks, Charles 226
Johnson, Philip 193, 229
Jones, Barbara 17, 50
journalism, architectural 225–6

Kardomah Coffee House 173, 242
Kingston University (formerly Polytechnic) 10, 11, 46, 172, 246
kitchen/diner 84–5, *85*, 89, *89*, 92, 99, 102, *146–7*, 162, 198, 222, 241
kitsch 197
knowledge 2, 6, 11–12, 18, 56, 70, 84, 101–2, 128, 130, 160, 188, 189, 193, 196–7, 201, 203, 232, 233, 236, 249
Koolhaas, Rem 224
KOYA Construction 6, 97, 101, 161
Kristeva, Julia 121
Kucharek, Jan-Carlos 6, 246
Kyoto protocol 163
Kyte, Peter 15, 16, 48, 49

laboratory 229
landscape 69
larder 24, *25*, 97, 102, *107*, *109*, 110, *145*, *148–9*, 241
l'Augier, l'Abbé Marc Antione 200
LBC News radio 53
Le Corbusier vii, 86, 88
Leaman, Adrian 179
LEED 179
leisure 67, 68–9, 242
library tower vii, 22, 24, *24*, *25*, 25, 26, 28, *32*, 44, 50, 51, 93, 97, 98, 101, 107, *107*, *109*, 109–10, 116, 174, 187, 198, 201, 234, 241, 243
lighting system 103
lime plaster 241, 243
Linnaeus, Carl 84
live-nearby approach 89, 91
live-with approach 89
live/work environment 67–70, 84–95, *85*, 106, 120, 171–4

polycarbonate sheeting 18, 54, 56, 69, 123, 127, 132, 133, 243; rodent guard 243; use of 16, 17–18
substantial architecture 1, 197, 198
Sudjic, Deyan 88
sustainable living *104*, 132, 200, 202
sustainability 53, 106, 112, 116, 133, 200, 202, 231
Symbolic order 123

Tabor, Phil 197
Talkback 58, 59
technology 97–9, 102–3, 163, 167
temporality 200
Thatcherism 228
Third Way, the 228
theory 5, 6, 10–11, 191, 195, 224, 225, 236, 245
Thomas, Randall 22
Till, Jeremy 3–4, 10, 13, 15, 21, 27, *33*, 97, 120, 127, 128, 130, 131, 161, 193, 194, 195, 198, 199, 247; architectural ethics 231; *Architecture Depends* 228; response to Tony Currivan 133; workspace 93
timeline chart 97
Tozer, William 195
Tree Trunk Order xi
treetop perch *89*, 89

U-valves 178
UK Energy Consumption Guide 19 (ECG 19) 181, 182, 183
unfinished 1, 27, 200, 225, 226
users 5, 6, 11, 61–2, 106, 112, 164–5, 166, 178, 188–9, 231
Use Class Order 93
utility meters 189

Vale, Brenda and Robert 106, 112, 183
ventilation 103, 109–10, 243
vertical louvres 109
Vesely, Dalibor 199
vibration reduction 17, 23, 107, 108, 125, 242
Villa dal'Ava 224
Vitruvius xi; *De Architectura* 234

Ware, Martyn 222, 228
Warmcell insulation 26, 96–7
waste 103
water systems 183, 195

wattle hurdles 69
weather, weathering 3, 29, 27, 62, 112, 125
Weldon, Huw 226
Weller, Edward: map of London *222*
Wigglesworth, Sarah 97, 120, 127, 130, 131, 161, *170*, 199, 247; response to Tony Currivan 133; Sarah Wigglesworth Architects 160–1; workspace 93
Williams-Ellis, Clough 222
Wilson, Colin St John 194, 198–9, 202; 'The Historical Sense' 197
willow *see* wattle hurdles
wind turbines 103
windows 54, 55, 91, 109; orientation 174; in sandbag wall *153, 154, 155*; south-west elevation *135*
wood-burning stove 111
workhomes 5, 84–95
workplace, use of term 84
Worsley, Giles 174
Wotton, Henry: *The Elements of Architecture* 232, 234
Wright, Frank Lloyd vii, 193
Wright Mills, C. 202

XML 103

Yaneva, Albena vii, 172

zero-carbon buildings 179
zoning 5, 93, 95, 106